Battle POPE
Mayhem

CREATED BY
ROBERT KIRKMAN
& TONY MOORE

London Borough of Hackney

Askews	Woo
	£8.50
	06/466

Robert Kirkman
writer, layout artist, letterer, penciller (19-25) inker (26-27)

Matthew Roberts
penciller (49-51, 61-104)

Tony Moore
penciller (5-18, 26-29, 33-34, 40-41, 45-48, 52-60) inker (26-27)

Mark Kidwell
penciller (30-32)

Brian Despain
penciller, inker (35-39)

Shane White
penciller, inker (42-44)

Val Staples
colorist

IMAGE COMICS, INC.
Erik Larsen - *Publisher*
Todd McFarlane - *President*
Marc Silvestri - *CEO*
Jim Valentino - *Vice-President*

Eric Stephenson - *Executive Director*
Jim Demonakos - *PR & Marketing Coordinator*
Mia MacHatton - *Accounts Manager*
Traci Hui - *Administrative Assistant*
Joe Keatinge - *Traffic Manager*
Allen Hui - *Production Manager*
Jonathan Chan - *Production Artist*
Drew Gill - *Production Artist*
Chris Giarrusso - *Production Artist*
www.imagecomics.com

BATTLE POPE VOL.2: MAYHEM. 2006. Published by Image Comics, Inc., Office of publication: 1942 University Avenue, Suite 305, Berkeley, California 94704.

Battle Pope changed my life.

Changed. My. Life. MY LIFE.

Some six or whatever years ago when I was a stripling of eleven years of age, I made regular forays into the world of electrical corkboards transmitted through the air on what I assume is television particles. Specifically, such corkboards that were themed towards horrible, depressing, sub-amateurish comic book art. It was at such a place that I "met" Robert Kirkman and Tony Moore.

I recall seeing some of Tony's drawings of the Teenage Mutant Ninja Turtles, and having grown up fond of the characters, I felt compelled to tell him I thought he was the cat's pajamas. I had a ton of the Turtles action figures when I was a kid. Man, this one time we had this secret Santa crap in school, and I made the mistake of buying something I wanted, rather than some crappy model car or a jigsaw puzzle. It was Wyrm, you know the yellow leech guy? I totally wanted him so hard, but I had to give him away, and the kid who I swapped with gave me a jigsaw puzzle of a model car. So Tony told me that he was working on a comic that was coming out that year called Battle Pope. Battle Pope! Just like you did at one time, I chortled at the first thought of the name. But then my thoughts quickly moved to the idea that I knew a person who was making an actual comic book! (It was later when I figured out that it wasn't a REAL comic book. I mean, it was printed on newsprint or something, uff.)

So I was a fan before the book came out. Take that you damn Johnny-come-lately-and-coloredly-and-published-at-Imagelies. Oh man, did you wait for this to come out in trade too? You asshole. Anyway, when the book did come out, I loved it. It was funny, and it was a little dirty and ribald. It kind of made me feel the way reading Mad Magazine did in fourth grade before I figured out Mad Magazine wasn't funny or offensive in the least. ...Ass Venturda. Good one. Well, I guess you get the picture, since I'll assume you've read the first volume and are back for seconds. Who wants to read introductions that just hype up the book you're already set on reading? Let's talk about me some more.

At the time, I was doing dopey comic strips or something, because I'm sure my attention span couldn't manage any kind of normal sequential narrative. I like to think it was less my spindley, supple frame and more a sign of promising potential that caught Robert Kirkman's eye. Whatever it was, he and Tony took me under and into their collective wing and fold. When Battle Pope: Mayhem was gestating, Robert axed me to whip together a couple of shorts to put in the back of each issue. I just about shat. There is one slightly notable omission from this collection and it is those backups. Which is okay, because they're kind of terrible, not TOO terrible, but not worth the bother. It was my first ever published work, and I was only at the ripe age of seven. Robert even wrote a flattering introduction for me. It is more important that you know what was written in that introduction than it is for you to know what he was introducing. He said he wants to work for me one day. Now that he rides in limosines with Joe Quesada, I wonder how he thinks that's going to play out.

But now it was official, I was in the club, I was one of the guys. I finally got to sit BEHIND the booth at conventions. Even though at the first convention I ever went to I sat behind the Funk-o-Tron booth... I guess if you just imagined I had attended years of conventions prior to that, and that there was some big buildup about the glitz and glam of being part of a comic book creative team... or something. I sat next to Erik Larsen on the way to the airport one time and I didn't even know who he was. In contrast, Benito Cereno, who was driving the car and has been reading comics since he fell off the caravan, was peeing himself. Anyway, I was one of the guys, but not one of the guys guys. I was the wunderkind, the tagalong, the precocious young scamp. I was sitting in the sidecar and enjoying the ride. I got to meet and know great artists and okay guys like Matt Roberts and Cory Walker, and I got to watch them grow and improve over the years and learn from them in turn. I had a front row seat to the meteoric rise to comic book pseudo-fame. Which is weird, because Robert is still Robert, ...but now he writes Marvel books. Lucky for me, right?

So Robert put myself and Benito in issues of Invincible until he told us to knock it off and make our own book and we went and made Hector Plasm: De Mortuis, which might not have ever been picked up or published if it weren't for his good word (Which maybe isn't exactly true, since its a pretty GREAT comic, to paraphrase people who are not me). Who knows what I would be doing if it weren't for him? Probably finishing my degree or something useless like that. So, I owe a lot to Robert and Tony and their Popey business. Rest assured, enthralled reader, that your thirteen or whatever dollars are going to a great guy, a good person, a pure heart and a giving soul.

By the way, the character of mine that he was really into was an aborted zombie fetus.

Nate Bellegarde
Age 14

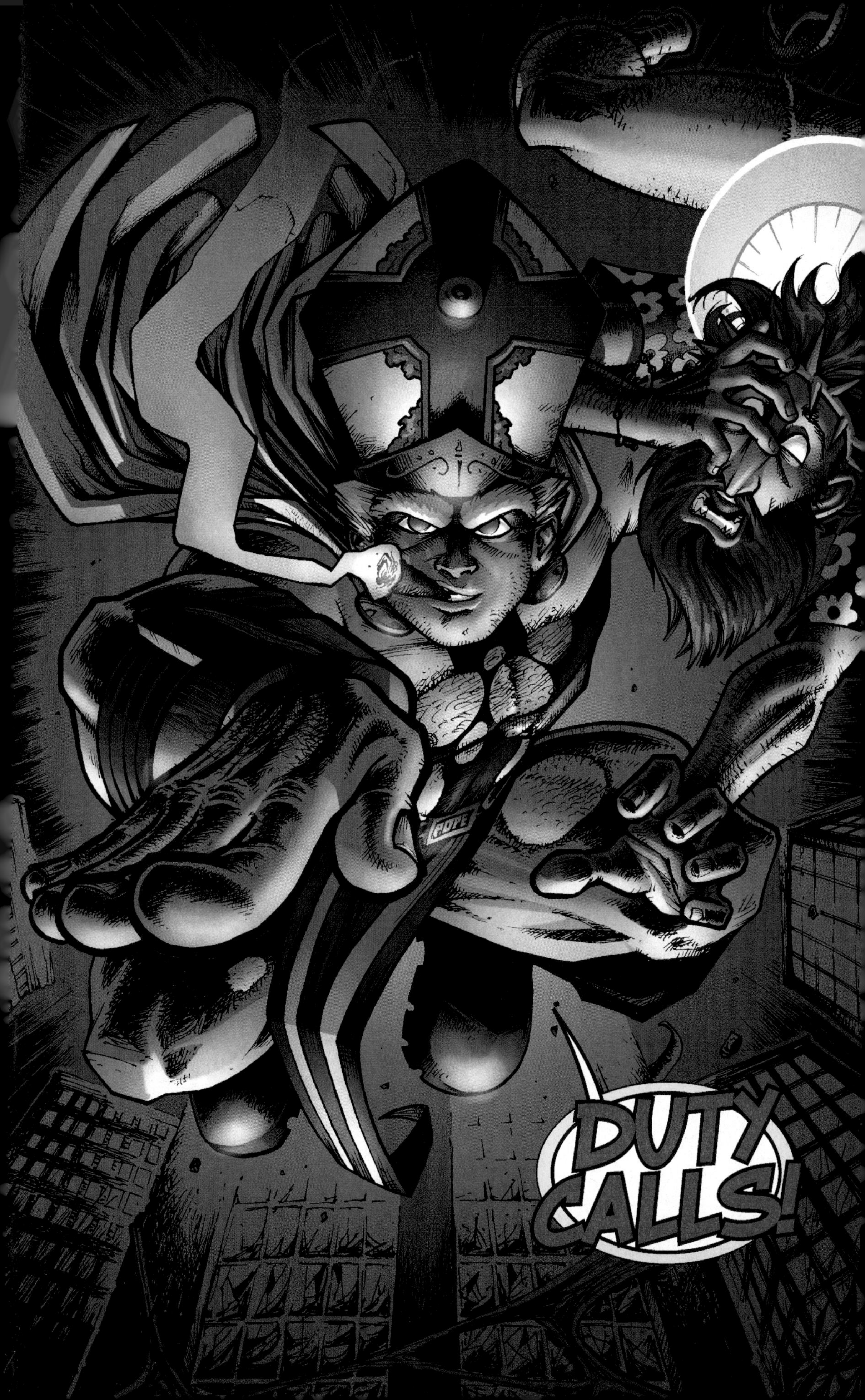
POPE
DUTY CALLS!

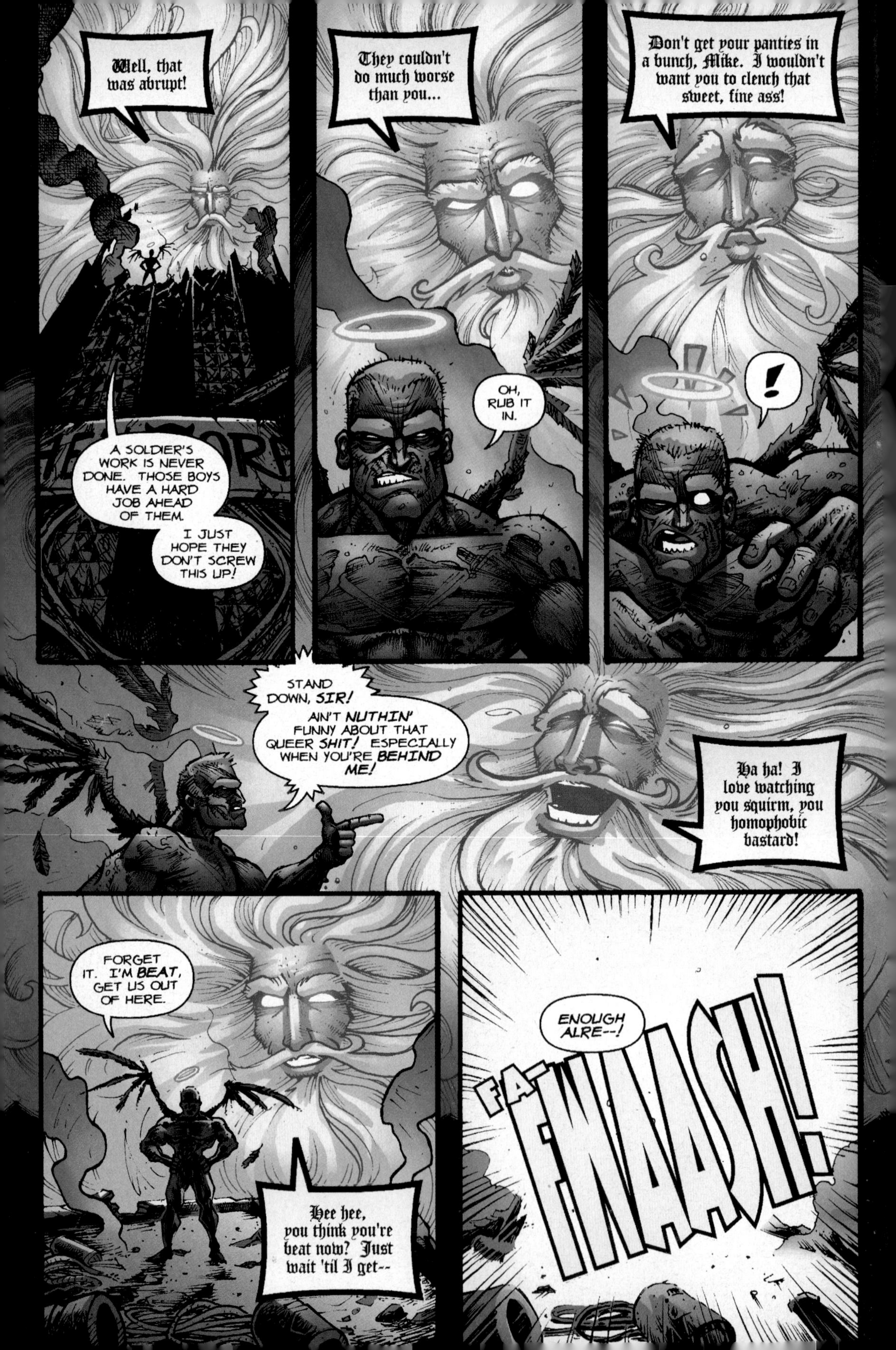
Well, that was abrupt!
A SOLDIER'S WORK IS NEVER DONE. THOSE BOYS HAVE A HARD JOB AHEAD OF THEM.
I JUST HOPE THEY DON'T SCREW THIS UP!
They couldn't do much worse than you...
OH, RUB IT IN.
Don't get your panties in a bunch, Mike. I wouldn't want you to clench that sweet, fine ass!
!
STAND DOWN, SIR!
AIN'T NUTHIN' FUNNY ABOUT THAT QUEER SHIT! ESPECIALLY WHEN YOU'RE BEHIND ME!
Ha ha! I love watching you squirm, you homophobic bastard!
FORGET IT. I'M BEAT, GET US OUT OF HERE.
Hee hee, you think you're beat now? Just wait 'til I get--
ENOUGH ALRE--!
FA-FWAASH!

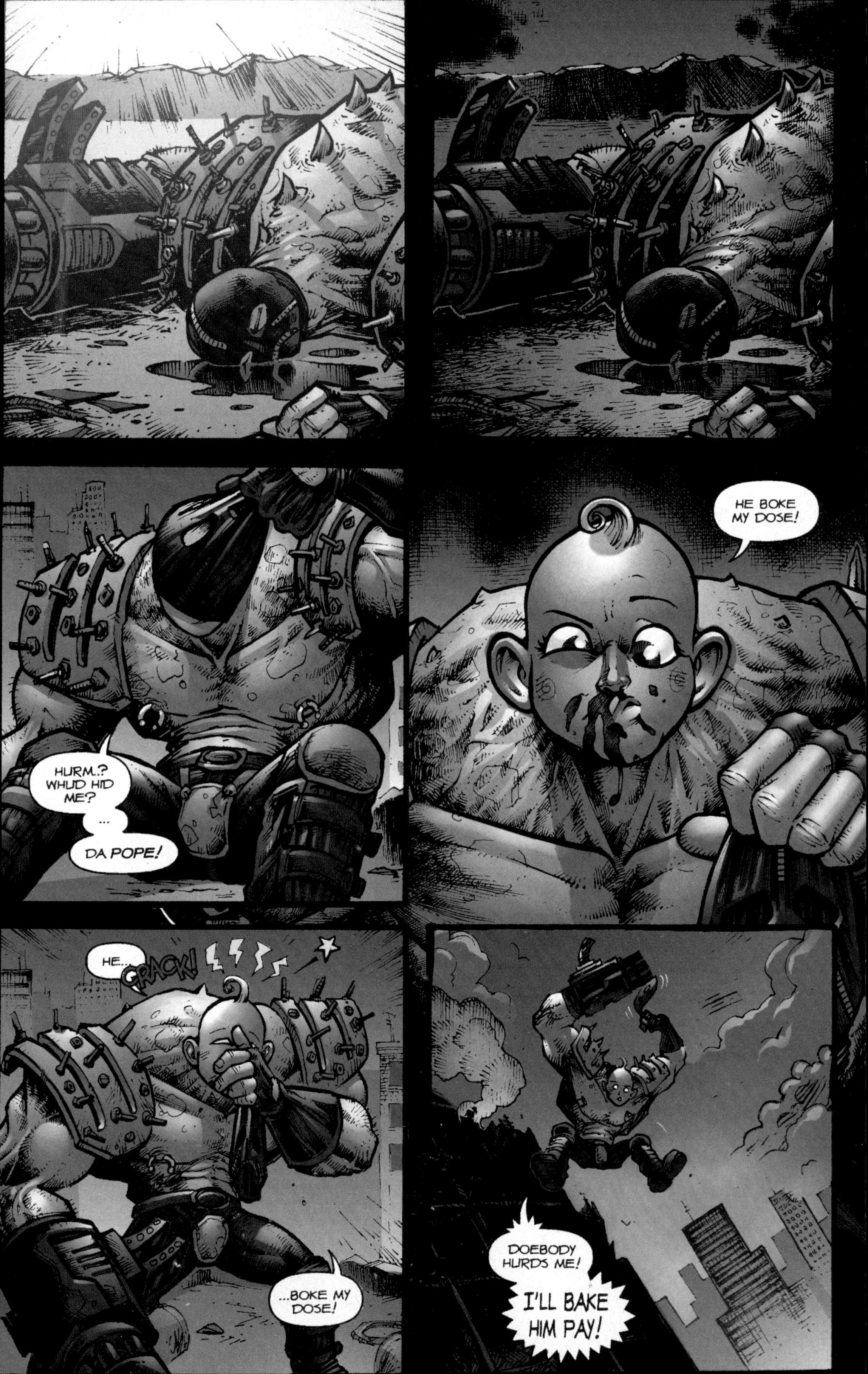
HURM..? WHUD HID ME?
...
DA POPE!
HE BOKE MY DOSE!
HE...
CRACK!
...BOKE MY DOSE!
DOEBODY HURDS ME!
I'LL BAKE HIM PAY!

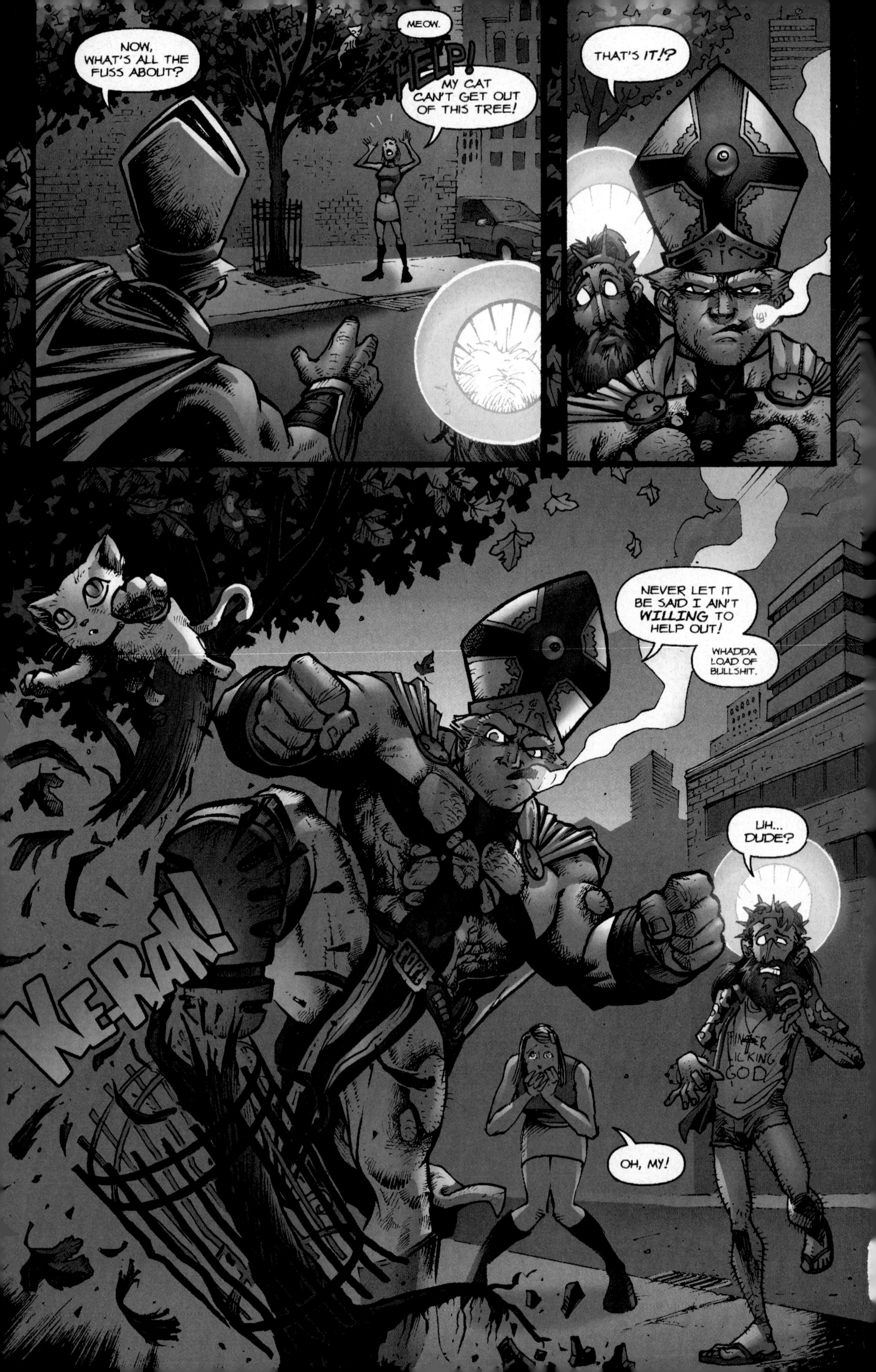
NOW, WHAT'S ALL THE FUSS ABOUT?
MEOW.
HELP!
MY CAT CAN'T GET OUT OF THIS TREE!
THAT'S IT!?
NEVER LET IT BE SAID I AIN'T WILLING TO HELP OUT!
WHADDA LOAD OF BULLSHIT.
UH... DUDE?
KE-RAK!
OH, MY!

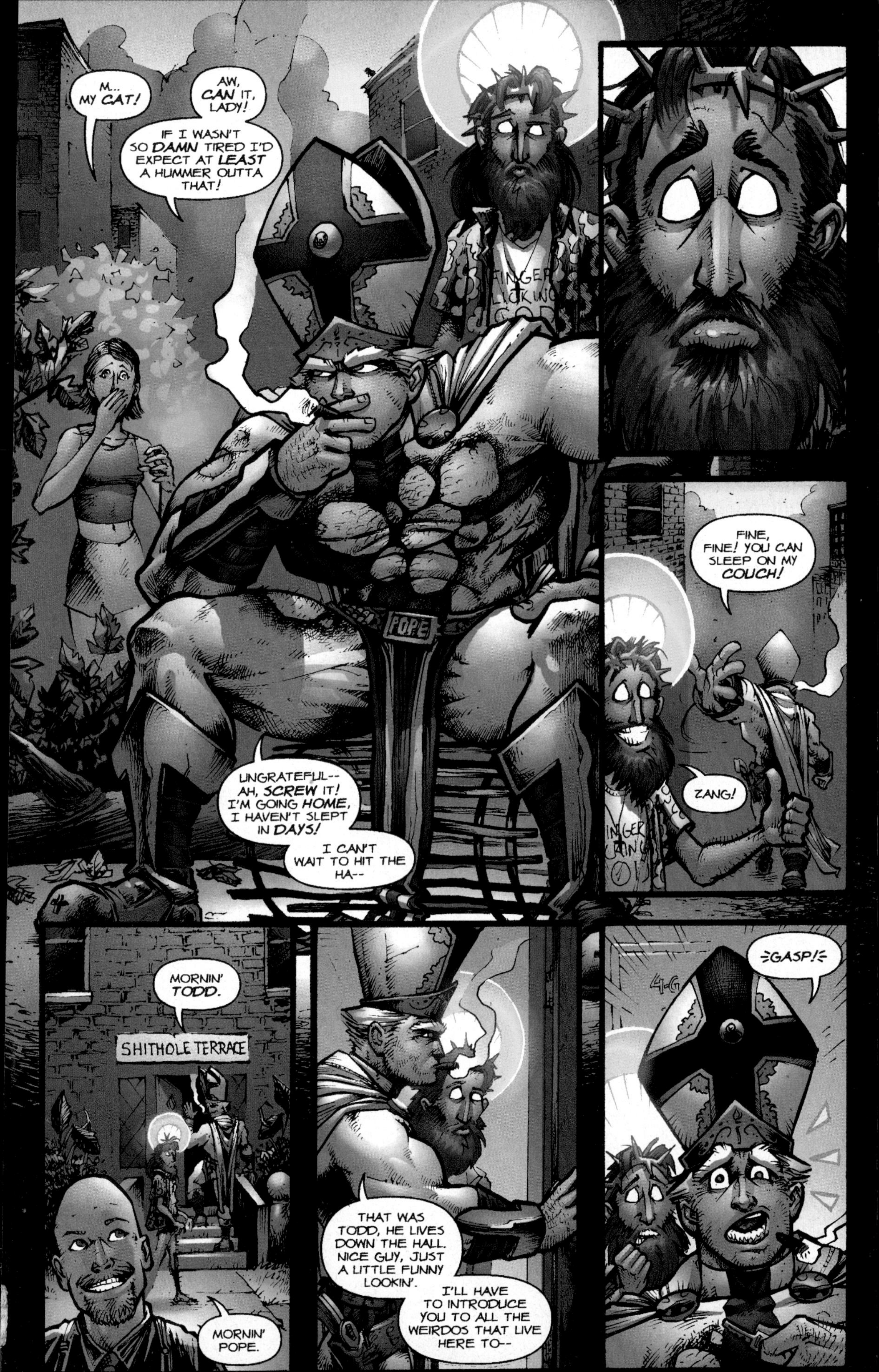
M... MY CAT!
AW, CAN IT, LADY!
IF I WASN'T SO DAMN TIRED I'D EXPECT AT LEAST A HUMMER OUTTA THAT!
UNGRATEFUL-- AH, SCREW IT! I'M GOING HOME, I HAVEN'T SLEPT IN DAYS!
I CAN'T WAIT TO HIT THE HA--
POPE
FINE, FINE! YOU CAN SLEEP ON MY COUCH!
ZANG!
MORNIN' TODD.
SHITHOLE TERRACE
MORNIN' POPE.
THAT WAS TODD, HE LIVES DOWN THE HALL. NICE GUY, JUST A LITTLE FUNNY LOOKIN'.
I'LL HAVE TO INTRODUCE YOU TO ALL THE WEIRDOS THAT LIVE HERE TO--
GASP!

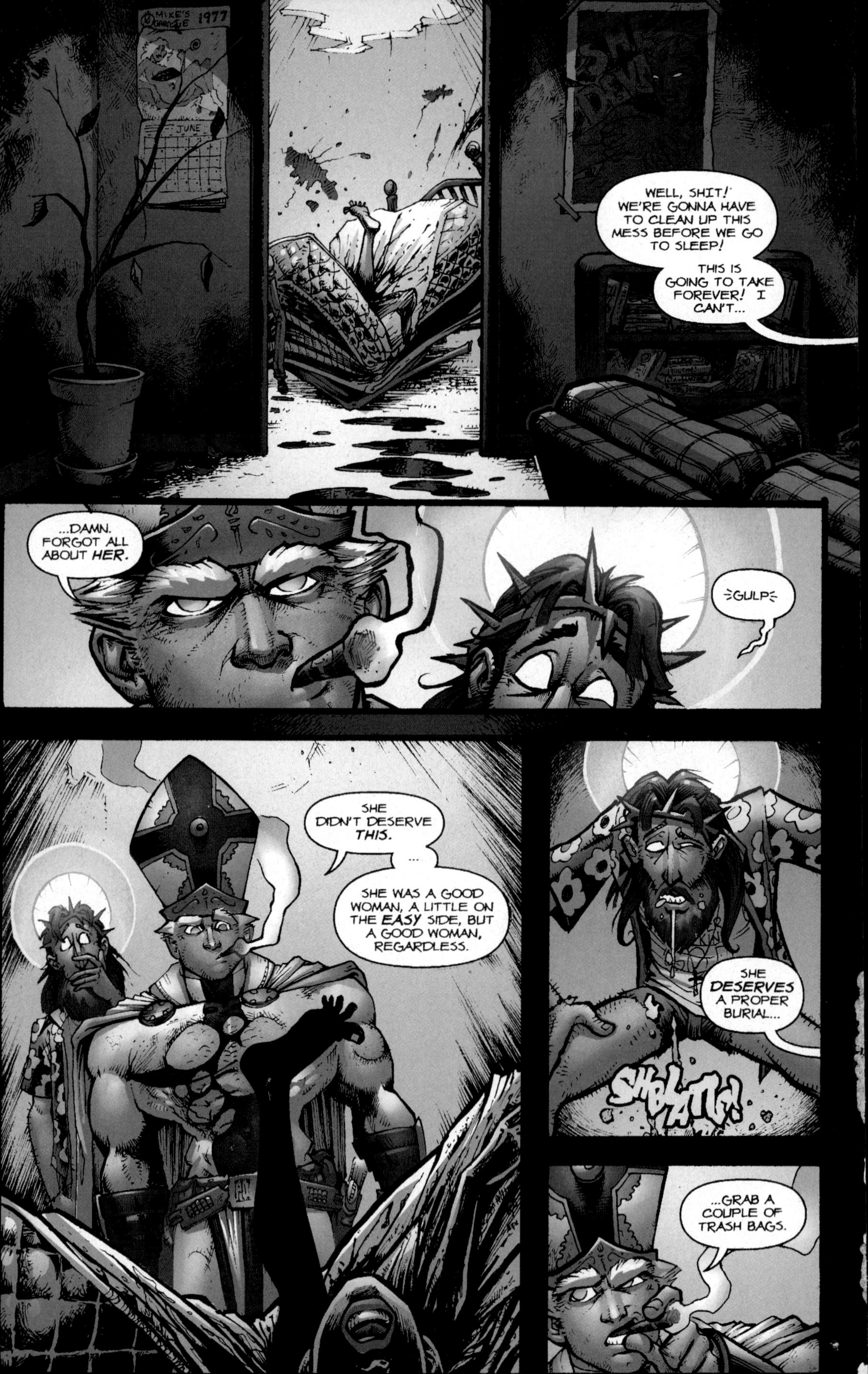

MIKE'S GARAGE 1977
JUNE
WELL, SHIT! WE'RE GONNA HAVE TO CLEAN UP THIS MESS BEFORE WE GO TO SLEEP!
THIS IS GOING TO TAKE FOREVER! I CAN'T...
...DAMN. FORGOT ALL ABOUT HER.
GULP
SHE DIDN'T DESERVE THIS.
...
SHE WAS A GOOD WOMAN, A LITTLE ON THE EASY SIDE, BUT A GOOD WOMAN, REGARDLESS.
SHE DESERVES A PROPER BURIAL...
SHBLATTG!
...GRAB A COUPLE OF TRASH BAGS.

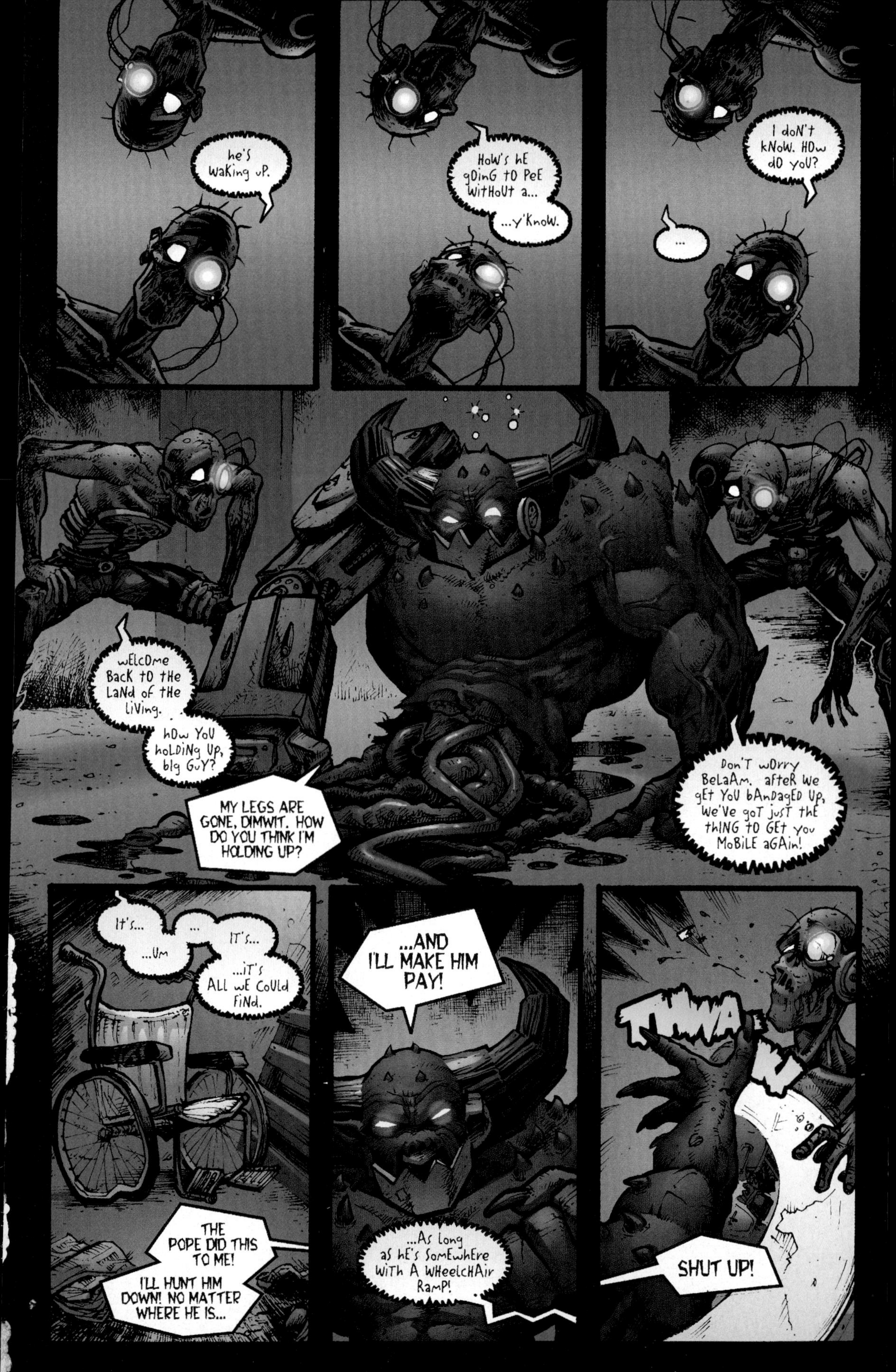
he's waking up.
How's he going to pee without a...
...y'know.
I don't know. How do you?
...
welcome back to the land of the living.
how you holding up, big guy?
MY LEGS ARE GONE, DIMWIT. HOW DO YOU THINK I'M HOLDING UP?
Don't worry Belaam. after we get you bandaged up, we've got just the thing to get you mobile again!
It's...
...um
...
It's...
...it's all we could find.
THE POPE DID THIS TO ME!
I'LL HUNT HIM DOWN! NO MATTER WHERE HE IS...
...AND I'LL MAKE HIM PAY!
...As long as he's somewhere with a wheelchair ramp!
THWAK
SHUT UP!

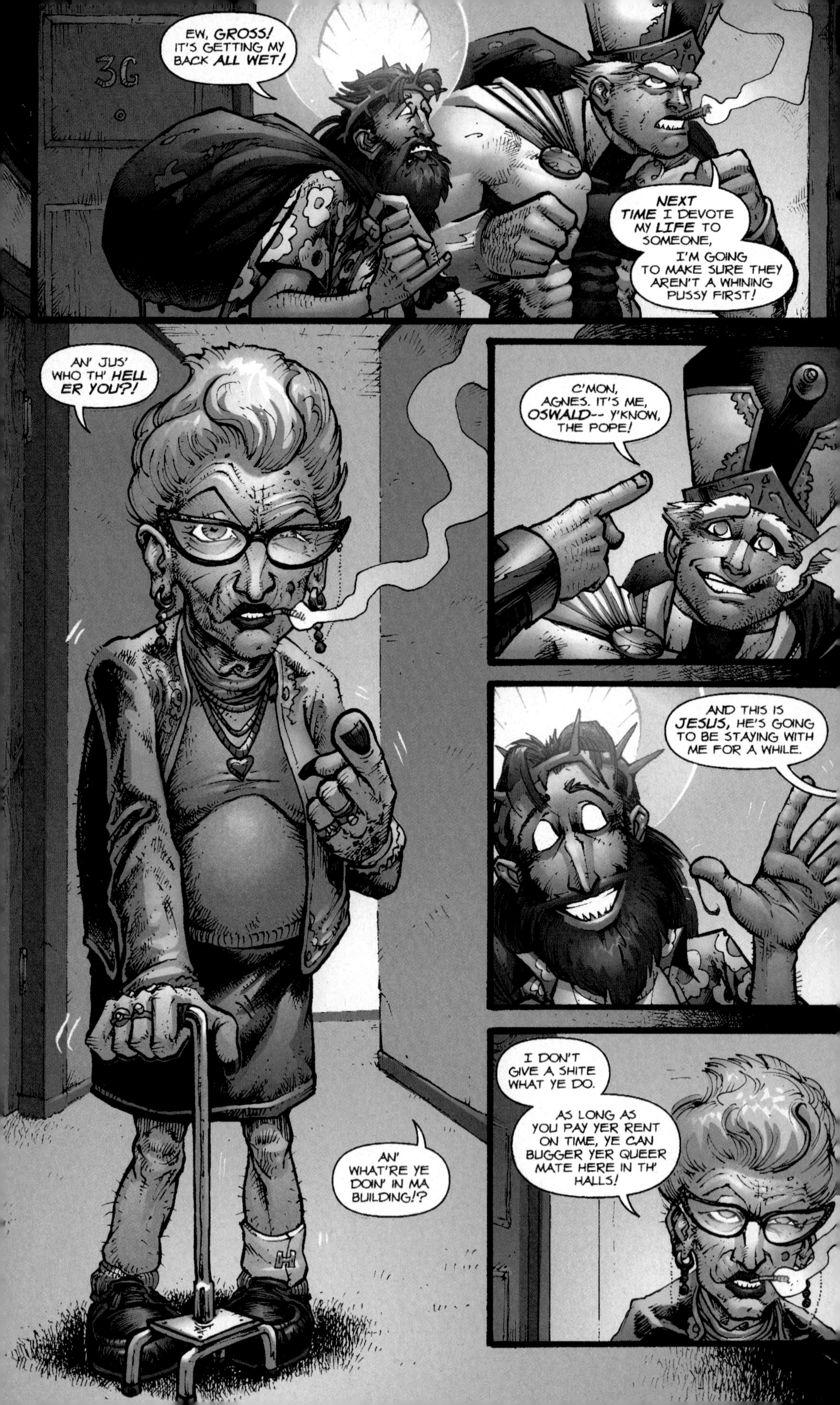

3G
EW, GROSS! IT'S GETTING MY BACK ALL WET!
NEXT TIME I DEVOTE MY LIFE TO SOMEONE, I'M GOING TO MAKE SURE THEY AREN'T A WHINING PUSSY FIRST!
AN' JUS' WHO TH' HELL ER YOU?!
C'MON, AGNES. IT'S ME, OSWALD-- Y'KNOW, THE POPE!
AND THIS IS JESUS, HE'S GOING TO BE STAYING WITH ME FOR A WHILE.
AN' WHAT'RE YE DOIN' IN MA BUILDING!?
I DON'T GIVE A SHITE WHAT YE DO.
AS LONG AS YOU PAY YER RENT ON TIME, YE CAN BUGGER YER QUEER MATE HERE IN TH' HALLS!

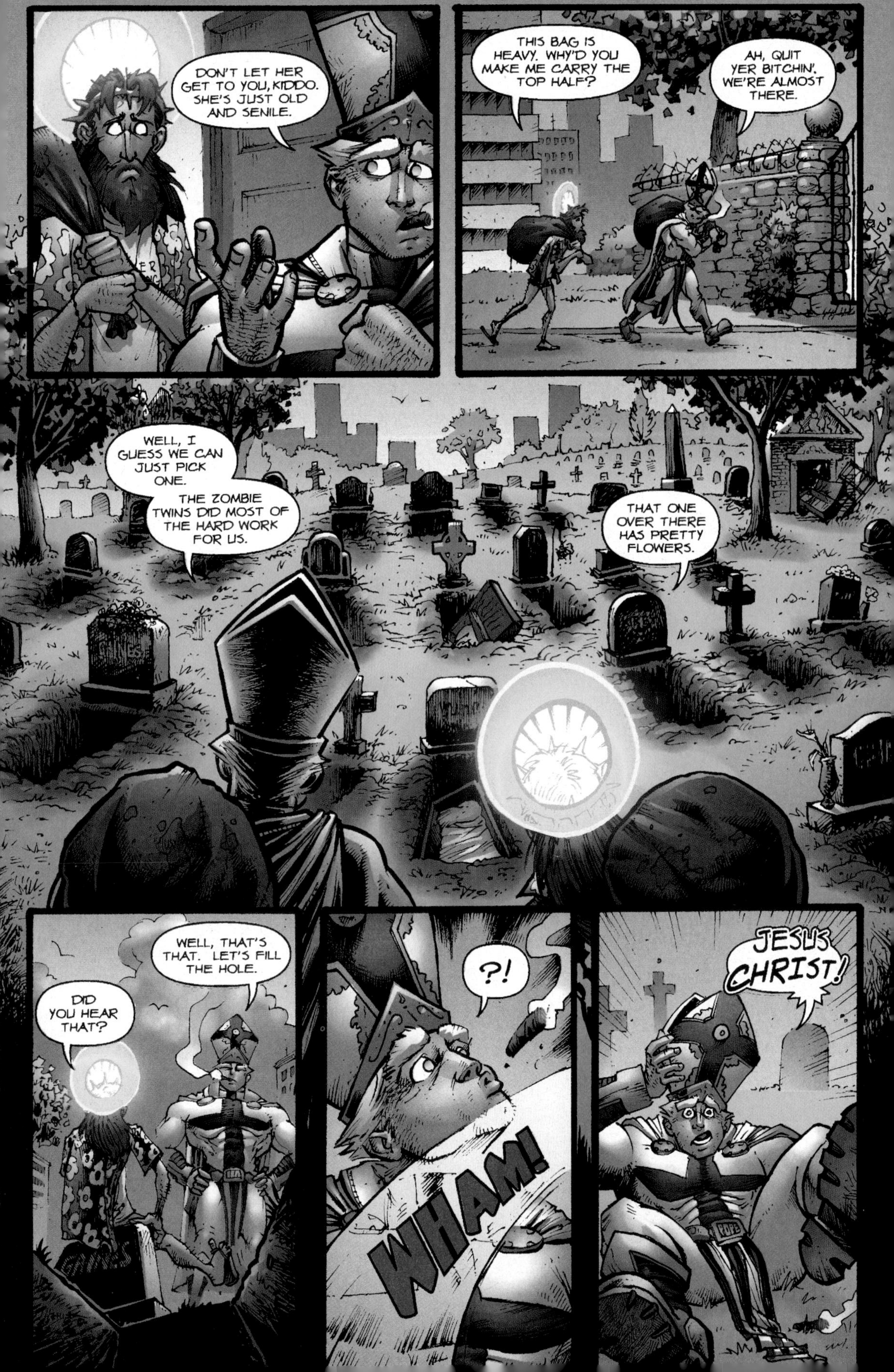
DON'T LET HER GET TO YOU, KIDDO. SHE'S JUST OLD AND SENILE.
THIS BAG IS HEAVY. WHY'D YOU MAKE ME CARRY THE TOP HALF?
AH, QUIT YER BITCHIN'. WE'RE ALMOST THERE.
WELL, I GUESS WE CAN JUST PICK ONE.
THE ZOMBIE TWINS DID MOST OF THE HARD WORK FOR US.
THAT ONE OVER THERE HAS PRETTY FLOWERS.
WELL, THAT'S THAT. LET'S FILL THE HOLE.
DID YOU HEAR THAT?
?!
WHAM!
JESUS CHRIST!

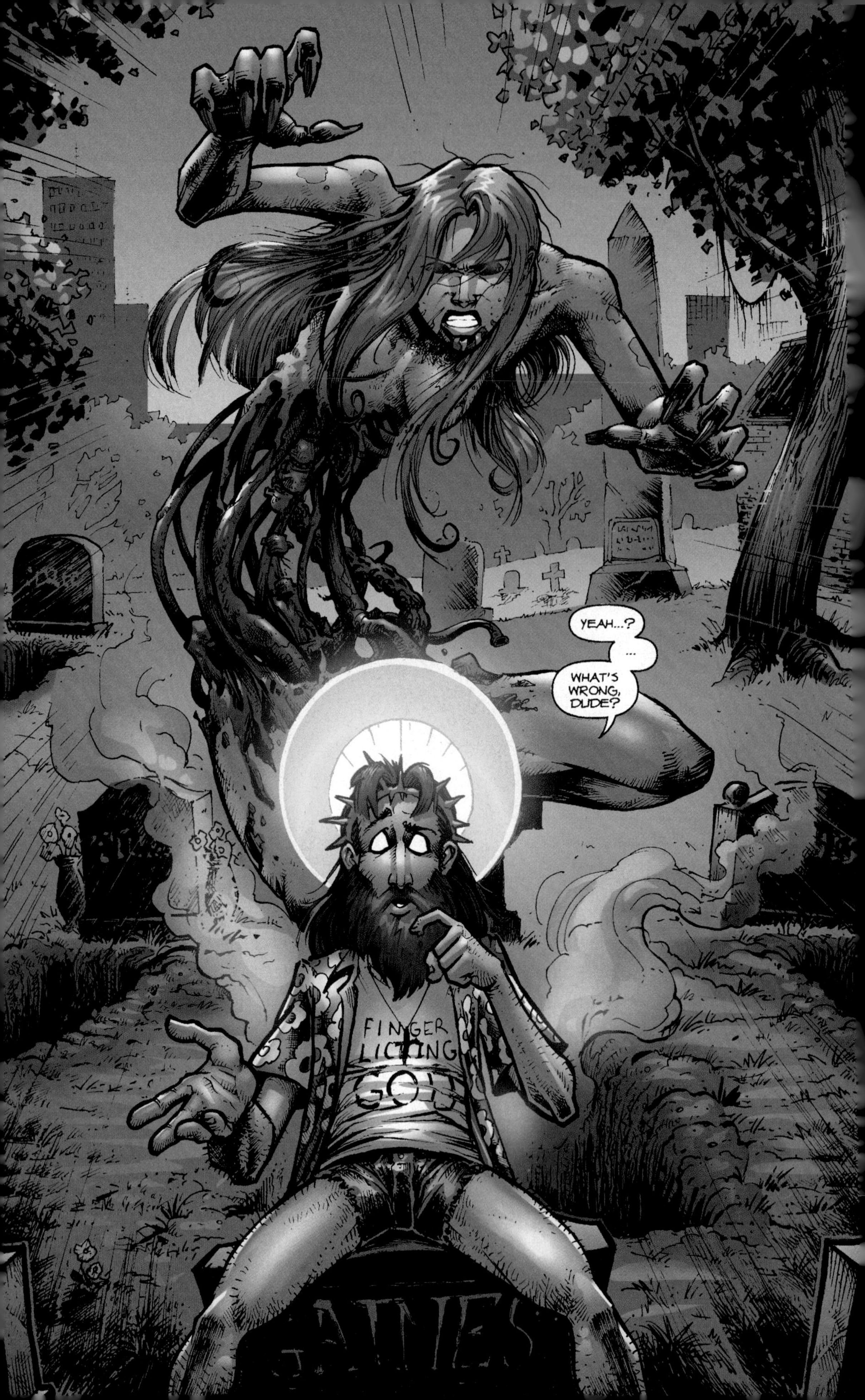
YEAH...?
...
WHAT'S WRONG, DUDE?
FINGER LICKING GOD

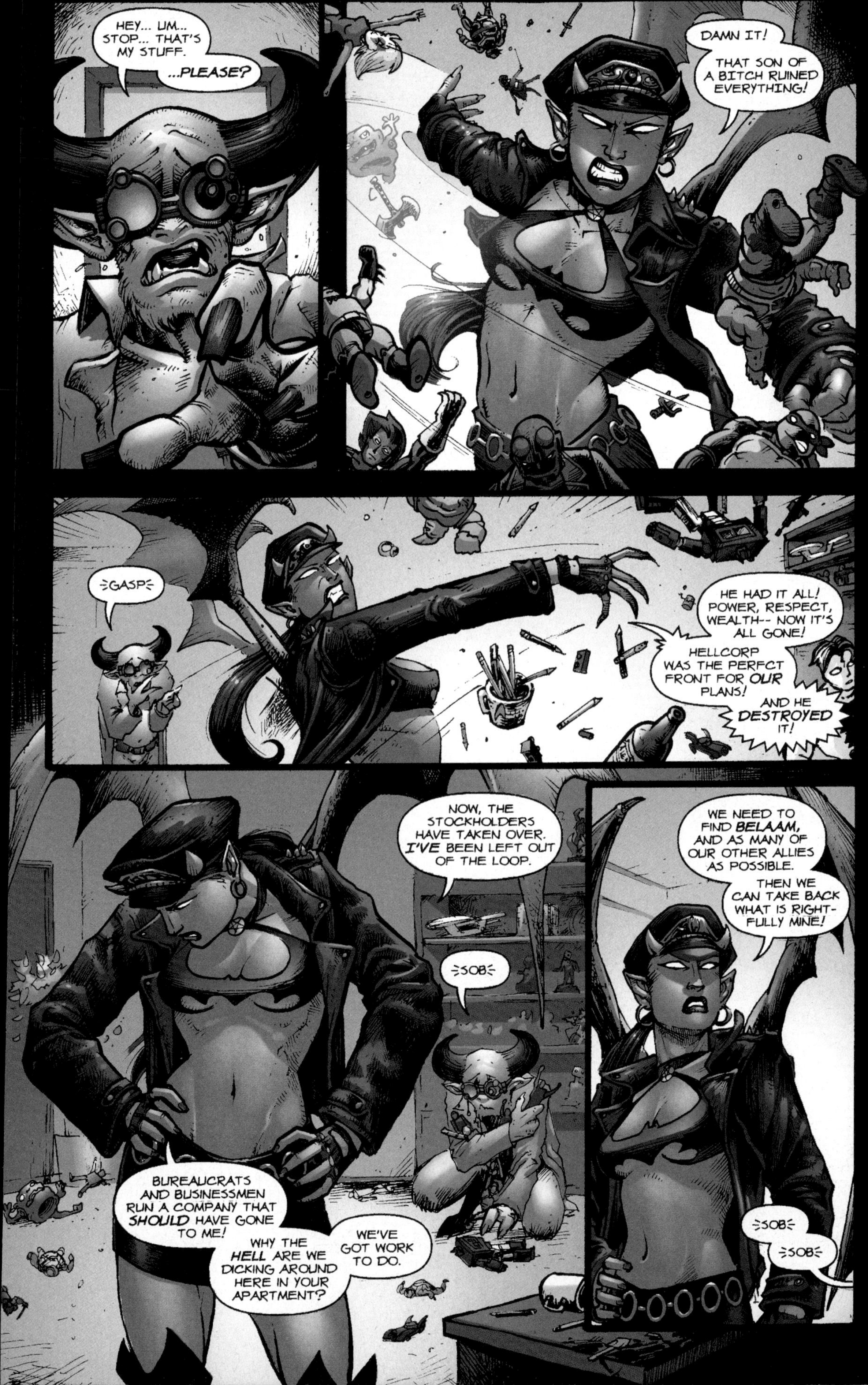
HEY... UM... STOP... THAT'S MY STUFF.
...PLEASE?
DAMN IT!
THAT SON OF A BITCH RUINED EVERYTHING!
GASP
HE HAD IT ALL! POWER, RESPECT, WEALTH-- NOW IT'S ALL GONE!
HELLCORP WAS THE PERFCT FRONT FOR OUR PLANS!
AND HE DESTROYED IT!
NOW, THE STOCKHOLDERS HAVE TAKEN OVER. I'VE BEEN LEFT OUT OF THE LOOP.
SOB
BUREAUCRATS AND BUSINESSMEN RUN A COMPANY THAT SHOULD HAVE GONE TO ME!
WHY THE HELL ARE WE DICKING AROUND HERE IN YOUR APARTMENT?
WE'VE GOT WORK TO DO.
WE NEED TO FIND BELAAM, AND AS MANY OF OUR OTHER ALLIES AS POSSIBLE.
THEN WE CAN TAKE BACK WHAT IS RIGHT-FULLY MINE!
SOB
SOB

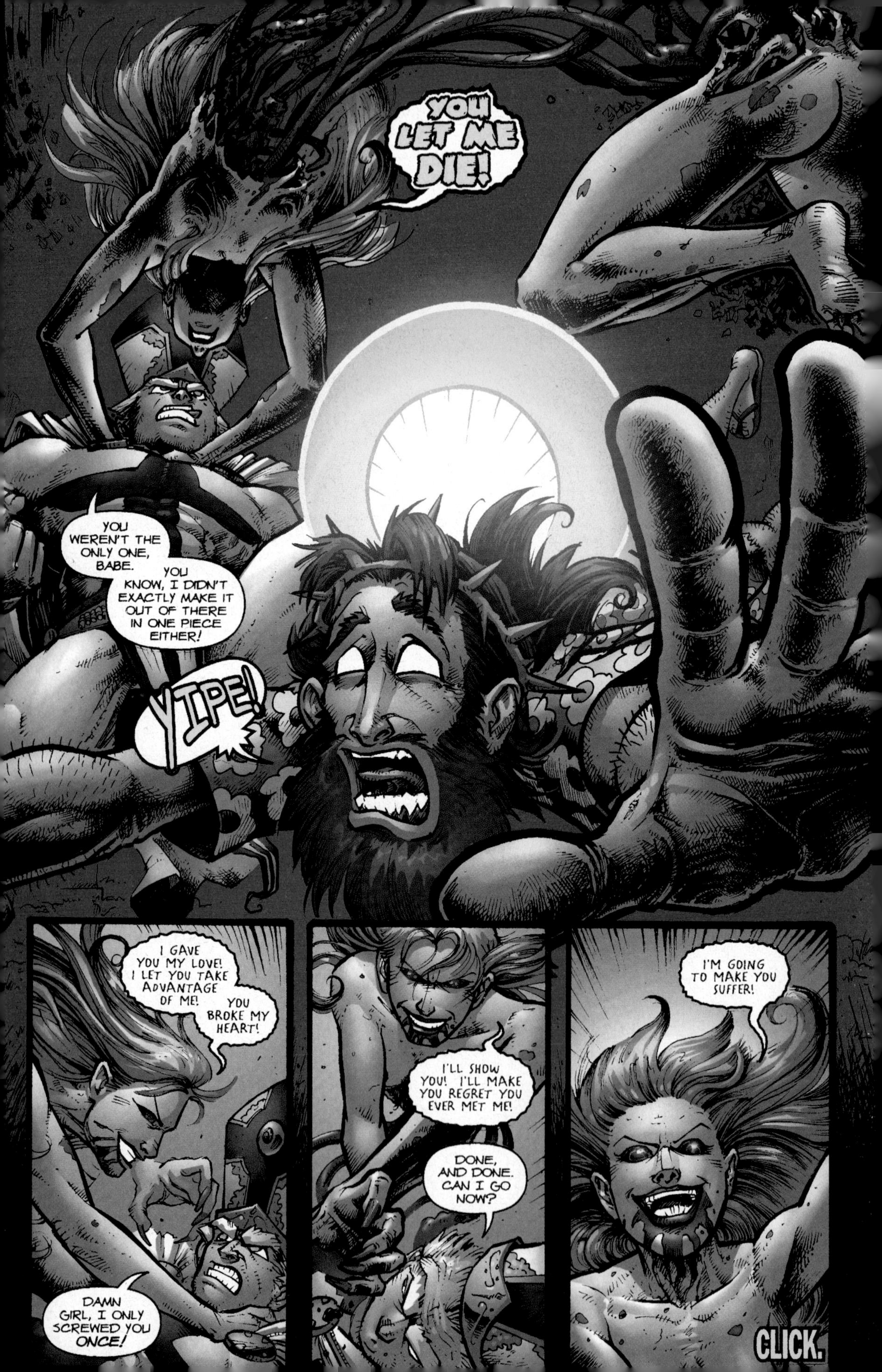
YOU LET ME DIE!
YOU WEREN'T THE ONLY ONE, BABE.
YOU KNOW, I DIDN'T EXACTLY MAKE IT OUT OF THERE IN ONE PIECE EITHER!
YIPE!
I GAVE YOU MY LOVE! I LET YOU TAKE ADVANTAGE OF ME!
YOU BROKE MY HEART!
DAMN GIRL, I ONLY SCREWED YOU ONCE!
I'LL SHOW YOU! I'LL MAKE YOU REGRET YOU EVER MET ME!
DONE, AND DONE. CAN I GO NOW?
I'M GOING TO MAKE YOU SUFFER!
CLICK.

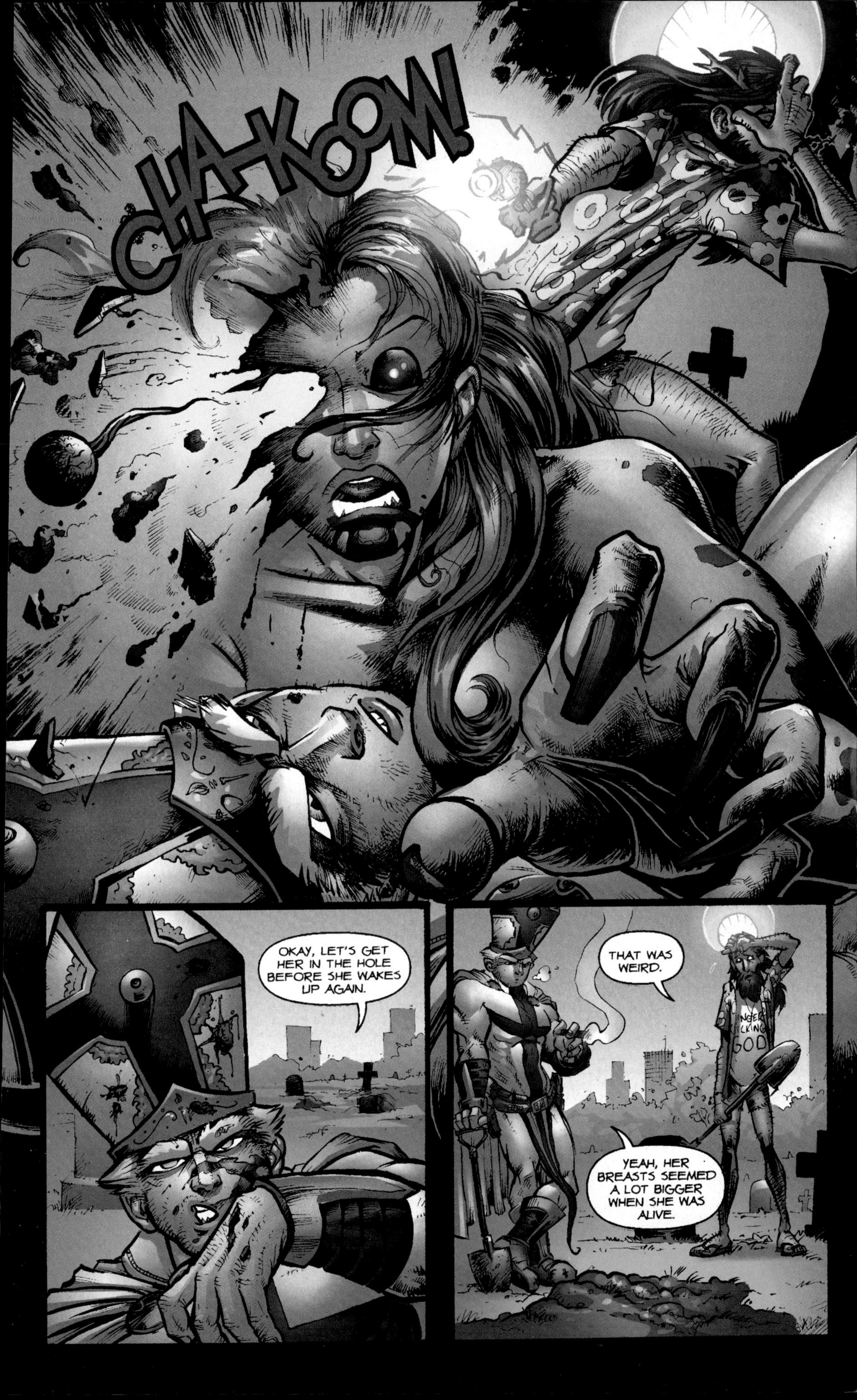
CHA-KOOM!
OKAY, LET'S GET HER IN THE HOLE BEFORE SHE WAKES UP AGAIN.
THAT WAS WEIRD.
YEAH, HER BREASTS SEEMED A LOT BIGGER WHEN SHE WAS ALIVE.

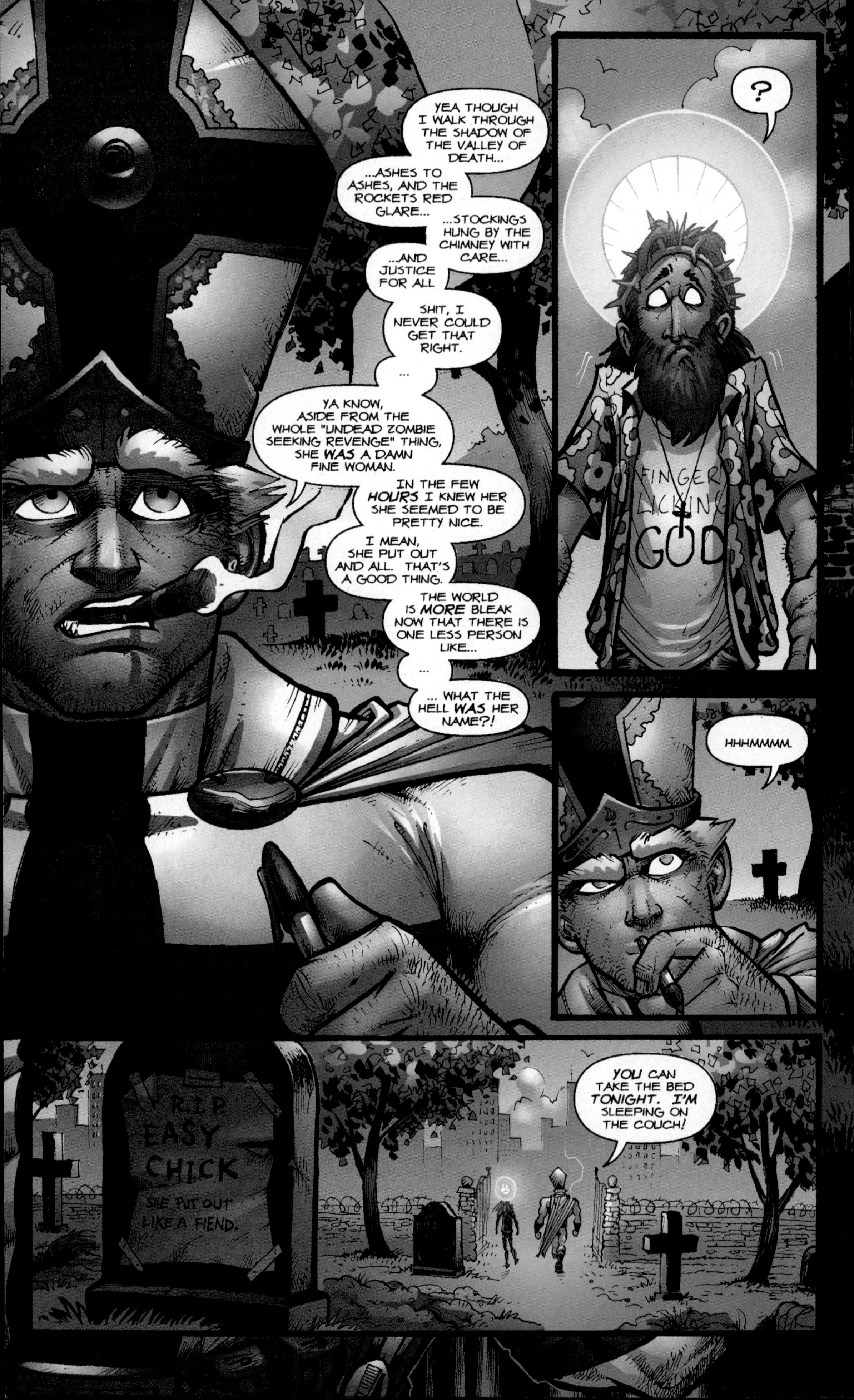
YEA THOUGH I WALK THROUGH THE SHADOW OF THE VALLEY OF DEATH...
...ASHES TO ASHES, AND THE ROCKETS RED GLARE...
...STOCKINGS HUNG BY THE CHIMNEY WITH CARE...
...AND JUSTICE FOR ALL
SHIT, I NEVER COULD GET THAT RIGHT.
...
YA KNOW, ASIDE FROM THE WHOLE "UNDEAD ZOMBIE SEEKING REVENGE" THING, SHE *WAS* A DAMN FINE WOMAN.
IN THE FEW *HOURS* I KNEW HER SHE SEEMED TO BE PRETTY NICE.
I MEAN, SHE PUT OUT AND ALL. THAT'S A GOOD THING.
THE WORLD IS *MORE* BLEAK NOW THAT THERE IS ONE LESS PERSON LIKE...
...
... WHAT THE HELL *WAS* HER NAME?!
?
FINGER LICKING GOD
HHHMMMM.
R.I.P. EASY CHICK
SHE PUT OUT LIKE A FIEND.
YOU CAN TAKE THE BED *TONIGHT. I'M* SLEEPING ON THE COUCH!

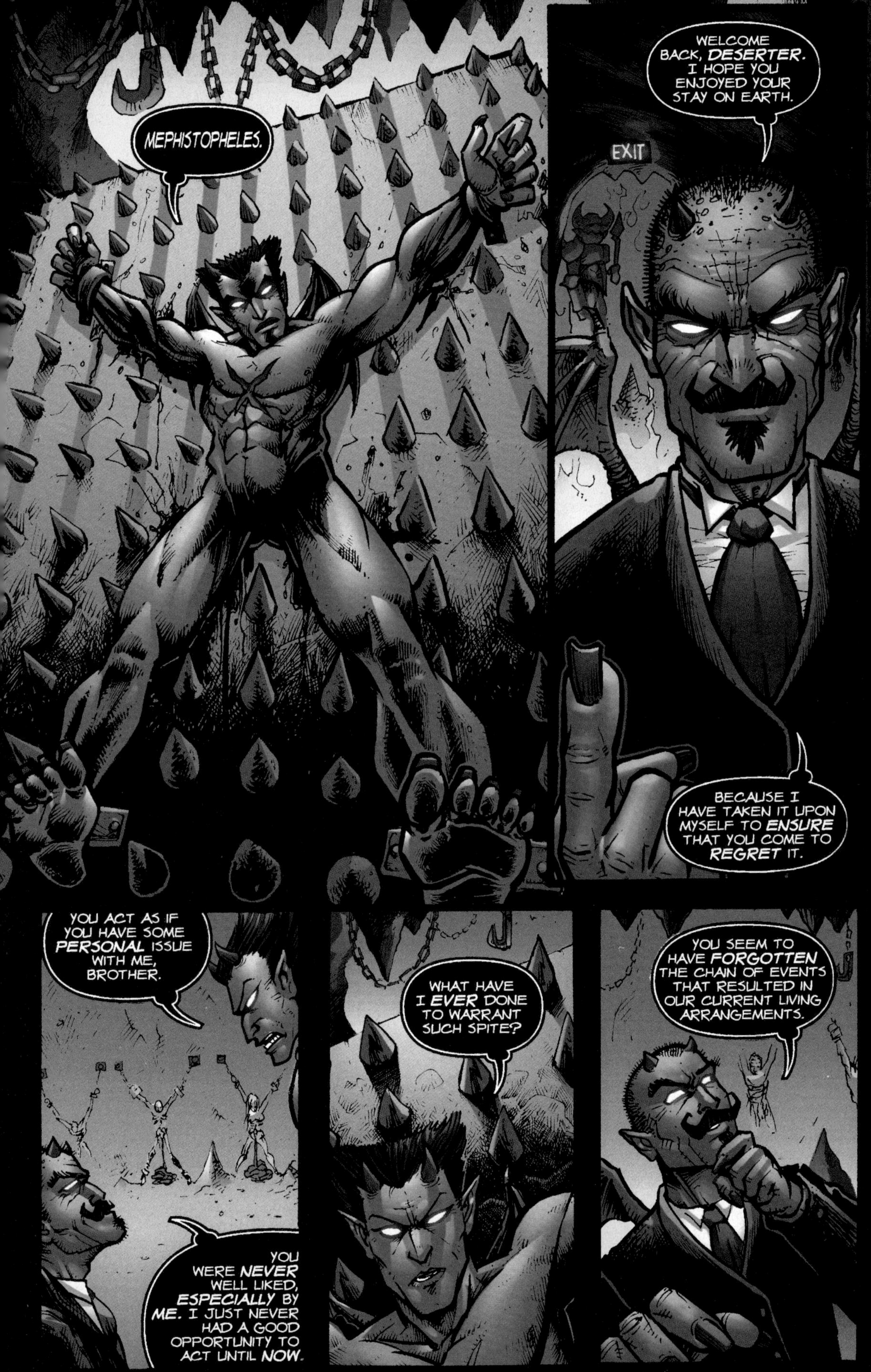
MEPHISTOPHELES.
WELCOME BACK, DESERTER. I HOPE YOU ENJOYED YOUR STAY ON EARTH.
EXIT
BECAUSE I HAVE TAKEN IT UPON MYSELF TO ENSURE THAT YOU COME TO REGRET IT.
YOU ACT AS IF YOU HAVE SOME PERSONAL ISSUE WITH ME, BROTHER.
YOU WERE NEVER WELL LIKED, ESPECIALLY BY ME. I JUST NEVER HAD A GOOD OPPORTUNITY TO ACT UNTIL NOW.
WHAT HAVE I EVER DONE TO WARRANT SUCH SPITE?
YOU SEEM TO HAVE FORGOTTEN THE CHAIN OF EVENTS THAT RESULTED IN OUR CURRENT LIVING ARRANGEMENTS.

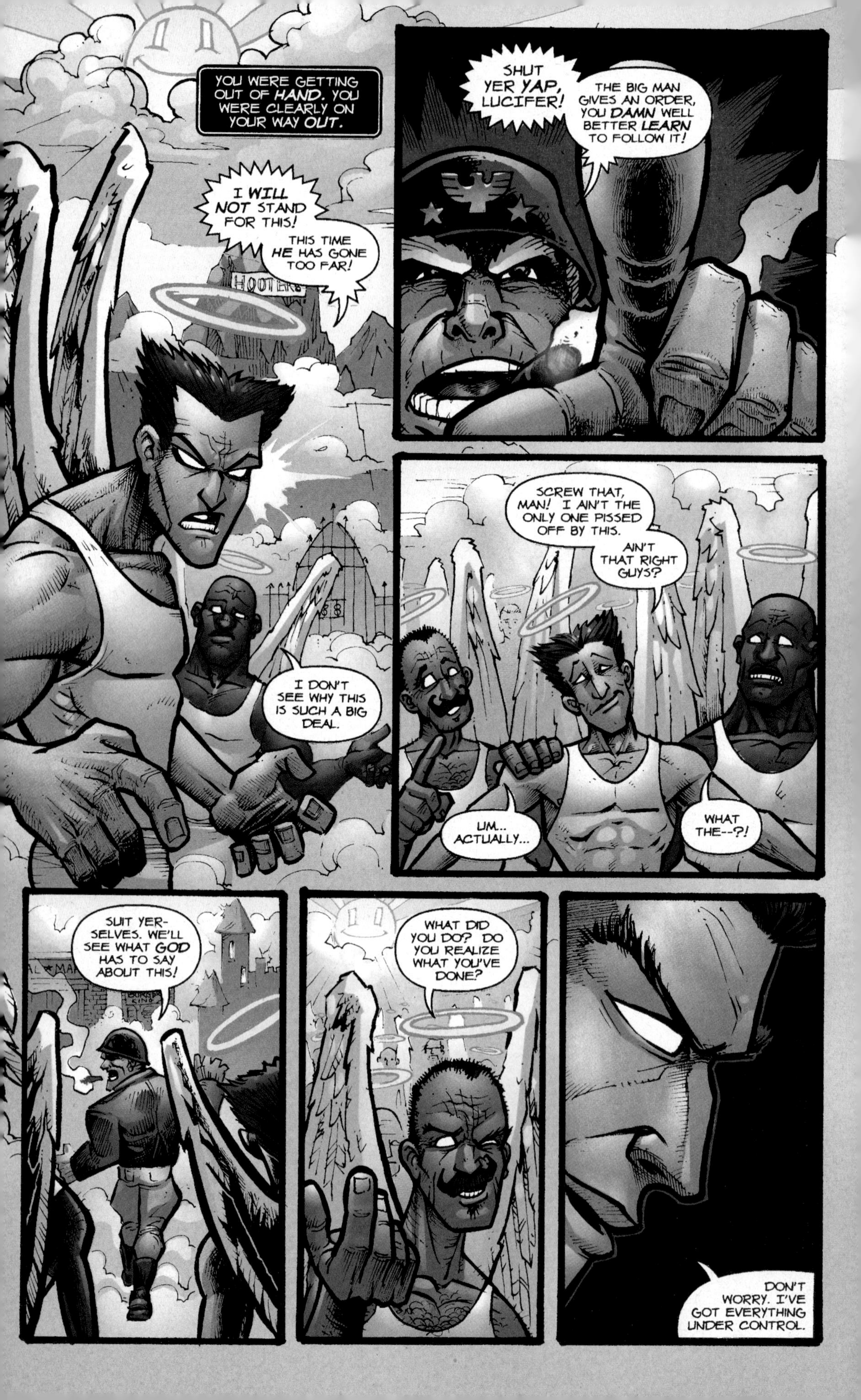
YOU WERE GETTING OUT OF HAND. YOU WERE CLEARLY ON YOUR WAY OUT.
SHUT YER YAP, LUCIFER!
THE BIG MAN GIVES AN ORDER, YOU DAMN WELL BETTER LEARN TO FOLLOW IT!
I WILL NOT STAND FOR THIS!
THIS TIME HE HAS GONE TOO FAR!
HOOTERS
I DON'T SEE WHY THIS IS SUCH A BIG DEAL.
SCREW THAT, MAN! I AIN'T THE ONLY ONE PISSED OFF BY THIS.
AIN'T THAT RIGHT GUYS?
UM.. ACTUALLY...
WHAT THE--?!
SUIT YER-SELVES. WE'LL SEE WHAT GOD HAS TO SAY ABOUT THIS!
WHAT DID YOU DO? DO YOU REALIZE WHAT YOU'VE DONE?
DON'T WORRY. I'VE GOT EVERYTHING UNDER CONTROL.

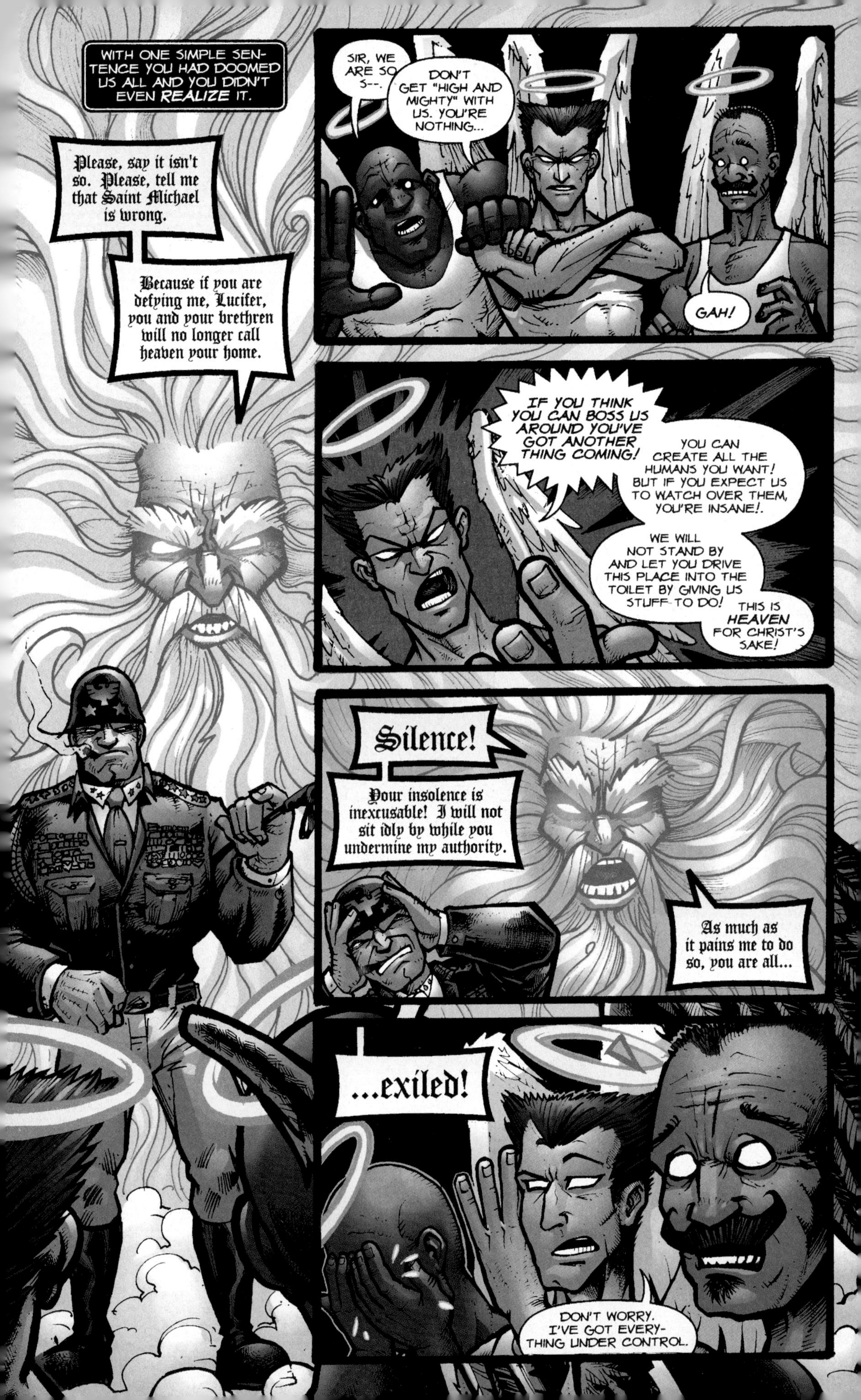

WITH ONE SIMPLE SENTENCE YOU HAD DOOMED US ALL AND YOU DIDN'T EVEN *REALIZE* IT.
Please, say it isn't so. Please, tell me that Saint Michael is wrong.
Because if you are defying me, Lucifer, you and your brethren will no longer call heaven your home.
SIR, WE ARE SO S--.
DON'T GET "HIGH AND MIGHTY" WITH US. YOU'RE NOTHING...
GAH!
IF YOU THINK YOU CAN BOSS US AROUND YOU'VE GOT ANOTHER THING COMING!
YOU CAN CREATE ALL THE HUMANS YOU WANT! BUT IF YOU EXPECT US TO WATCH OVER THEM, YOU'RE INSANE!.
WE WILL NOT STAND BY AND LET YOU DRIVE THIS PLACE INTO THE TOILET BY GIVING US STUFF TO DO!
THIS IS *HEAVEN* FOR CHRIST'S SAKE!
Silence!
Your insolence is inexcusable! I will not sit idly by while you undermine my authority.
As much as it pains me to do so, you are all...
...exiled!
DON'T WORRY. I'VE GOT EVERYTHING UNDER CONTROL.

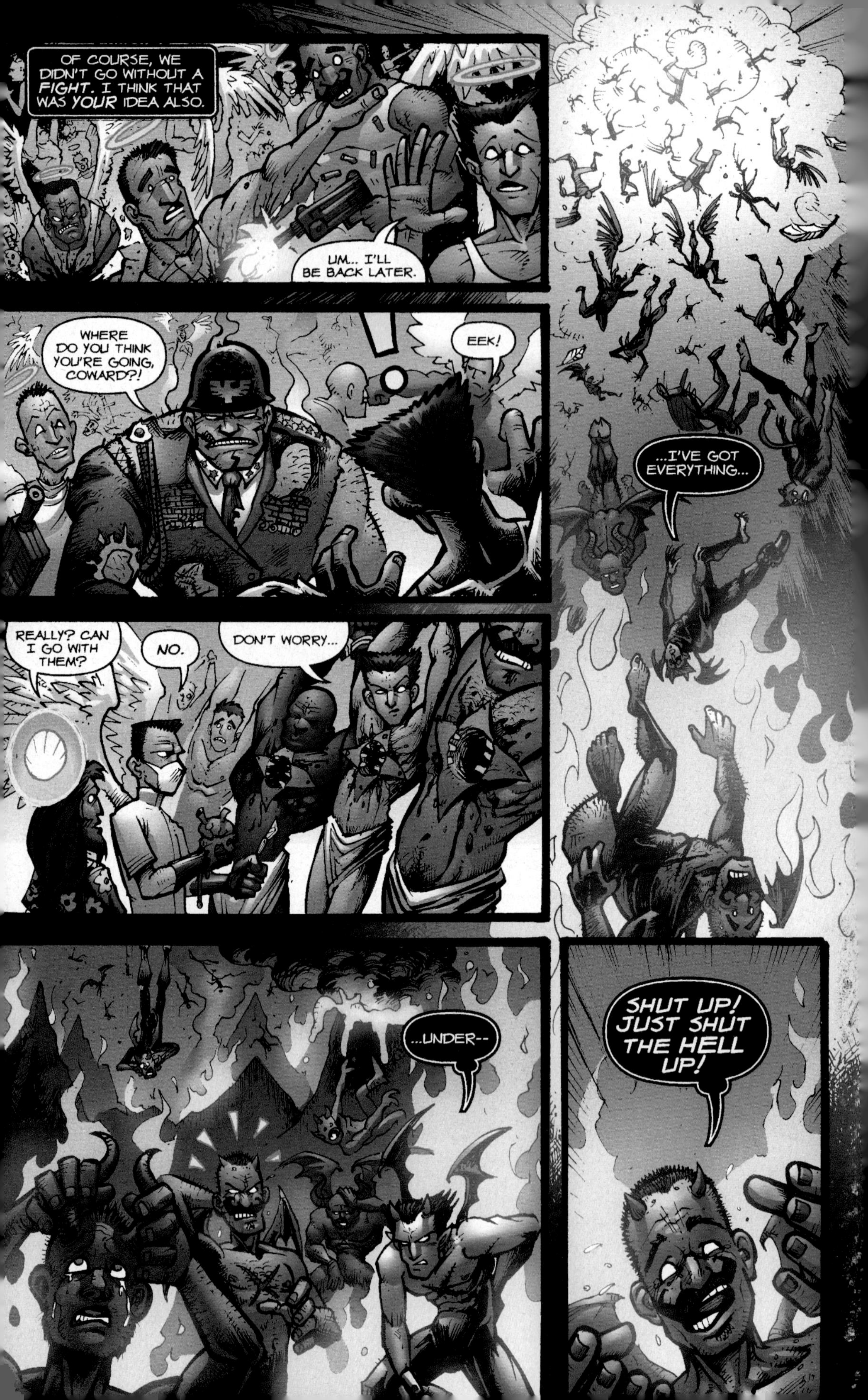
OF COURSE, WE DIDN'T GO WITHOUT A FIGHT. I THINK THAT WAS YOUR IDEA ALSO.
UM.. I'LL BE BACK LATER.
WHERE DO YOU THINK YOU'RE GOING, COWARD?!
EEK!
REALLY? CAN I GO WITH THEM?
NO.
DON'T WORRY...
...I'VE GOT EVERYTHING...
...UNDER--
SHUT UP! JUST SHUT THE HELL UP!

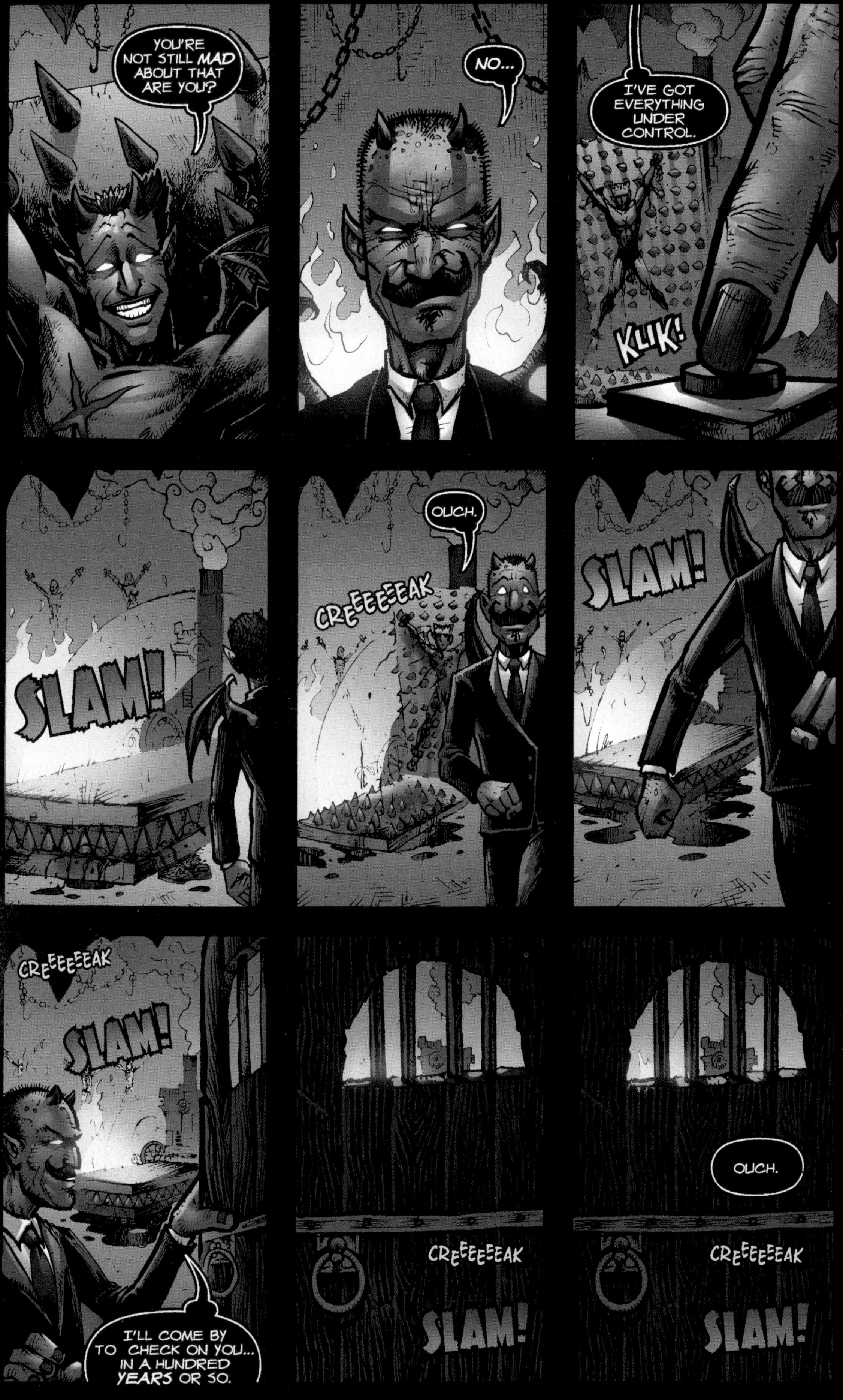
YOU'RE NOT STILL MAD ABOUT THAT ARE YOU?
NO...
I'VE GOT EVERYTHING UNDER CONTROL.
KLIK!
SLAM!
OUCH.
CREEEEEEAK
SLAM!
CREEEEEEAK
SLAM!
I'LL COME BY TO CHECK ON YOU... IN A HUNDRED YEARS OR SO.
CREEEEEEAK
SLAM!
OUCH.
CREEEEEEAK
SLAM!

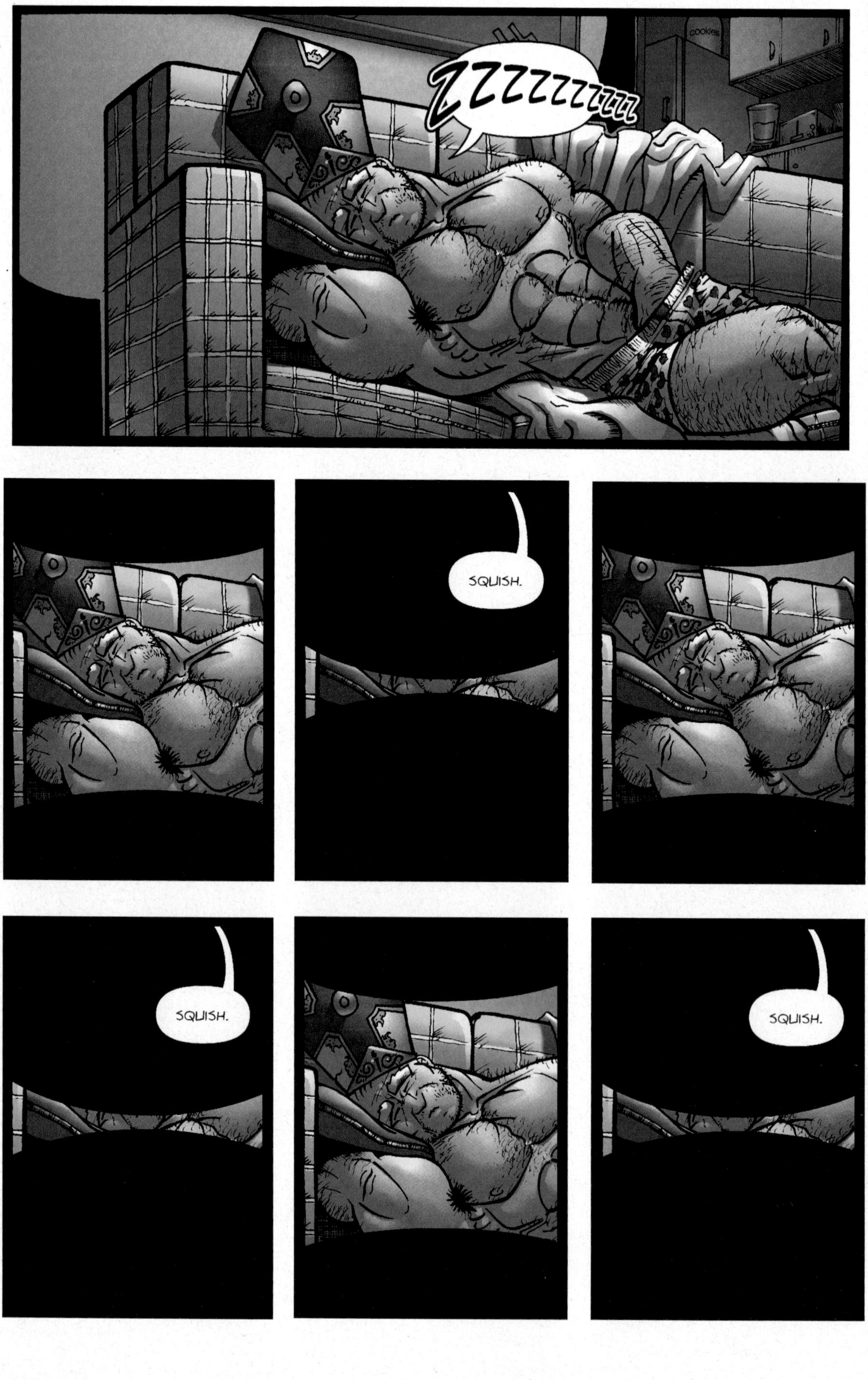
cookies
ZZZZZZZZZZZ
SQUISH.
SQUISH.
SQUISH.

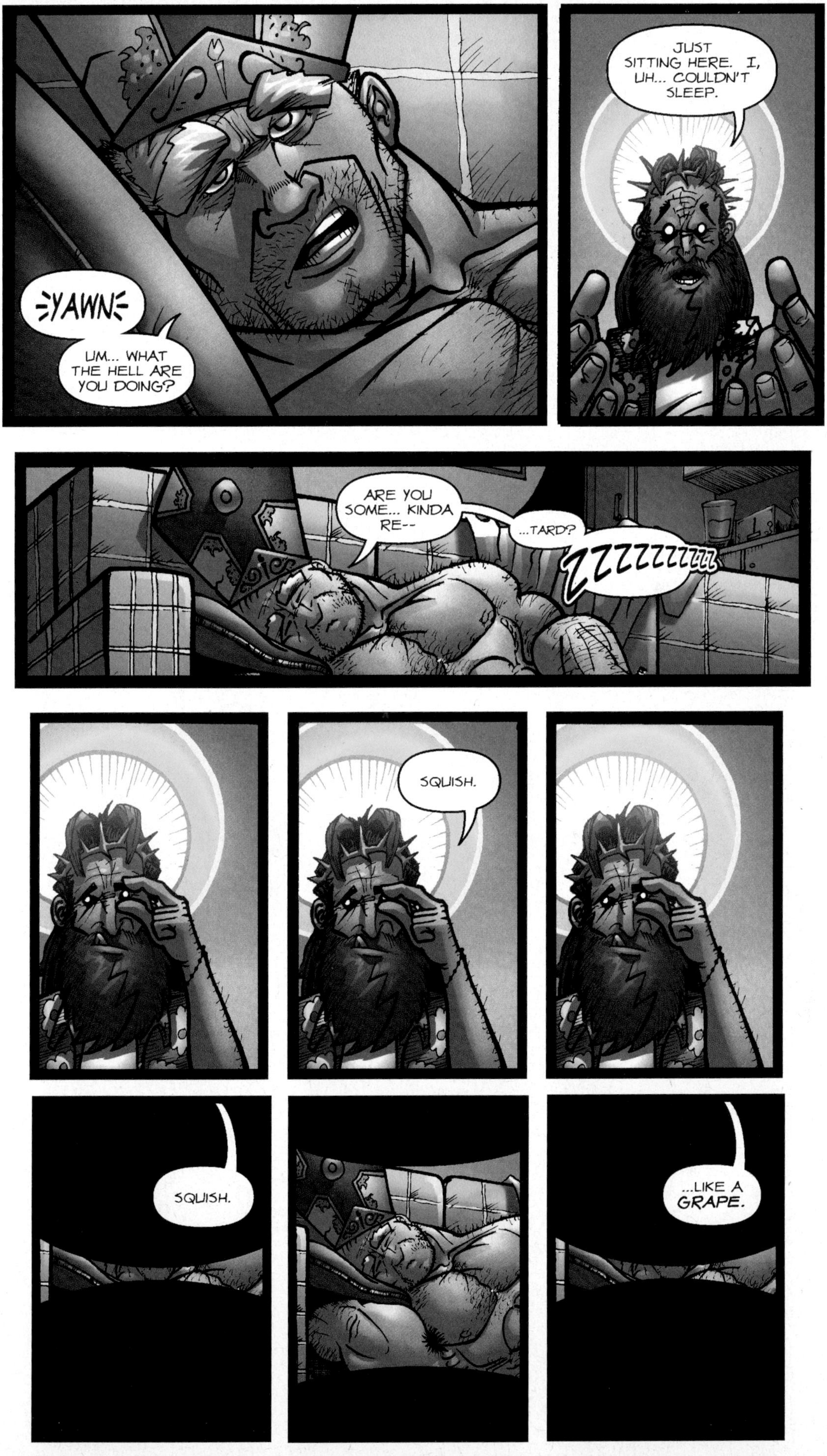
YAWN
UM... WHAT THE HELL ARE YOU DOING?
JUST SITTING HERE. I, UH... COULDN'T SLEEP.
ARE YOU SOME... KINDA RE--
...TARD?
ZZZZZZZZZZ
SQUISH.
SQUISH.
...LIKE A GRAPE.

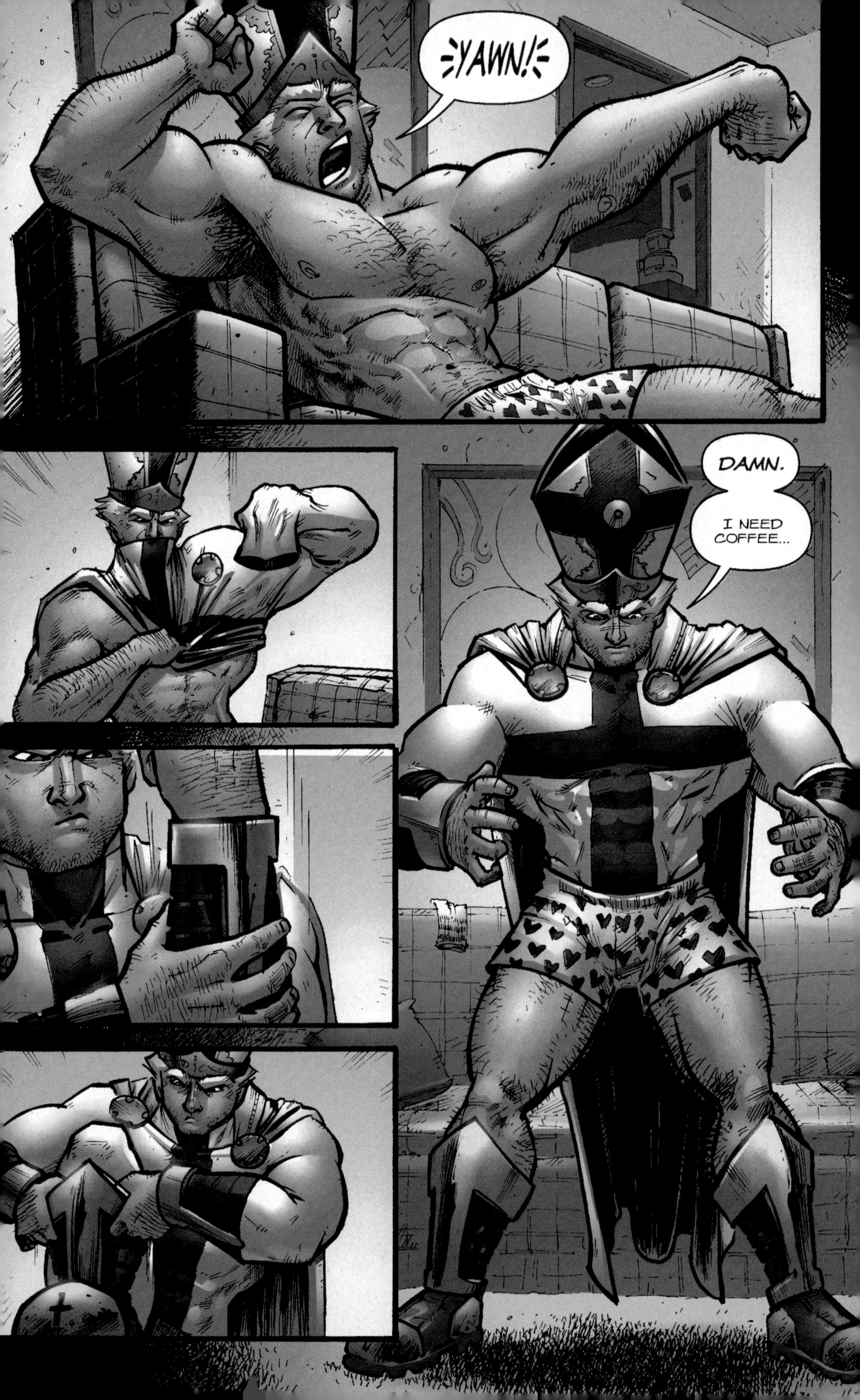
YAWN!
DAMN.
I NEED COFFEE...

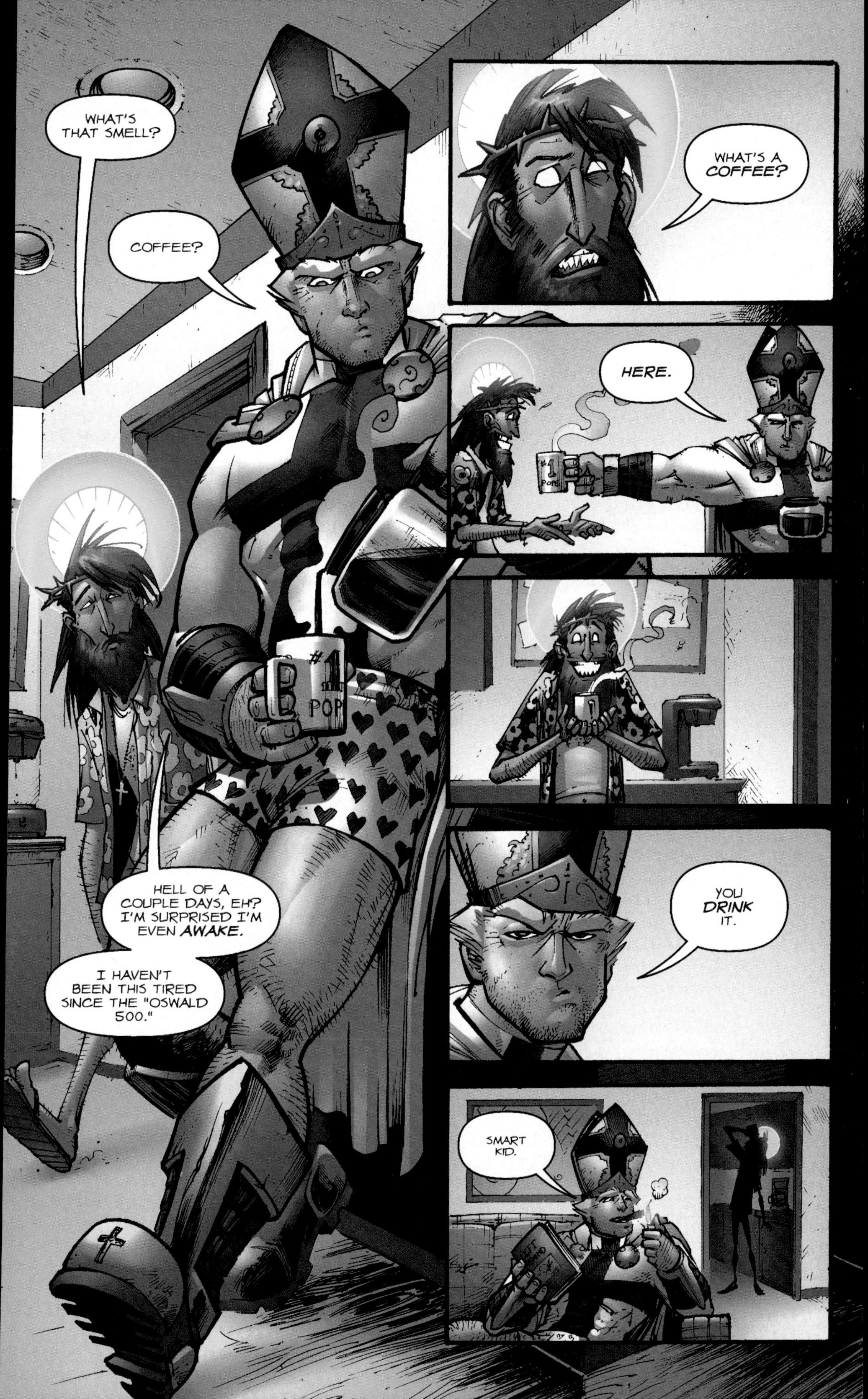
WHAT'S THAT SMELL?
COFFEE?
WHAT'S A COFFEE?
HERE.
HELL OF A COUPLE DAYS, EH? I'M SURPRISED I'M EVEN AWAKE.
I HAVEN'T BEEN THIS TIRED SINCE THE "OSWALD 500."
YOU DRINK IT.
SMART KID.

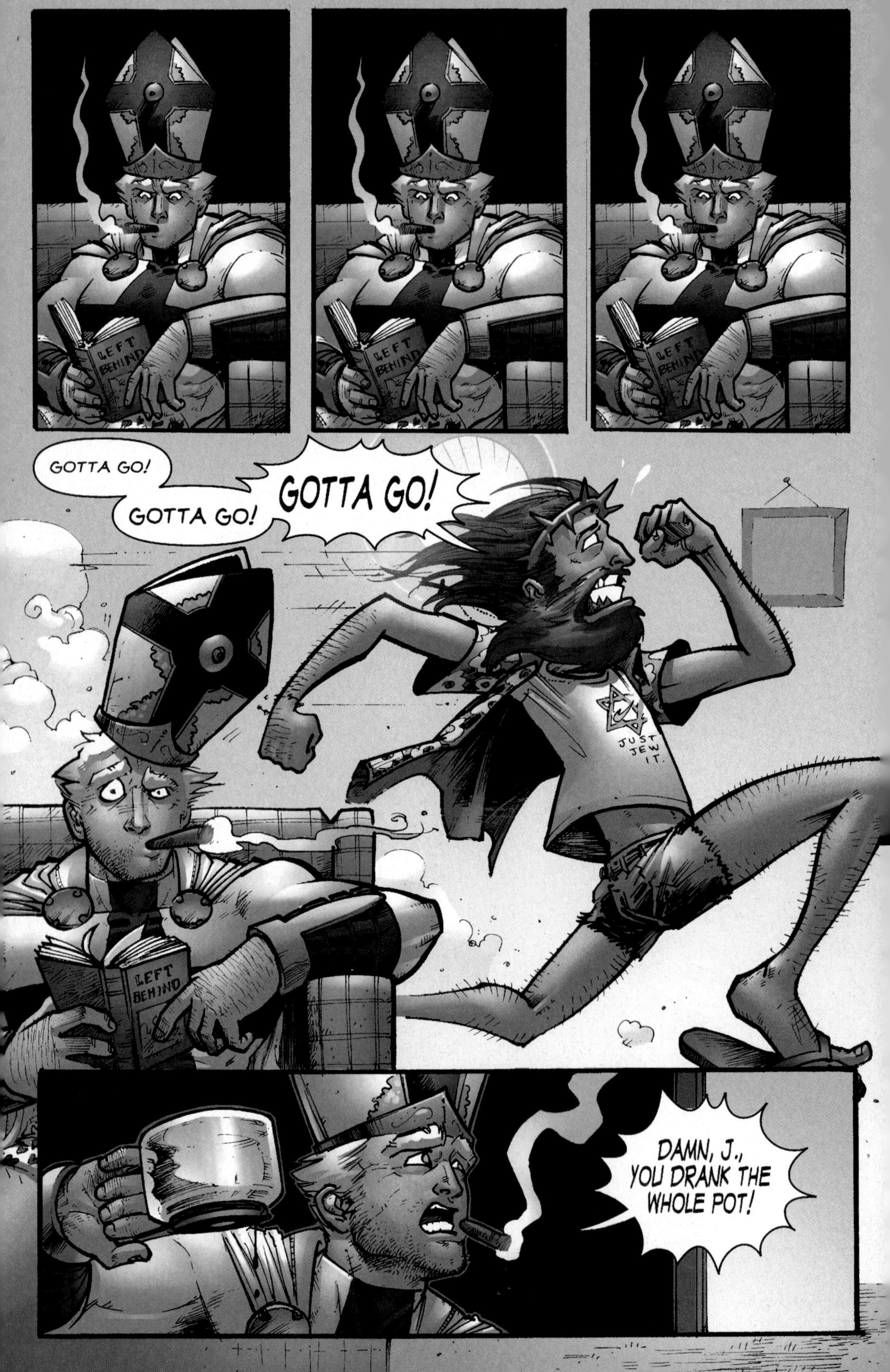
LEFT BEHIND
LEFT BEHIND
LEFT BEHIND
GOTTA GO!
GOTTA GO!
GOTTA GO!
JUST JEW IT.
LEFT BEHIND
DAMN, J., YOU DRANK THE WHOLE POT!

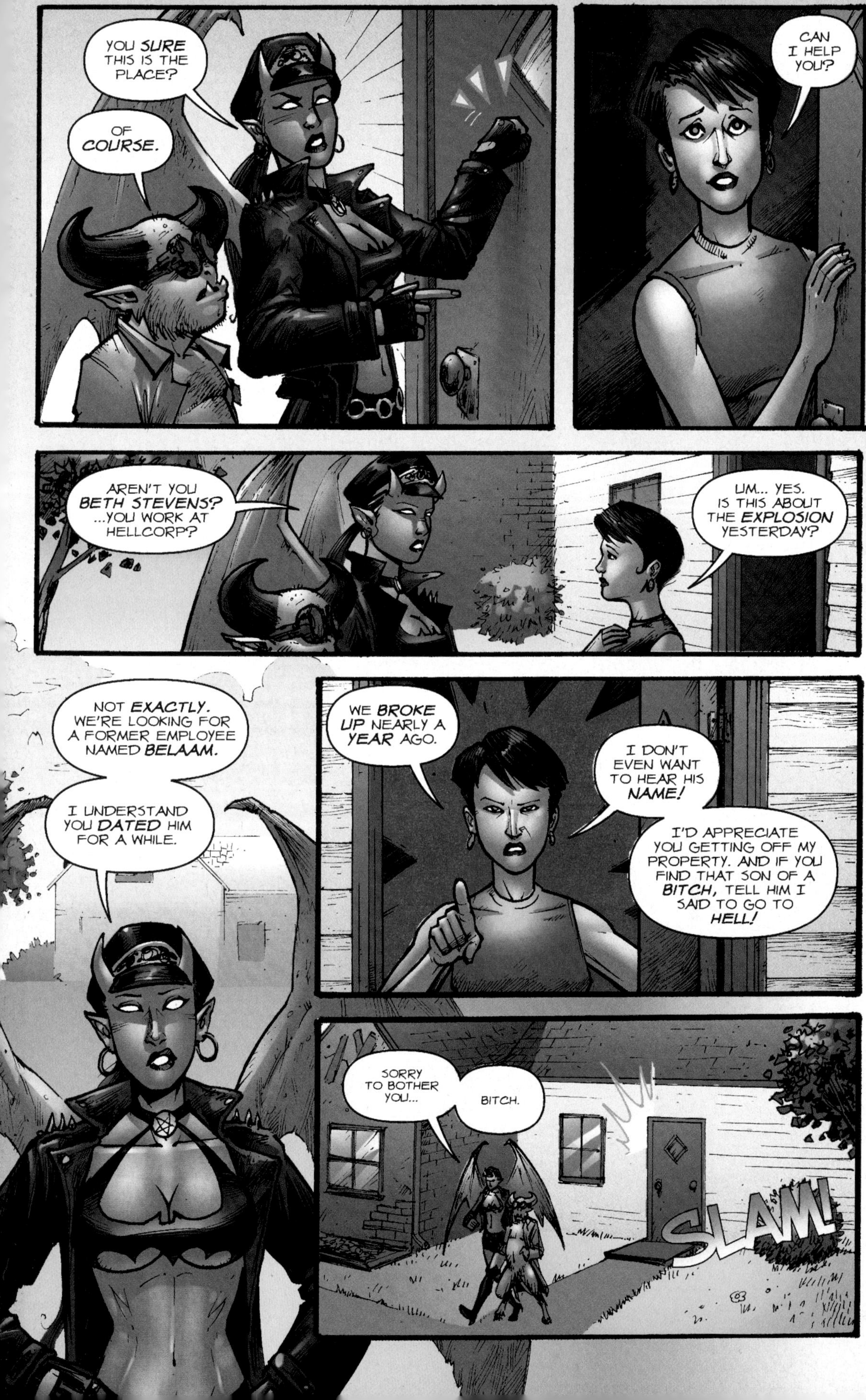

YOU SURE THIS IS THE PLACE?
OF COURSE.
CAN I HELP YOU?
AREN'T YOU BETH STEVENS? ...YOU WORK AT HELLCORP?
UM... YES. IS THIS ABOUT THE EXPLOSION YESTERDAY?
NOT EXACTLY. WE'RE LOOKING FOR A FORMER EMPLOYEE NAMED BELAAM.
I UNDERSTAND YOU DATED HIM FOR A WHILE.
WE BROKE UP NEARLY A YEAR AGO.
I DON'T EVEN WANT TO HEAR HIS NAME!
I'D APPRECIATE YOU GETTING OFF MY PROPERTY. AND IF YOU FIND THAT SON OF A BITCH, TELL HIM I SAID TO GO TO HELL!
SORRY TO BOTHER YOU...
BITCH.
SLAM!

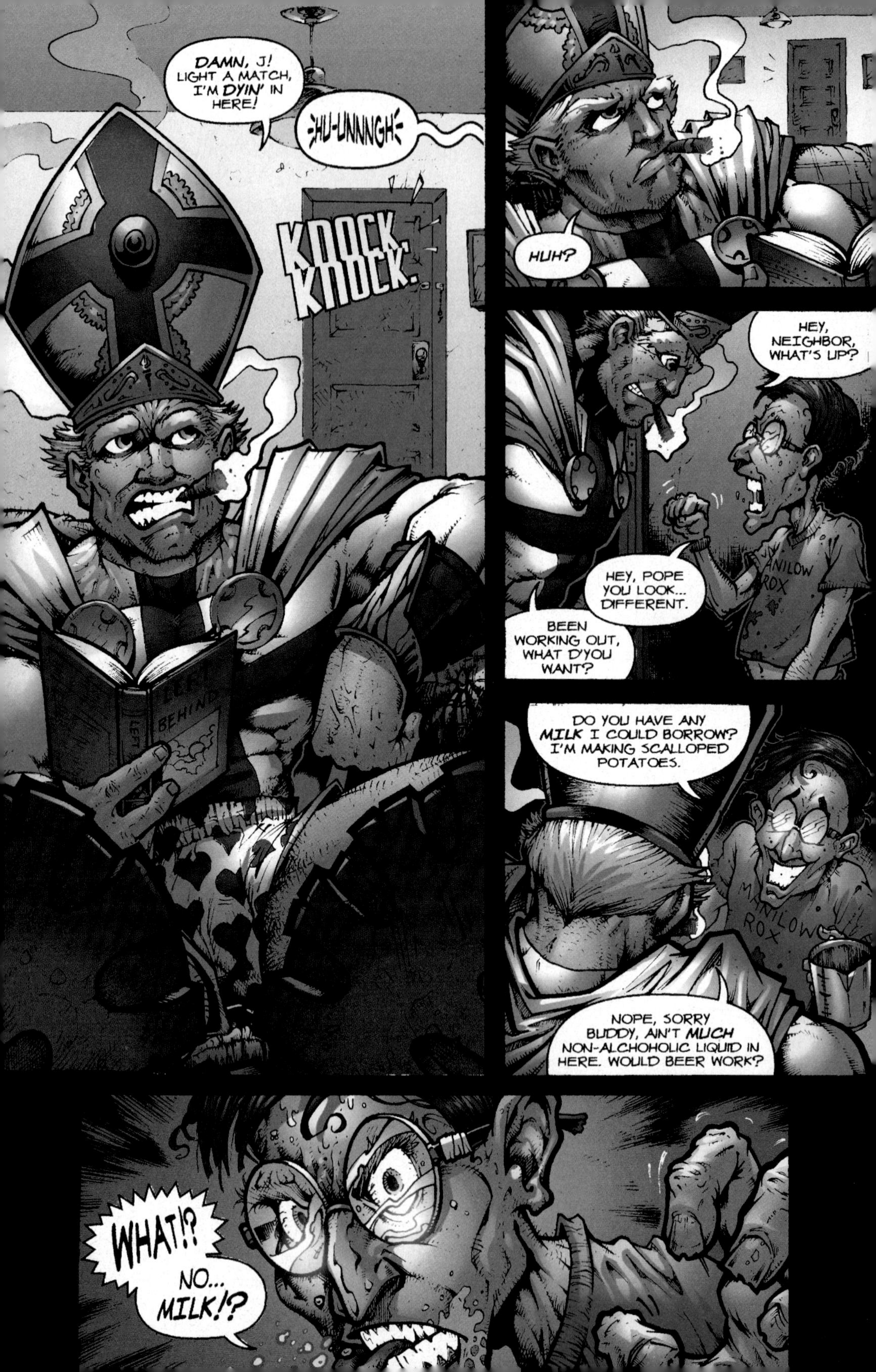
DAMN, J! LIGHT A MATCH, I'M DYIN' IN HERE!
HU-UNNNGH
KNOCK. KNOCK.
HUH?
HEY, NEIGHBOR, WHAT'S UP?
HEY, POPE YOU LOOK... DIFFERENT.
BEEN WORKING OUT, WHAT D'YOU WANT?
MANILOW ROX
DO YOU HAVE ANY MILK I COULD BORROW? I'M MAKING SCALLOPED POTATOES.
NOPE, SORRY BUDDY, AIN'T MUCH NON-ALCHOHOLIC LIQUID IN HERE. WOULD BEER WORK?
WHAT!?
NO... MILK!?

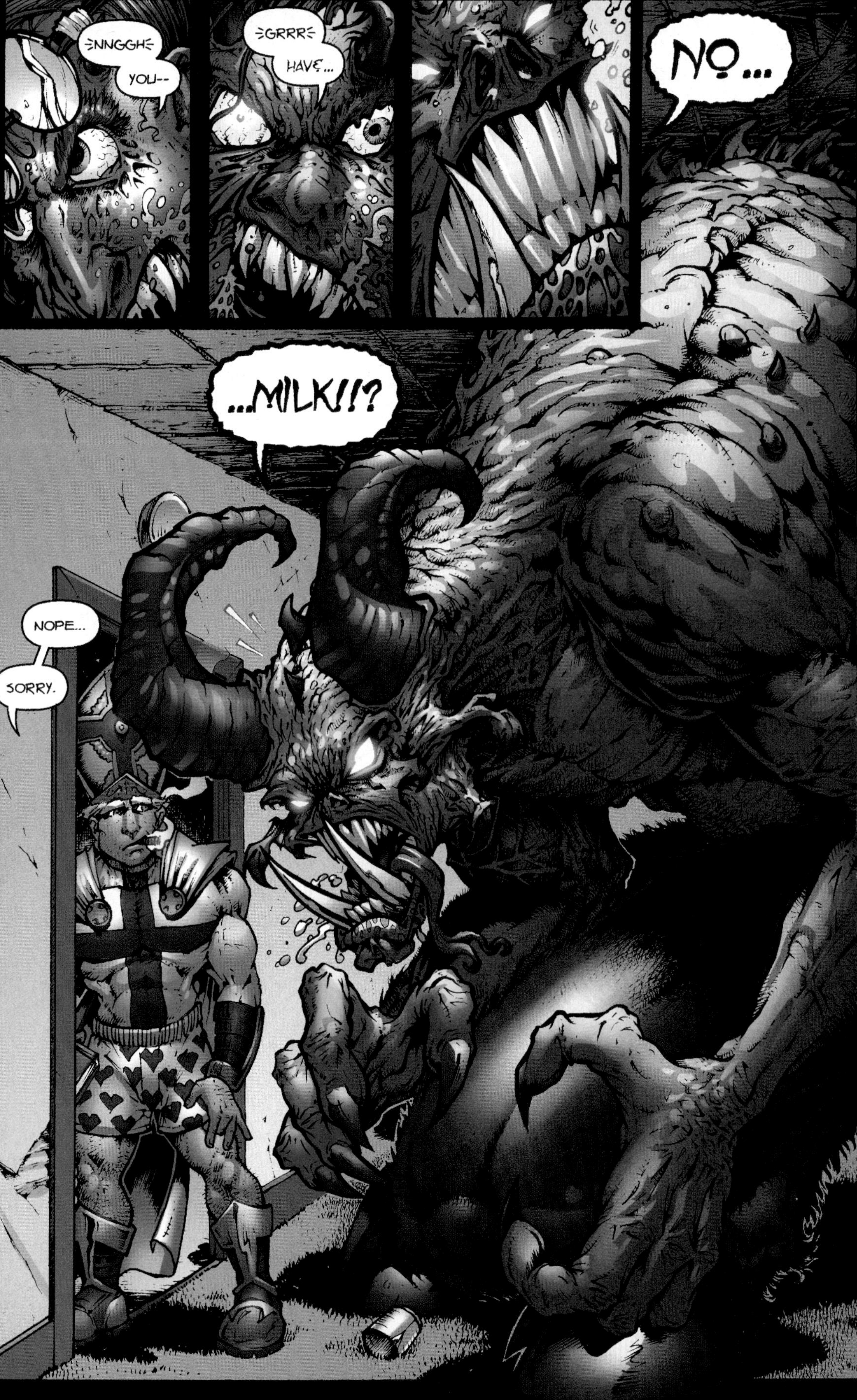

NNGGH
YOU--
GRRR
HAVE...
NO...
...MILK!!?
NOPE...
SORRY.

WE'RE ALL OUT.

OH. OKAY. I GUESS I'LL GO ASK TINA.

HEH, *THAT'LL BE GOOD FOR HER NERVES.*

KNOCK KNOCK.

HEY, TINA, DO YOU HAVE ANY—

AAAAOOOEEEEEEEMMM OOO

HAPPY EASTER, ASSHOLE!

=WHEW=

I THOUGHT DYING FOR YOUR SINS HURT!

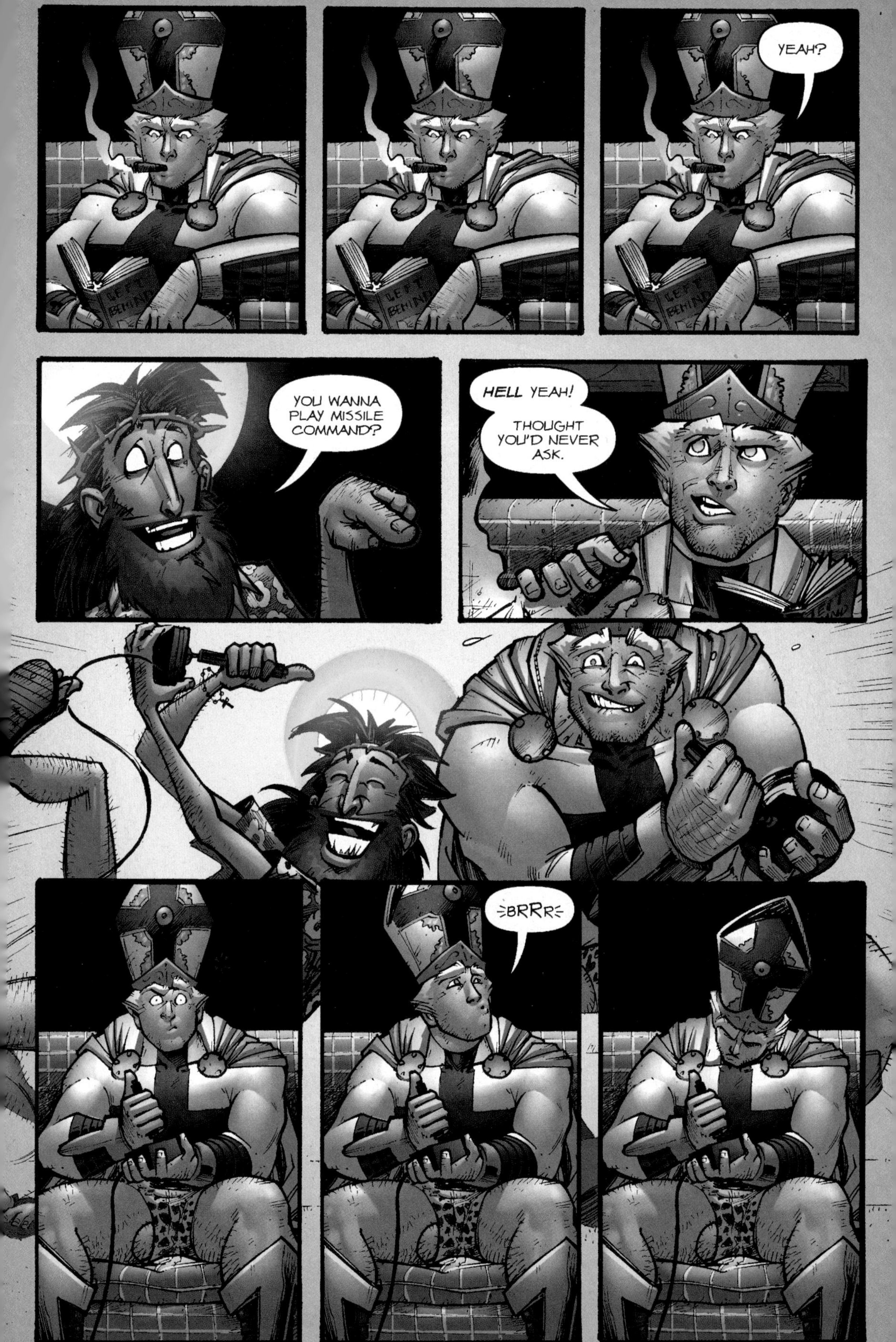
YEAH?
YOU WANNA PLAY MISSILE COMMAND?
HELL YEAH!
THOUGHT YOU'D NEVER ASK.
BRRR

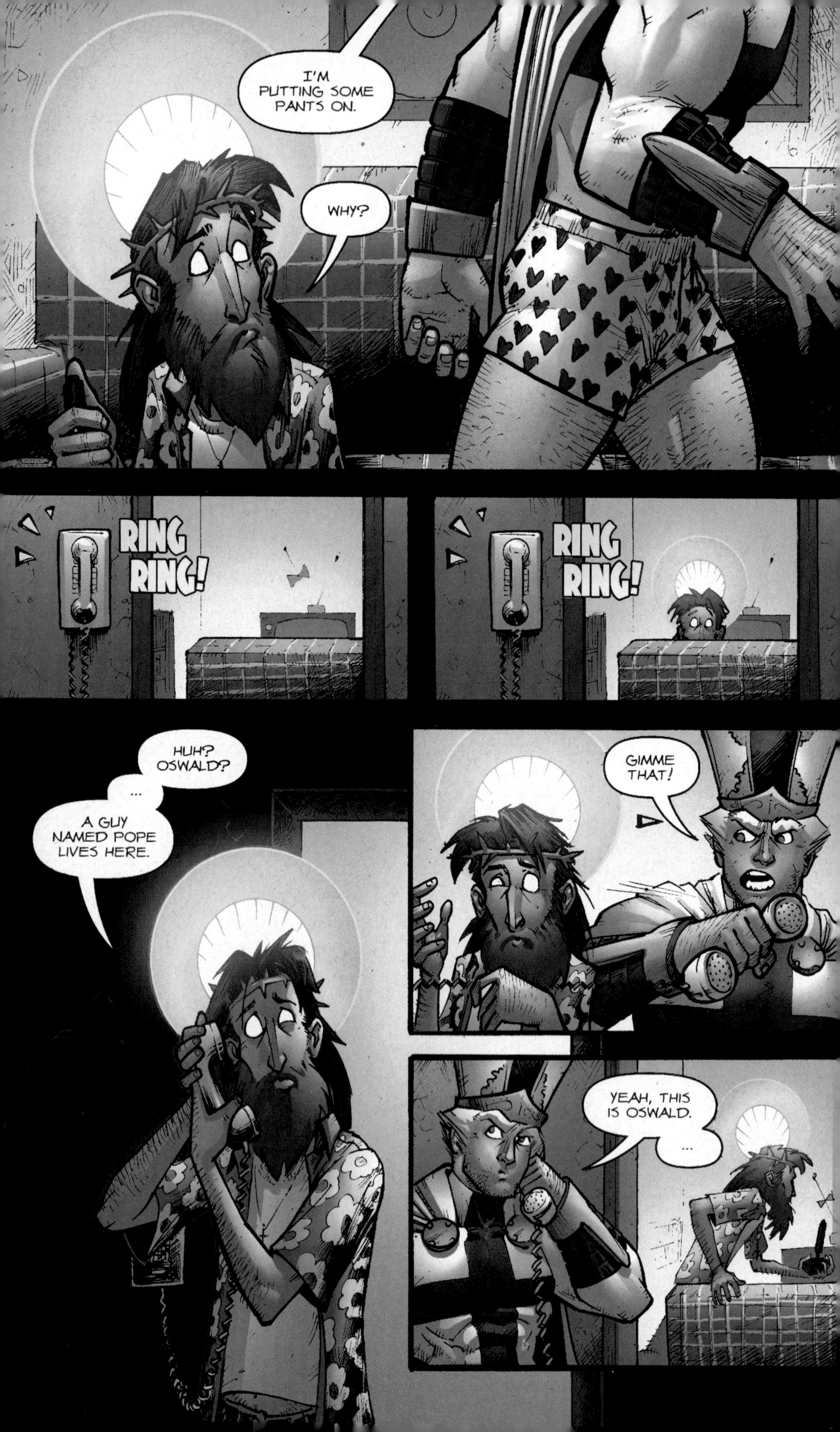
I'M PUTTING SOME PANTS ON.
WHY?
RING RING!
RING RING!
HUH? OSWALD?
...
A GUY NAMED POPE LIVES HERE.
GIMME THAT!
YEAH, THIS IS OSWALD.
...

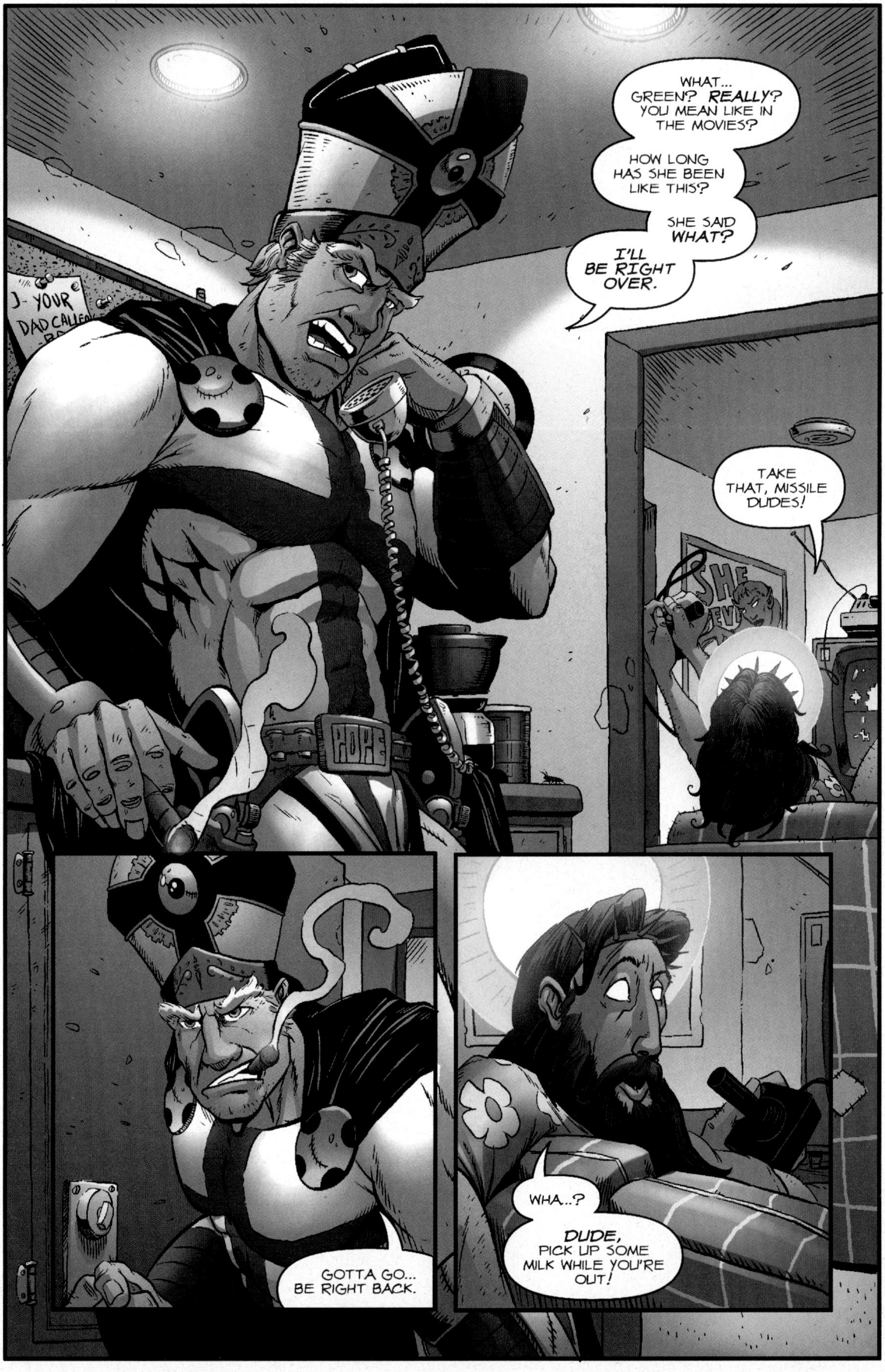
J- YOUR DAD CALLED
WHAT... GREEN? REALLY? YOU MEAN LIKE IN THE MOVIES?
HOW LONG HAS SHE BEEN LIKE THIS?
SHE SAID WHAT?
I'LL BE RIGHT OVER.
TAKE THAT, MISSILE DUDES!
POPE
GOTTA GO... BE RIGHT BACK.
WHA..?
DUDE, PICK UP SOME MILK WHILE YOU'RE OUT!

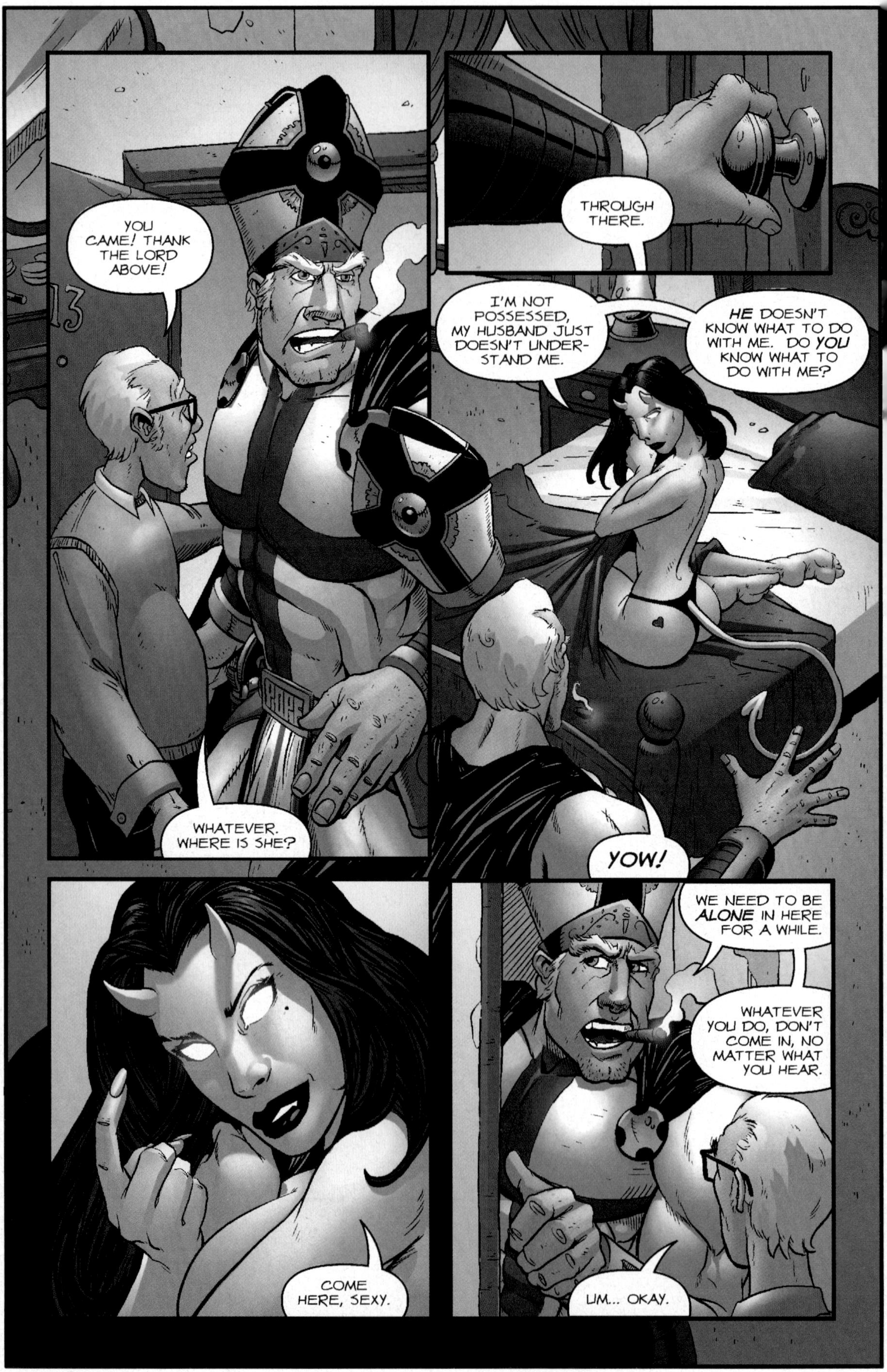

YOU CAME! THANK THE LORD ABOVE!
WHATEVER. WHERE IS SHE?
THROUGH THERE.
I'M NOT POSSESSED, MY HUSBAND JUST DOESN'T UNDER-STAND ME.
HE DOESN'T KNOW WHAT TO DO WITH ME. DO YOU KNOW WHAT TO DO WITH ME?
YOW!
COME HERE, SEXY.
WE NEED TO BE ALONE IN HERE FOR A WHILE.
WHATEVER YOU DO, DON'T COME IN, NO MATTER WHAT YOU HEAR.
UM... OKAY.

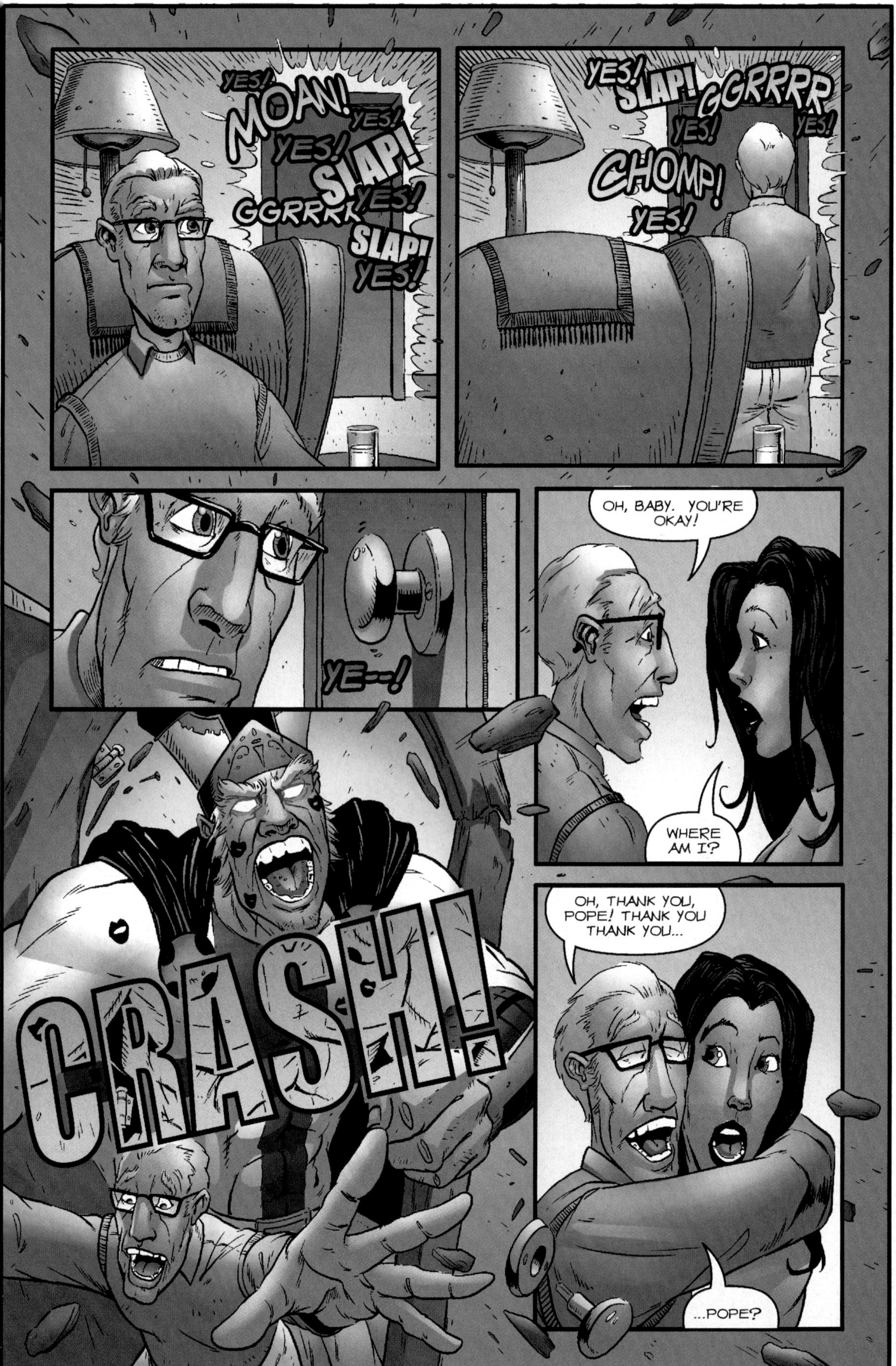
YES!
MOAN!
YES!
YES!
SLAP!
YES!
GGRRRR
SLAP!
YES!
YES!
SLAP!
GGRRRR
YES!
YES!
CHOMP!
YES!
YE--!
OH, BABY. YOU'RE OKAY!
WHERE AM I?
CRASH!
OH, THANK YOU, POPE! THANK YOU THANK YOU...
...POPE?

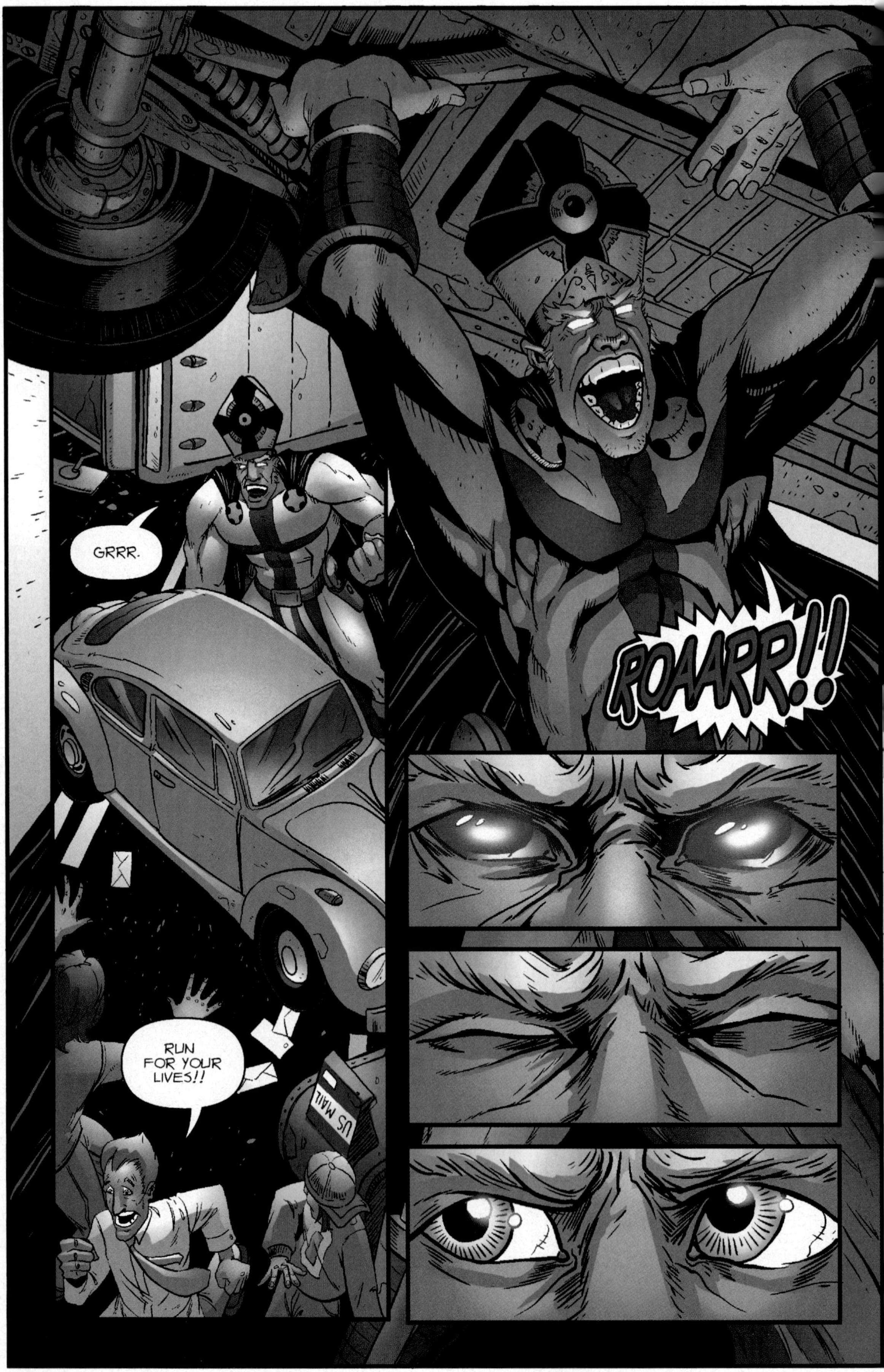
ROAARR!!
GRRR.
RUN FOR YOUR LIVES!!
US MAIL

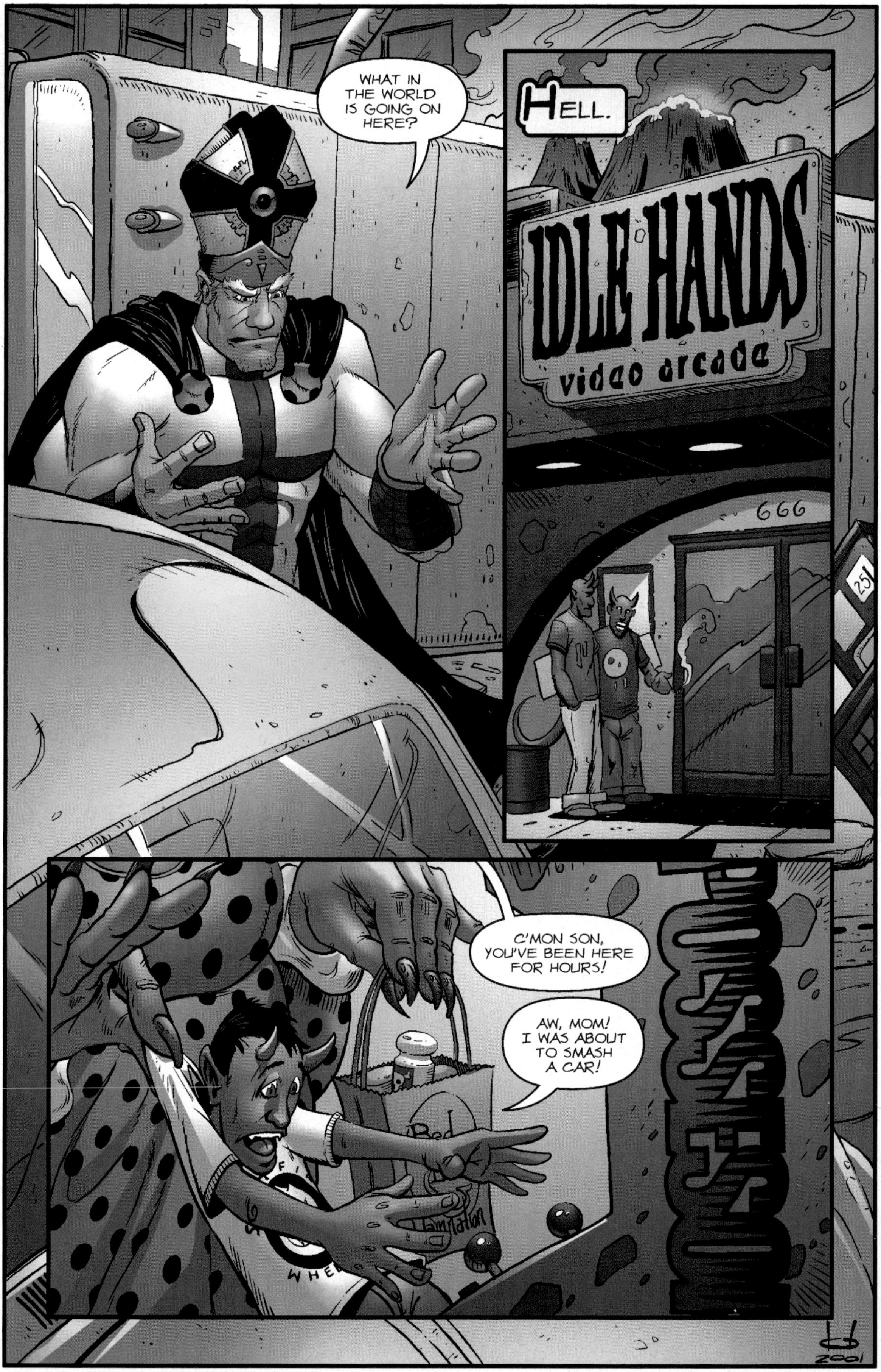
WHAT IN THE WORLD IS GOING ON HERE?
HELL.
IDLE HANDS
video arcade
666
C'MON SON, YOU'VE BEEN HERE FOR HOURS!
AW, MOM! I WAS ABOUT TO SMASH A CAR!
2001

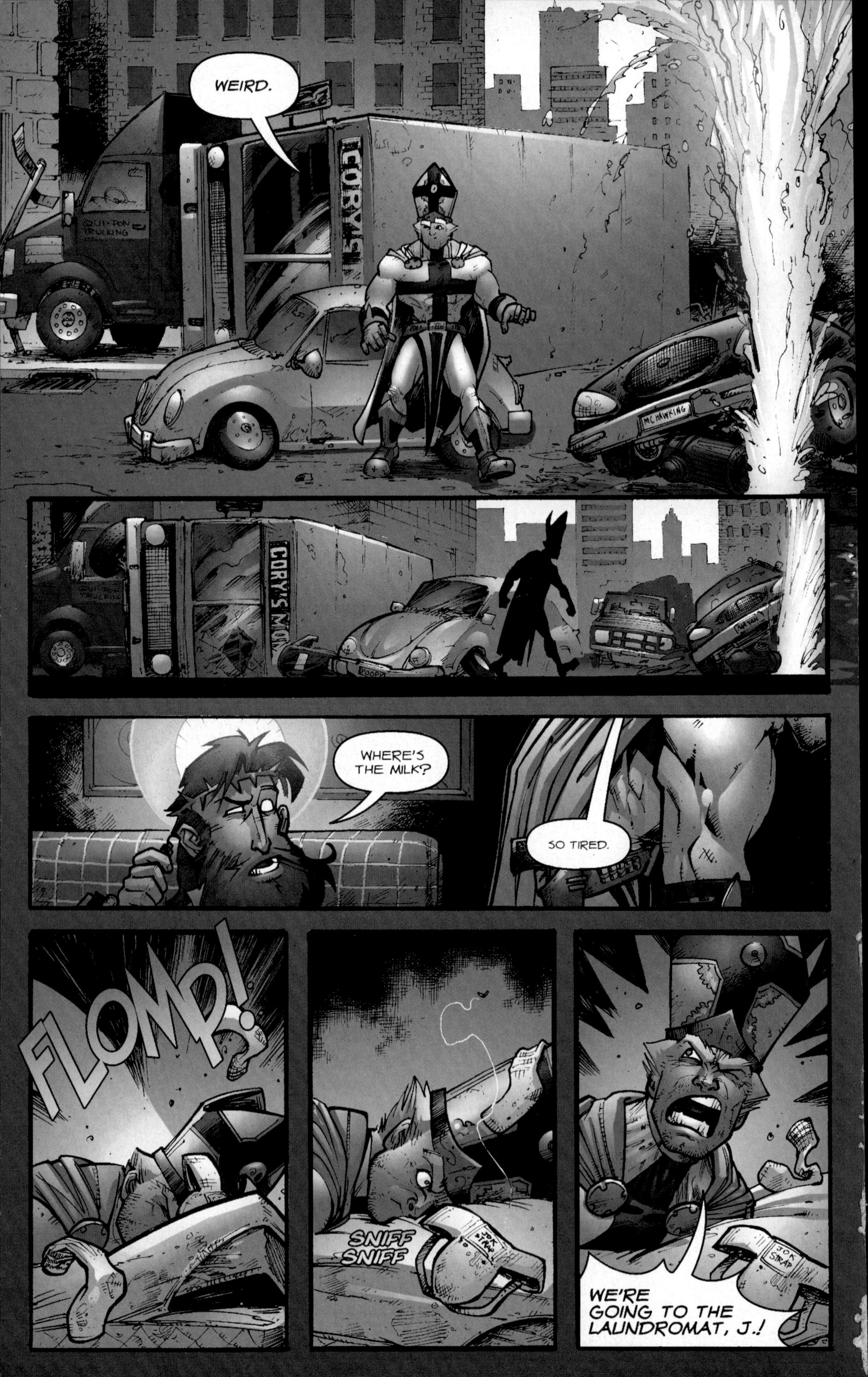
WEIRD.
CORY'S
QUI-PON TRUCKING
MC HAWKING
CORY'S MO
WHERE'S THE MILK?
SO TIRED.
FLOMP!
SNIFF SNIFF
JOK STRAP
WE'RE GOING TO THE LAUNDROMAT, J.!

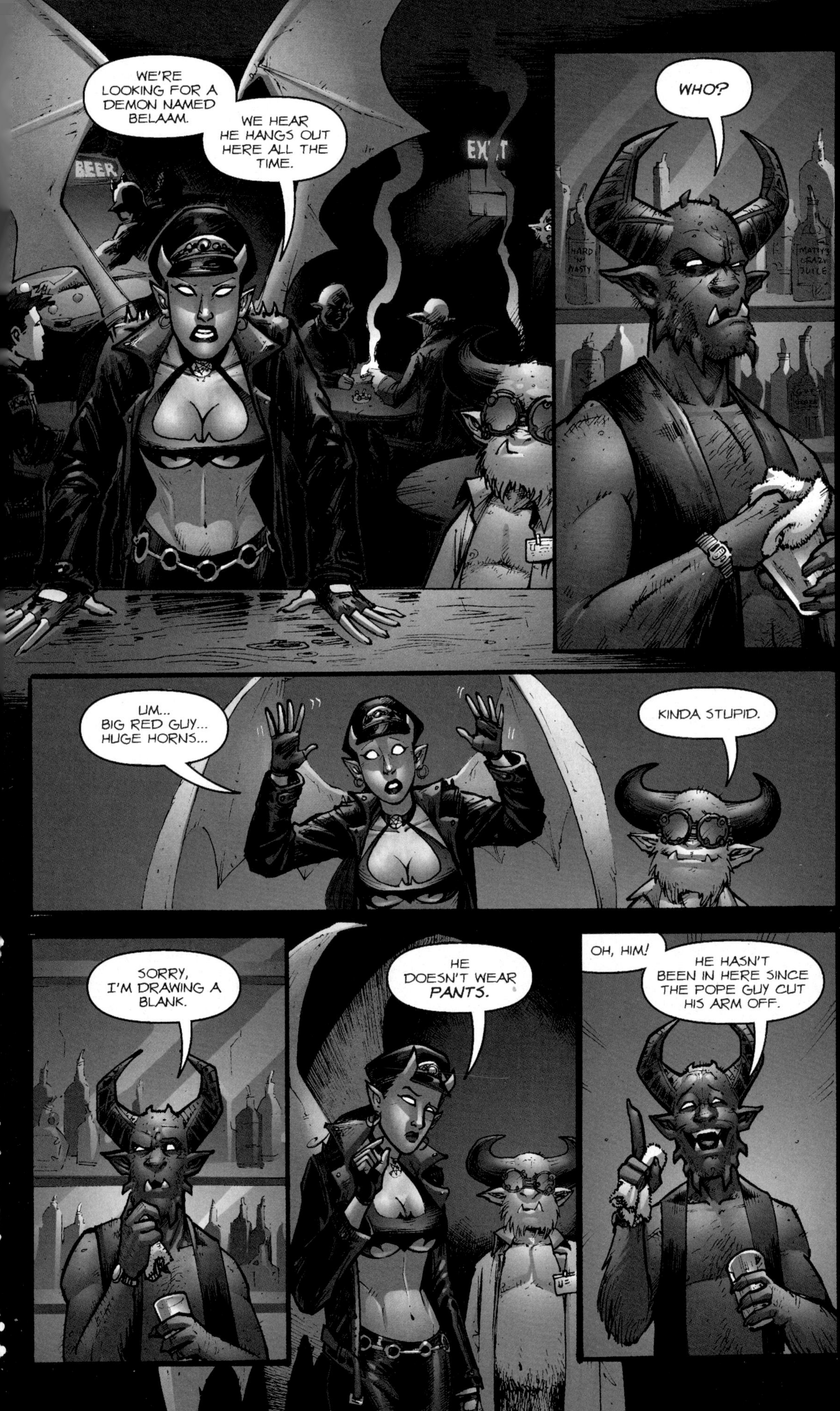
WE'RE LOOKING FOR A DEMON NAMED BELAAM.
WE HEAR HE HANGS OUT HERE ALL THE TIME.
BEER
EXIT
WHO?
HARD N' NASTY
MATTY'S CRAZY JUICE
UM... BIG RED GUY... HUGE HORNS...
KINDA STUPID.
SORRY, I'M DRAWING A BLANK.
HE DOESN'T WEAR PANTS.
OH, HIM!
HE HASN'T BEEN IN HERE SINCE THE POPE GUY CUT HIS ARM OFF.

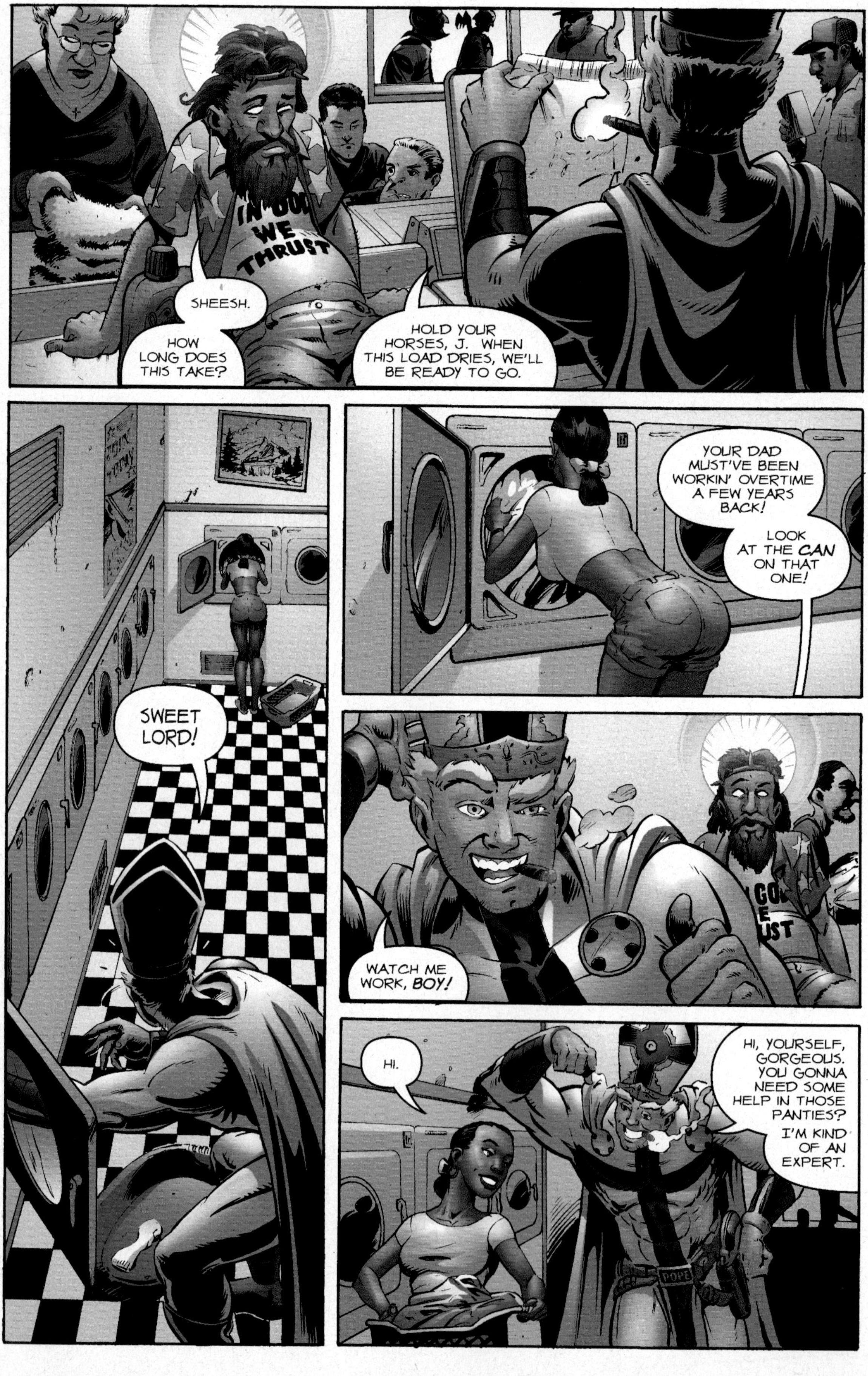
SHEESH.
HOW LONG DOES THIS TAKE?
HOLD YOUR HORSES, J. WHEN THIS LOAD DRIES, WE'LL BE READY TO GO.
IN GOD WE THRUST
SWEET LORD!
YOUR DAD MUST'VE BEEN WORKIN' OVERTIME A FEW YEARS BACK!
LOOK AT THE CAN ON THAT ONE!
WATCH ME WORK, BOY!
HI.
HI, YOURSELF, GORGEOUS. YOU GONNA NEED SOME HELP IN THOSE PANTIES?
I'M KIND OF AN EXPERT.
POPE

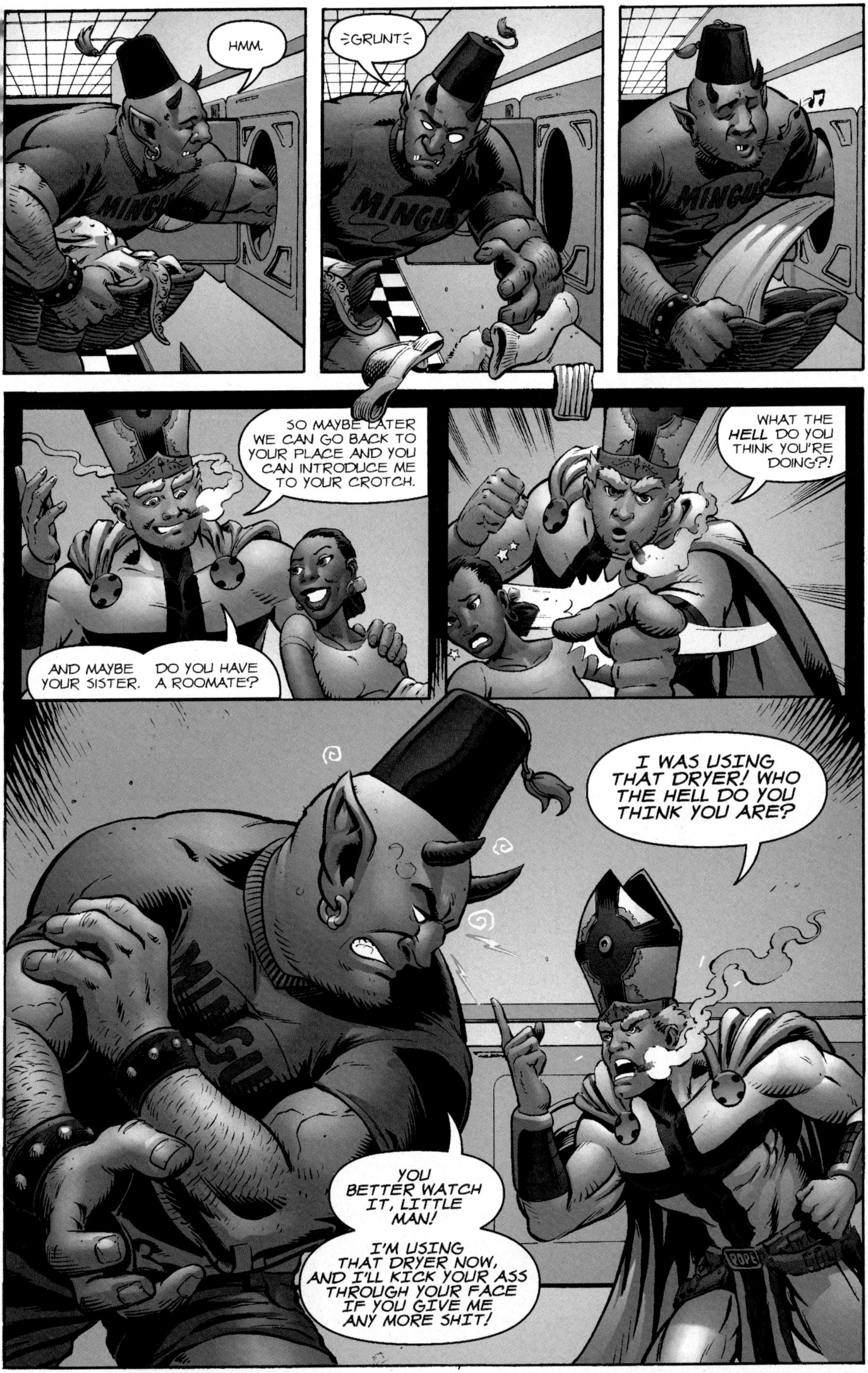
HMM.
GRUNT
SO MAYBE LATER WE CAN GO BACK TO YOUR PLACE AND YOU CAN INTRODUCE ME TO YOUR CROTCH.
AND MAYBE YOUR SISTER.
DO YOU HAVE A ROOMATE?
WHAT THE HELL DO YOU THINK YOU'RE DOING?!
I WAS USING THAT DRYER! WHO THE HELL DO YOU THINK YOU ARE?
YOU BETTER WATCH IT, LITTLE MAN!
I'M USING THAT DRYER NOW, AND I'LL KICK YOUR ASS THROUGH YOUR FACE IF YOU GIVE ME ANY MORE SHIT!

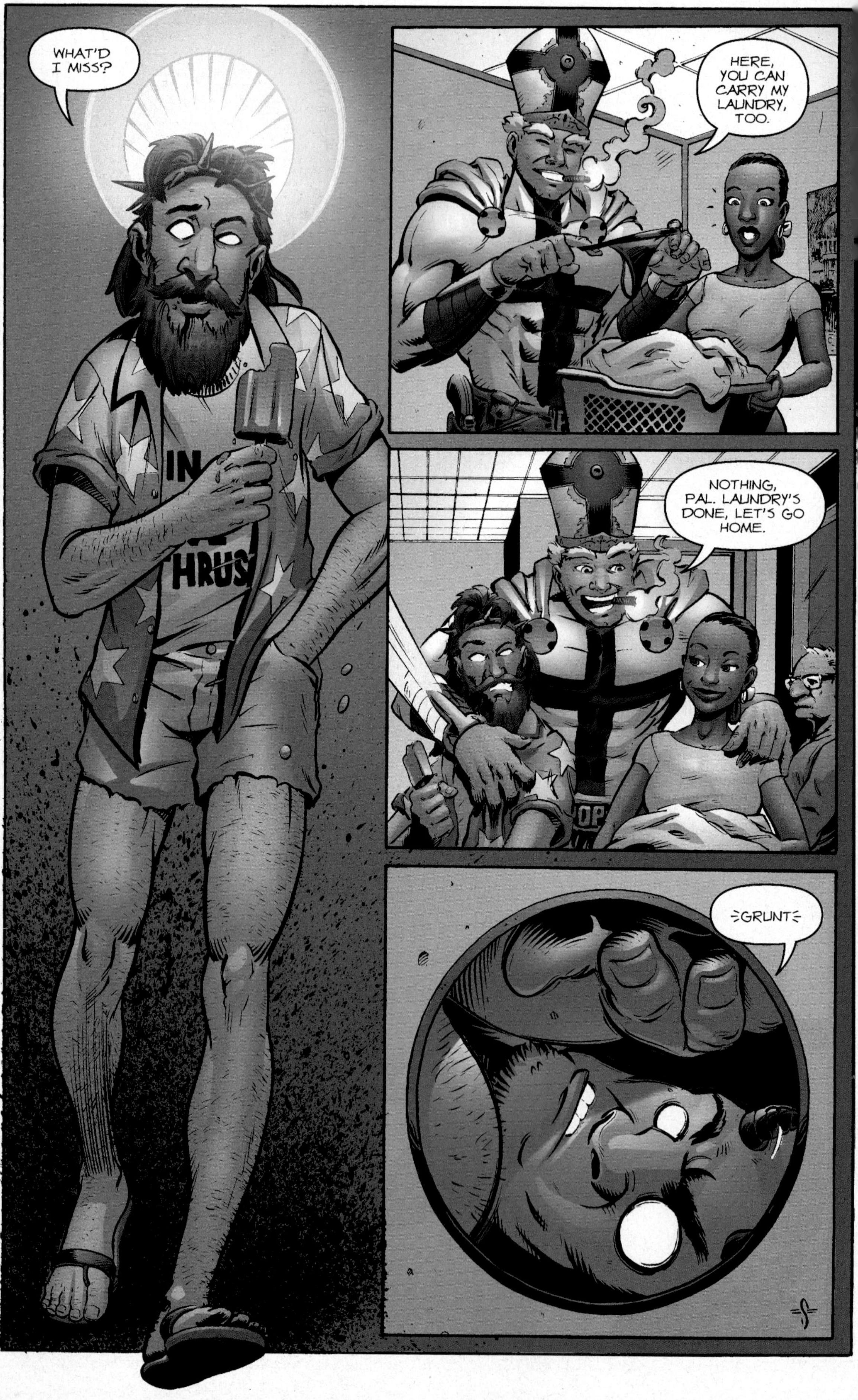
WHAT'D I MISS?
HERE, YOU CAN CARRY MY LAUNDRY, TOO.
NOTHING, PAL. LAUNDRY'S DONE, LET'S GO HOME.
GRUNT

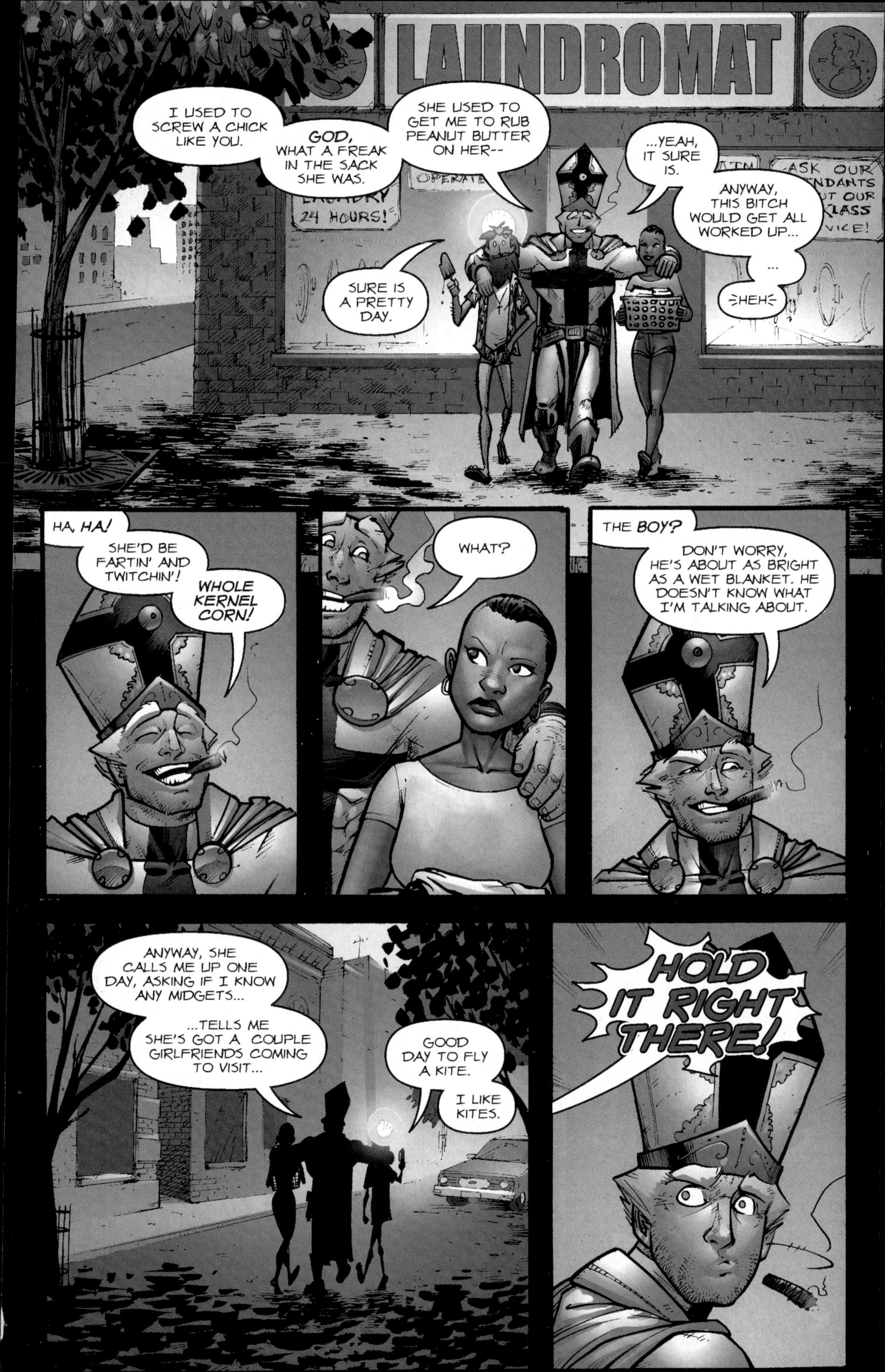
LAUNDROMAT
I USED TO SCREW A CHICK LIKE YOU.
GOD, WHAT A FREAK IN THE SACK SHE WAS.
SHE USED TO GET ME TO RUB PEANUT BUTTER ON HER--
...YEAH, IT SURE IS.
SURE IS A PRETTY DAY.
ANYWAY, THIS BITCH WOULD GET ALL WORKED UP...
...
HEH
HA, HA!
SHE'D BE FARTIN' AND TWITCHIN'!
WHOLE KERNEL CORN!
WHAT?
THE BOY?
DON'T WORRY, HE'S ABOUT AS BRIGHT AS A WET BLANKET. HE DOESN'T KNOW WHAT I'M TALKING ABOUT.
ANYWAY, SHE CALLS ME UP ONE DAY, ASKING IF I KNOW ANY MIDGETS...
...TELLS ME SHE'S GOT A COUPLE GIRLFRIENDS COMING TO VISIT...
GOOD DAY TO FLY A KITE.
I LIKE KITES.
HOLD IT RIGHT THERE!

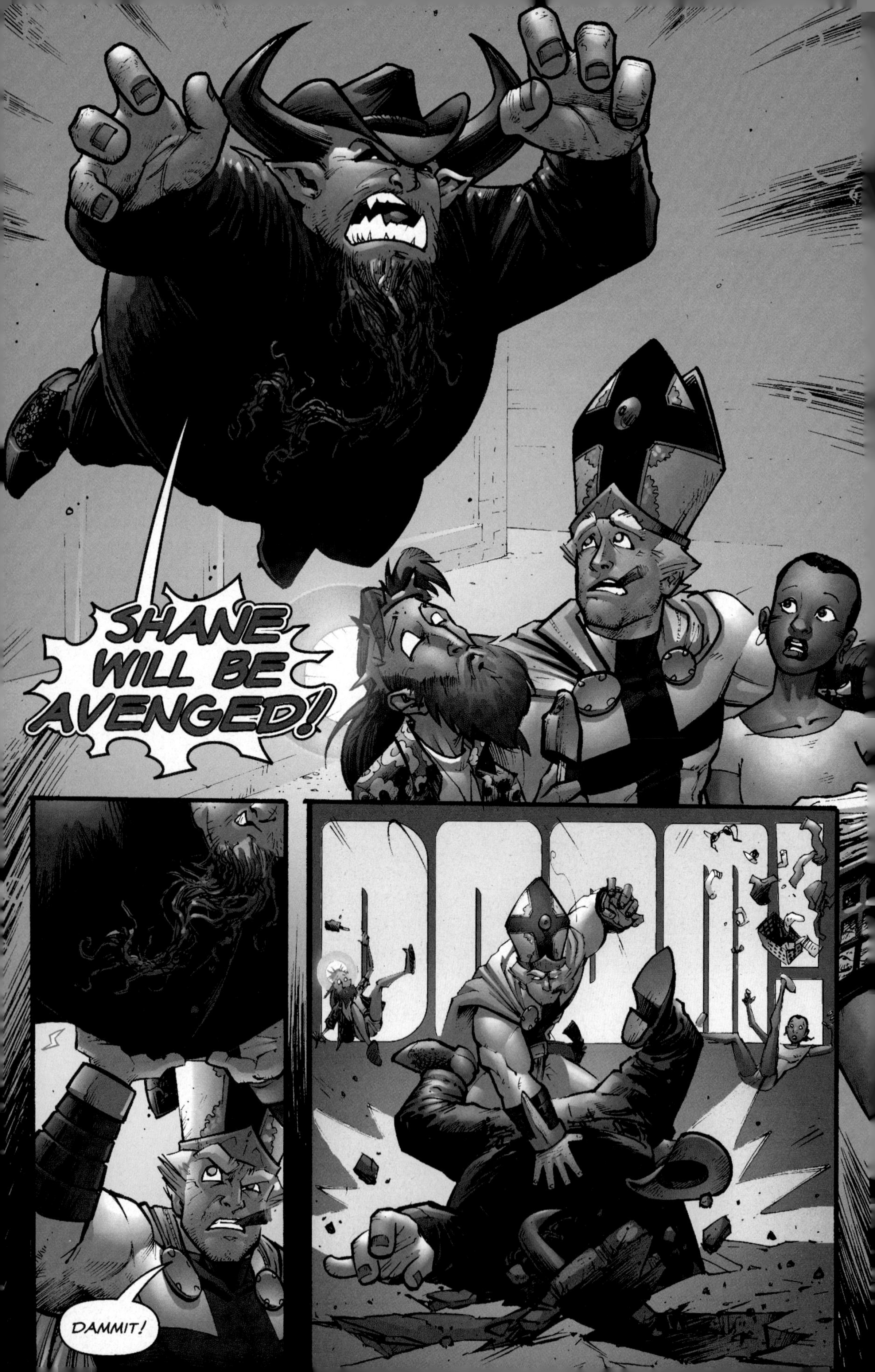
SHANE WILL BE AVENGED!
DAMMIT!

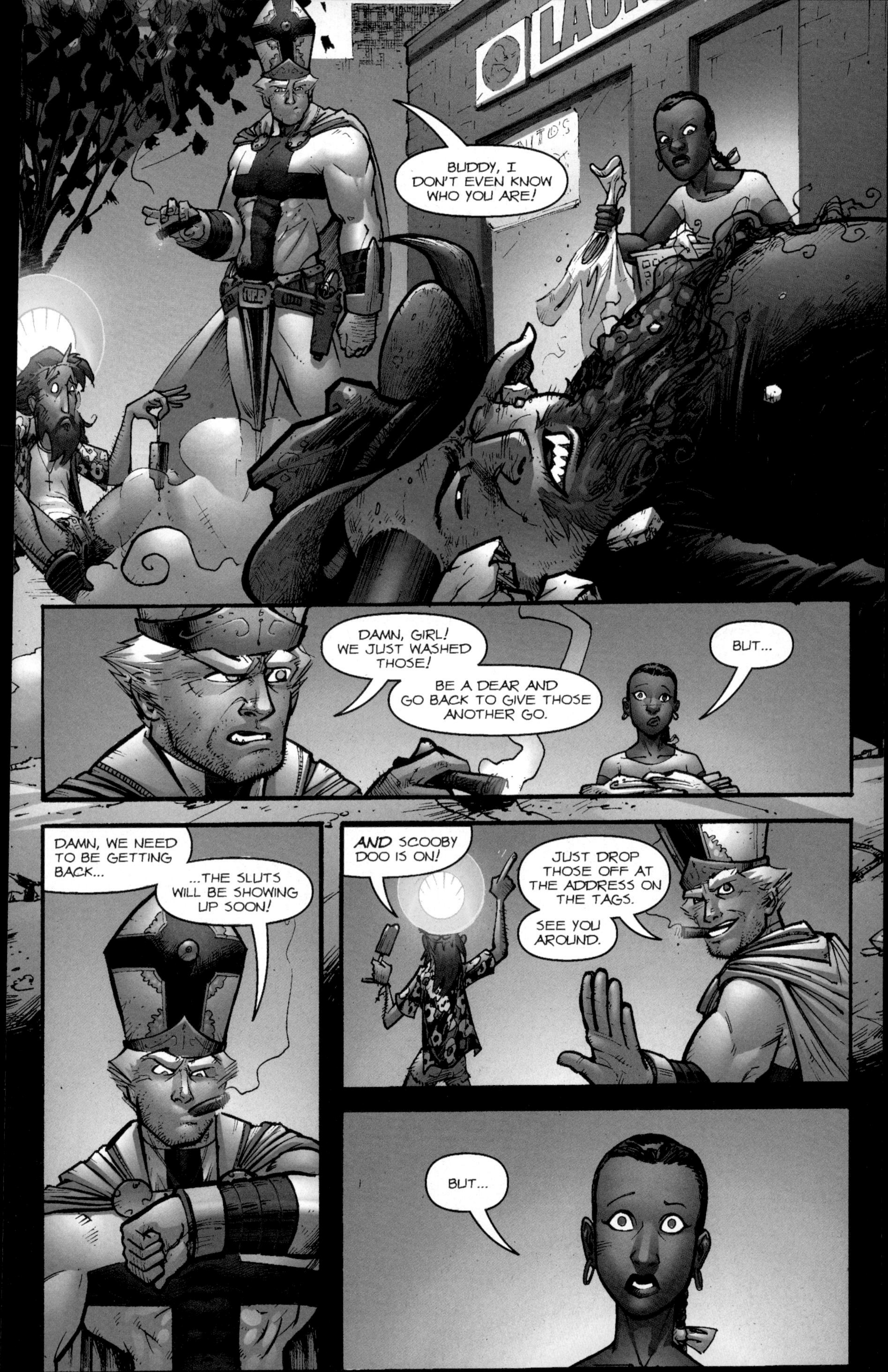
BUDDY, I DON'T EVEN KNOW WHO YOU ARE!
DAMN, GIRL! WE JUST WASHED THOSE!
BE A DEAR AND GO BACK TO GIVE THOSE ANOTHER GO.
BUT...
DAMN, WE NEED TO BE GETTING BACK...
...THE SLUTS WILL BE SHOWING UP SOON!
AND SCOOBY DOO IS ON!
JUST DROP THOSE OFF AT THE ADDRESS ON THE TAGS.
SEE YOU AROUND.
BUT...

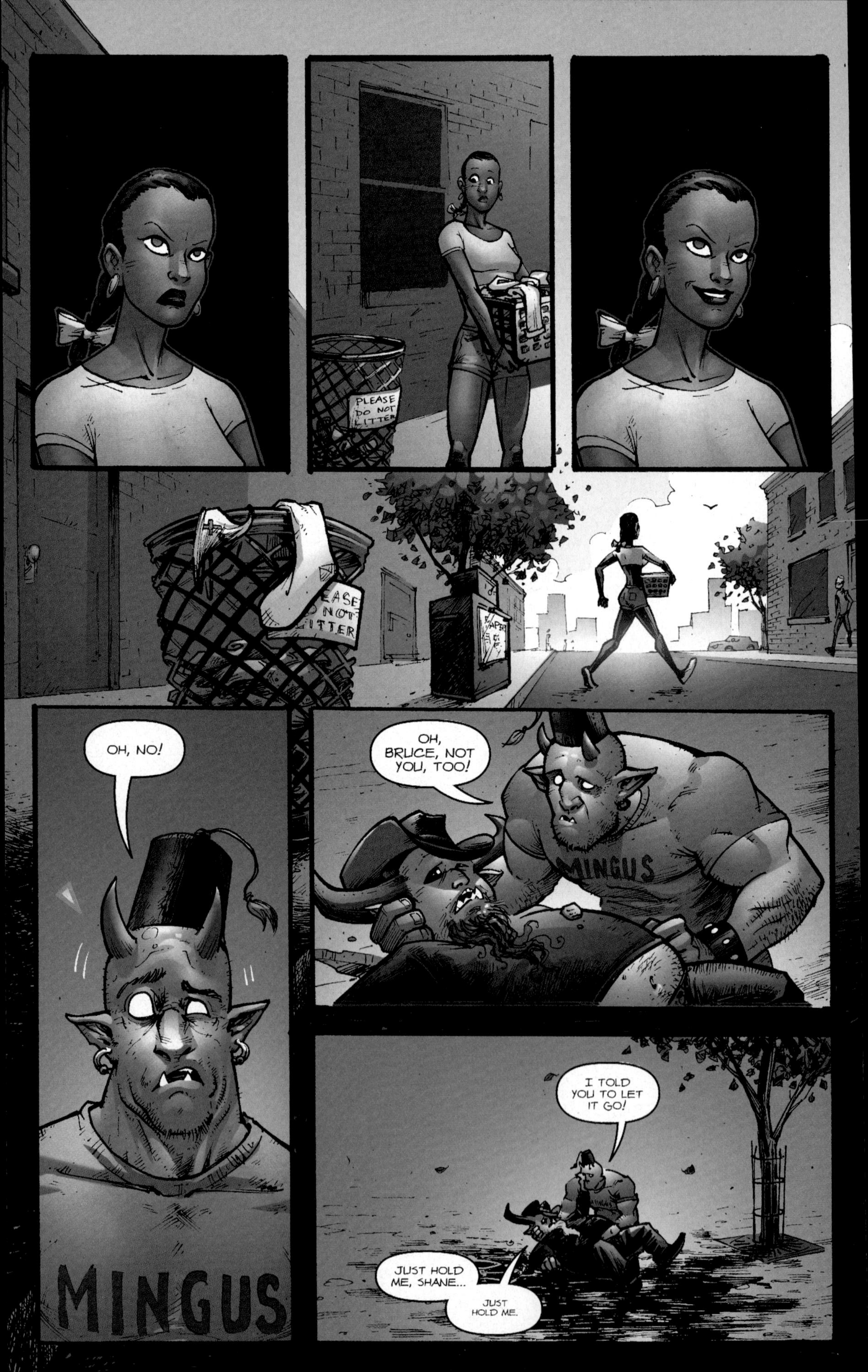
PLEASE DO NOT LITTER
OH, NO!
OH, BRUCE, NOT YOU, TOO!
MINGUS
I TOLD YOU TO LET IT GO!
JUST HOLD ME, SHANE...
JUST HOLD ME.
MINGUS

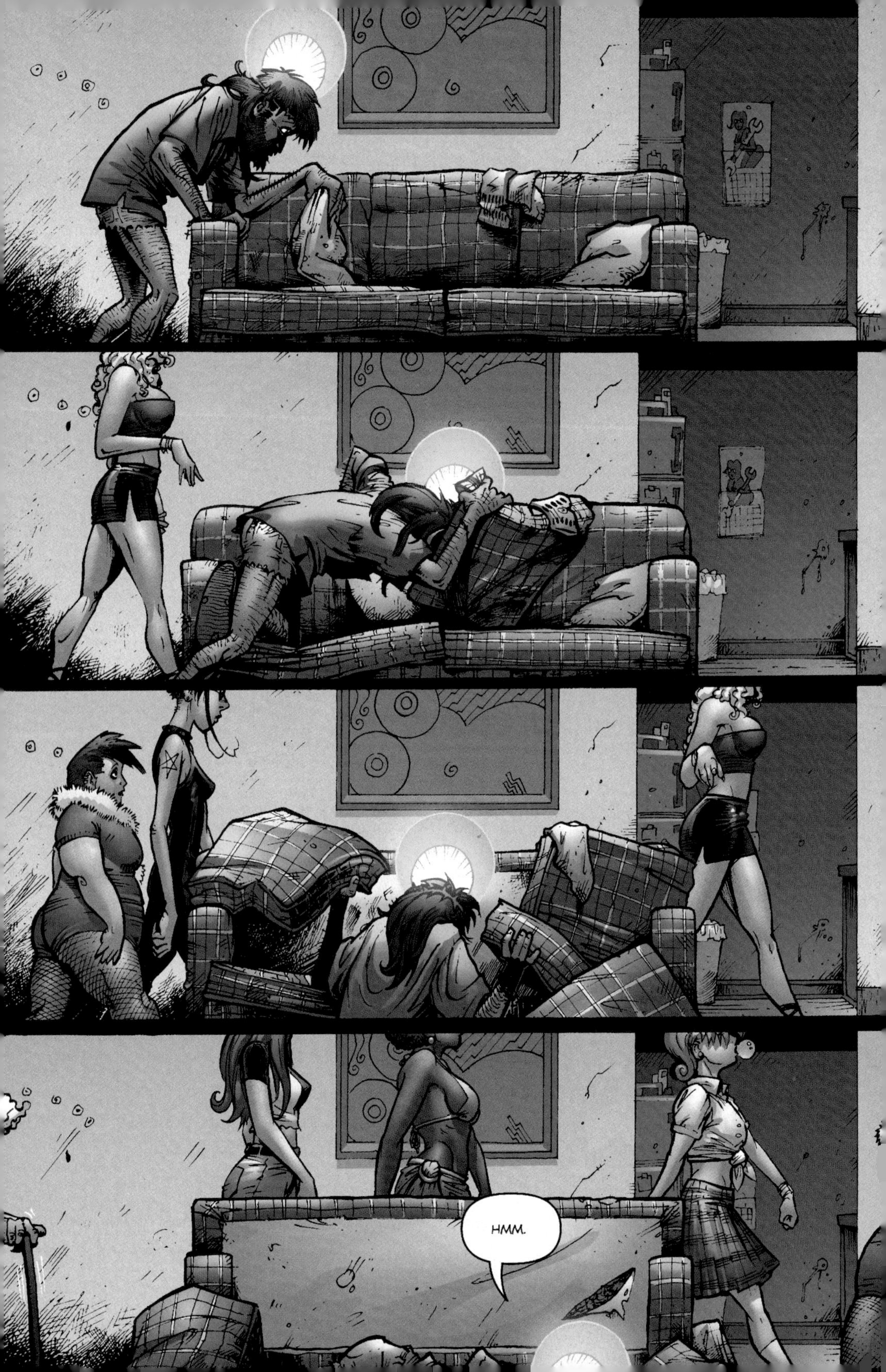
HMM.

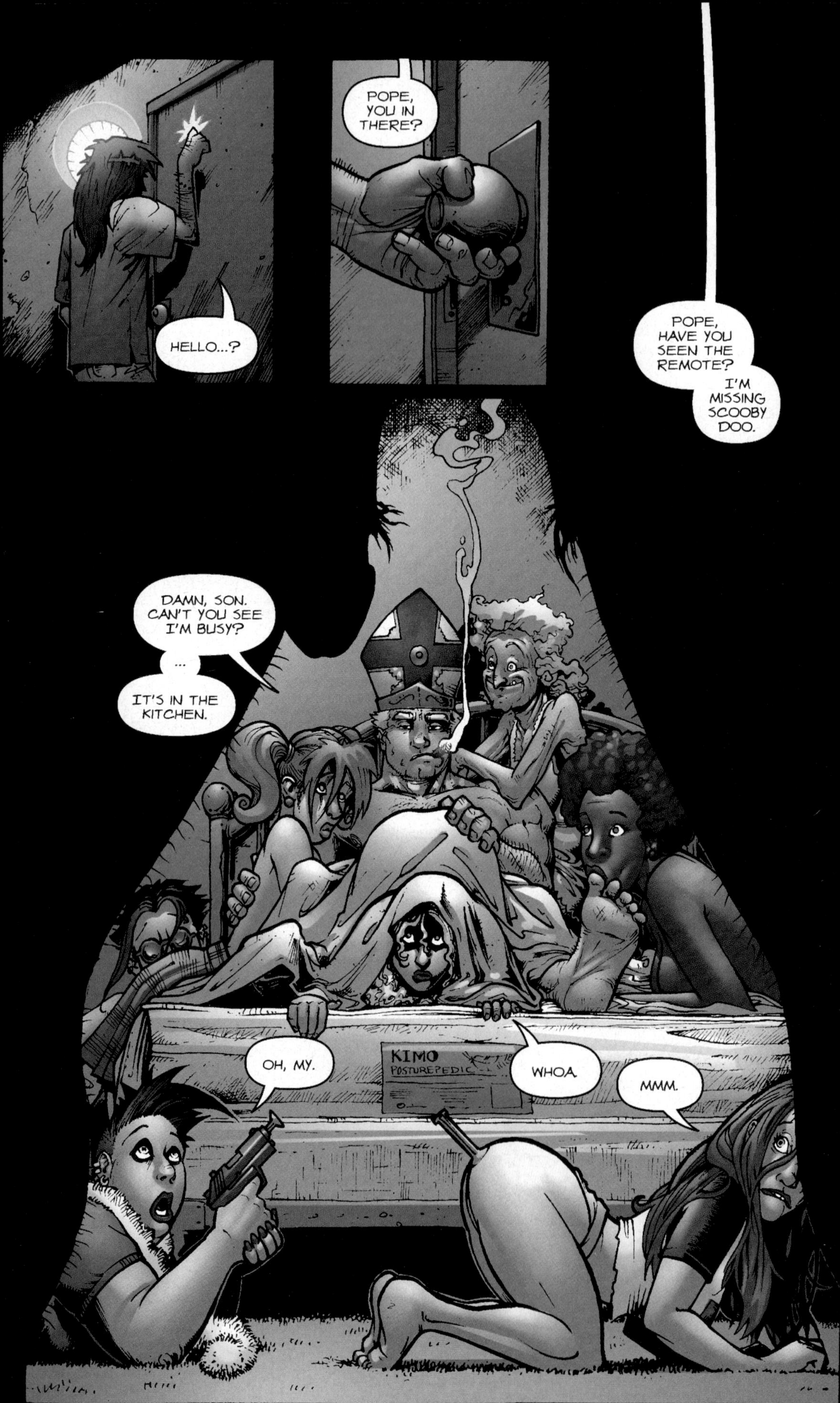
HELLO...?
POPE, YOU IN THERE?
POPE, HAVE YOU SEEN THE REMOTE?
I'M MISSING SCOOBY DOO.
DAMN, SON. CAN'T YOU SEE I'M BUSY?
...
IT'S IN THE KITCHEN.
KIMO POSTUREPEDIC
OH, MY.
WHOA
MMM.

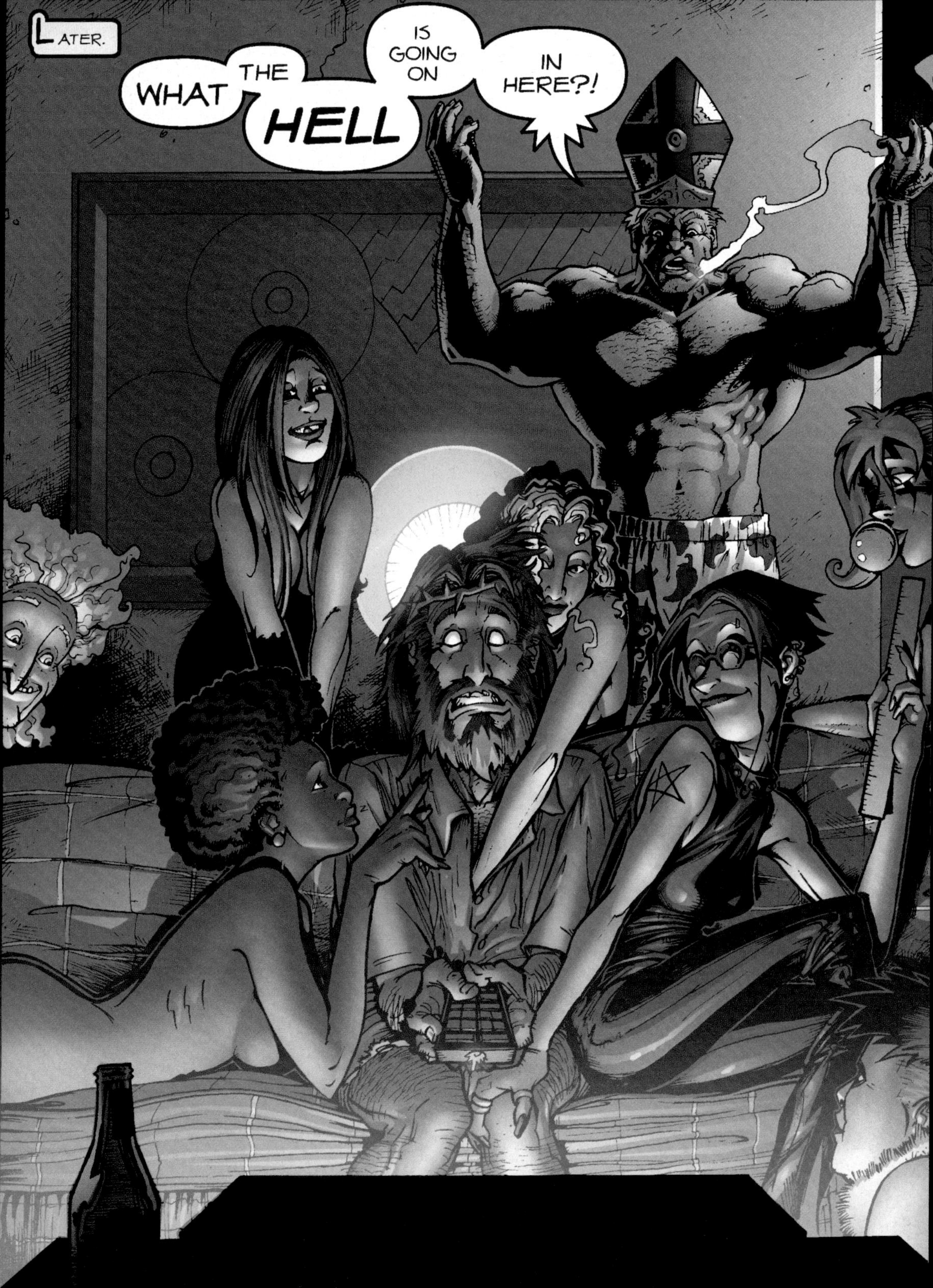
LATER.
WHAT THE HELL IS GOING ON IN HERE?!

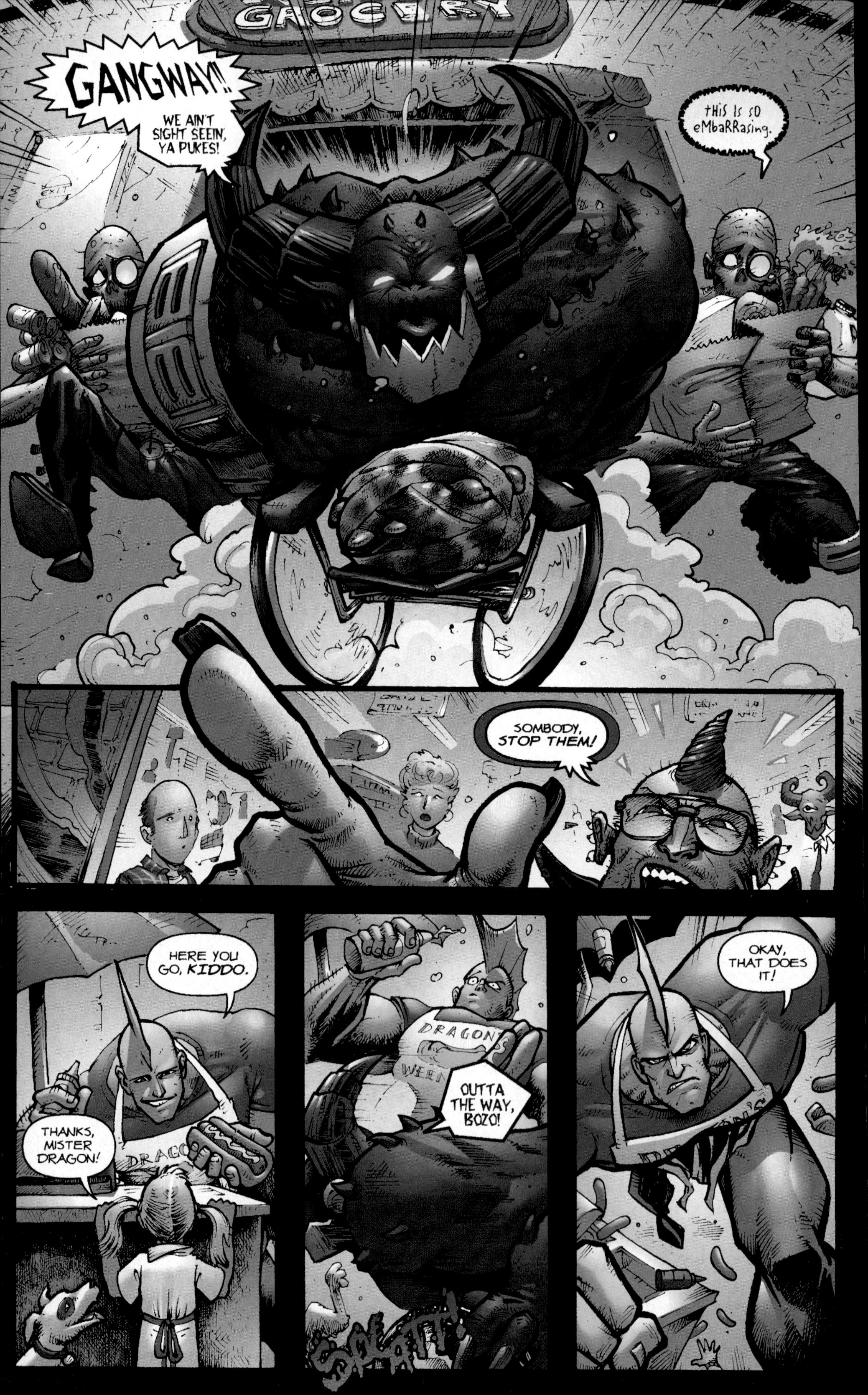
GROCERY
GANGWAY!!
WE AIN'T SIGHT SEEIN', YA PUKES!
tHIS Is sO eMbaRRasing.
SOMBODY, STOP THEM!
HERE YOU GO, KIDDO.
THANKS, MISTER DRAGON!
DRAGON'S WEEN
OUTTA THE WAY, BOZO!
SPLATT!
OKAY, THAT DOES IT!

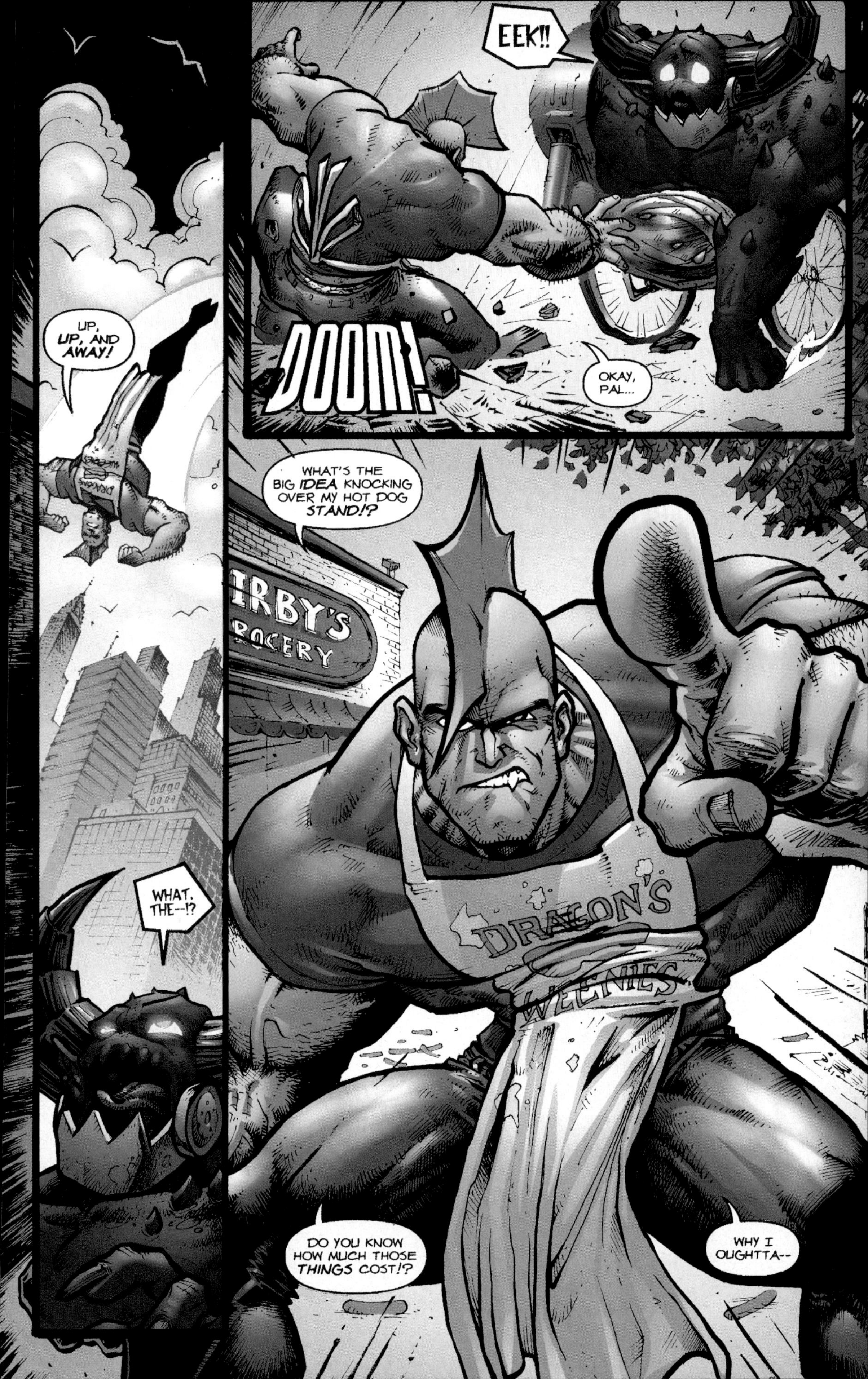
UP, UP, AND AWAY!
WHAT THE--!?
EEK!!
DOOM!
OKAY, PAL...
WHAT'S THE BIG IDEA KNOCKING OVER MY HOT DOG STAND!?
IRBY'S ROCERY
DRAGON'S WEENIES
DO YOU KNOW HOW MUCH THOSE THINGS COST!?
WHY I OUGHTTA--

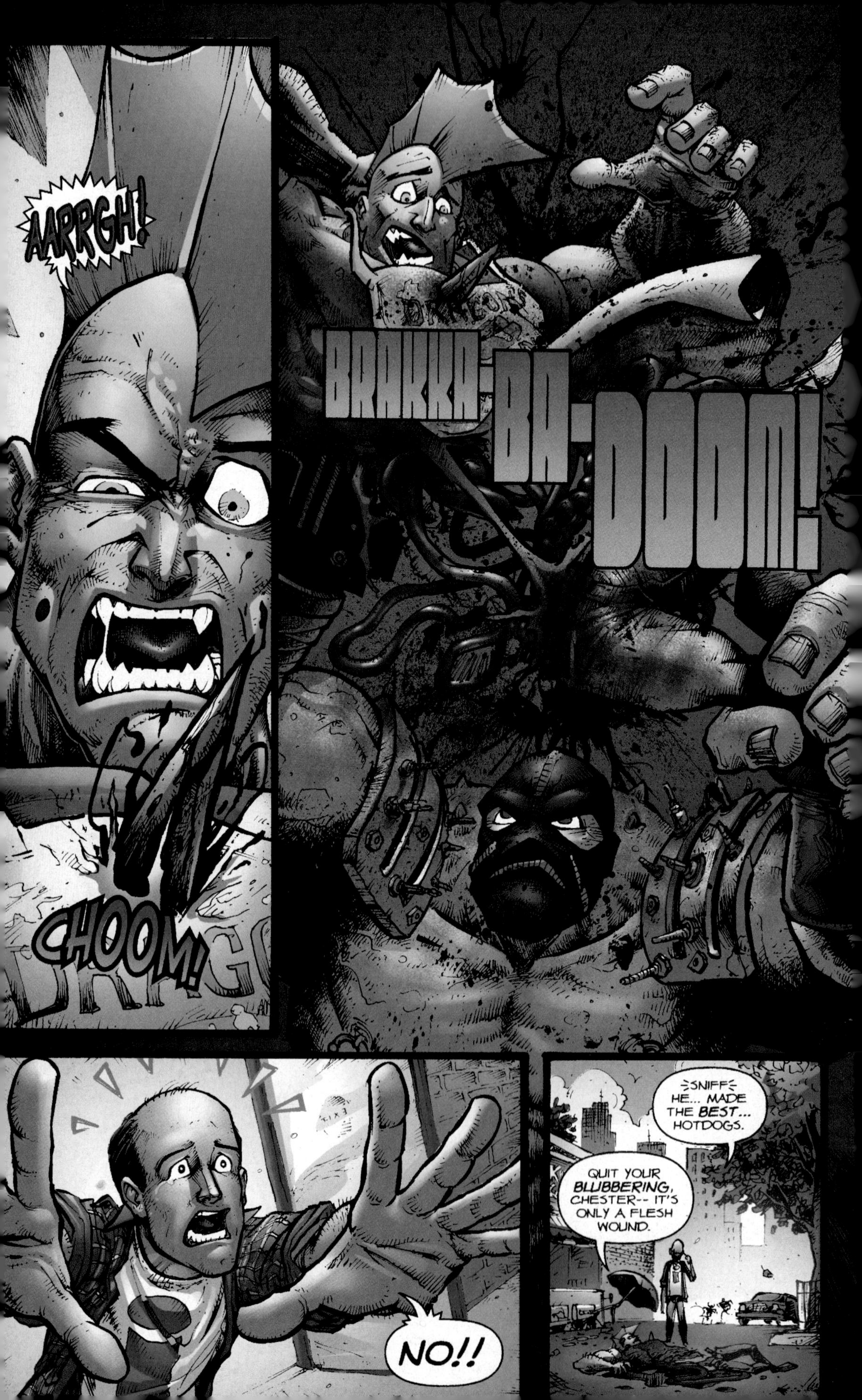

AARRGH!
CHOOM!
BRAKKA-BA-DOOM!
NO!!
SNIFF
HE... MADE THE BEST... HOTDOGS.
QUIT YOUR BLUBBERING, CHESTER-- IT'S ONLY A FLESH WOUND.

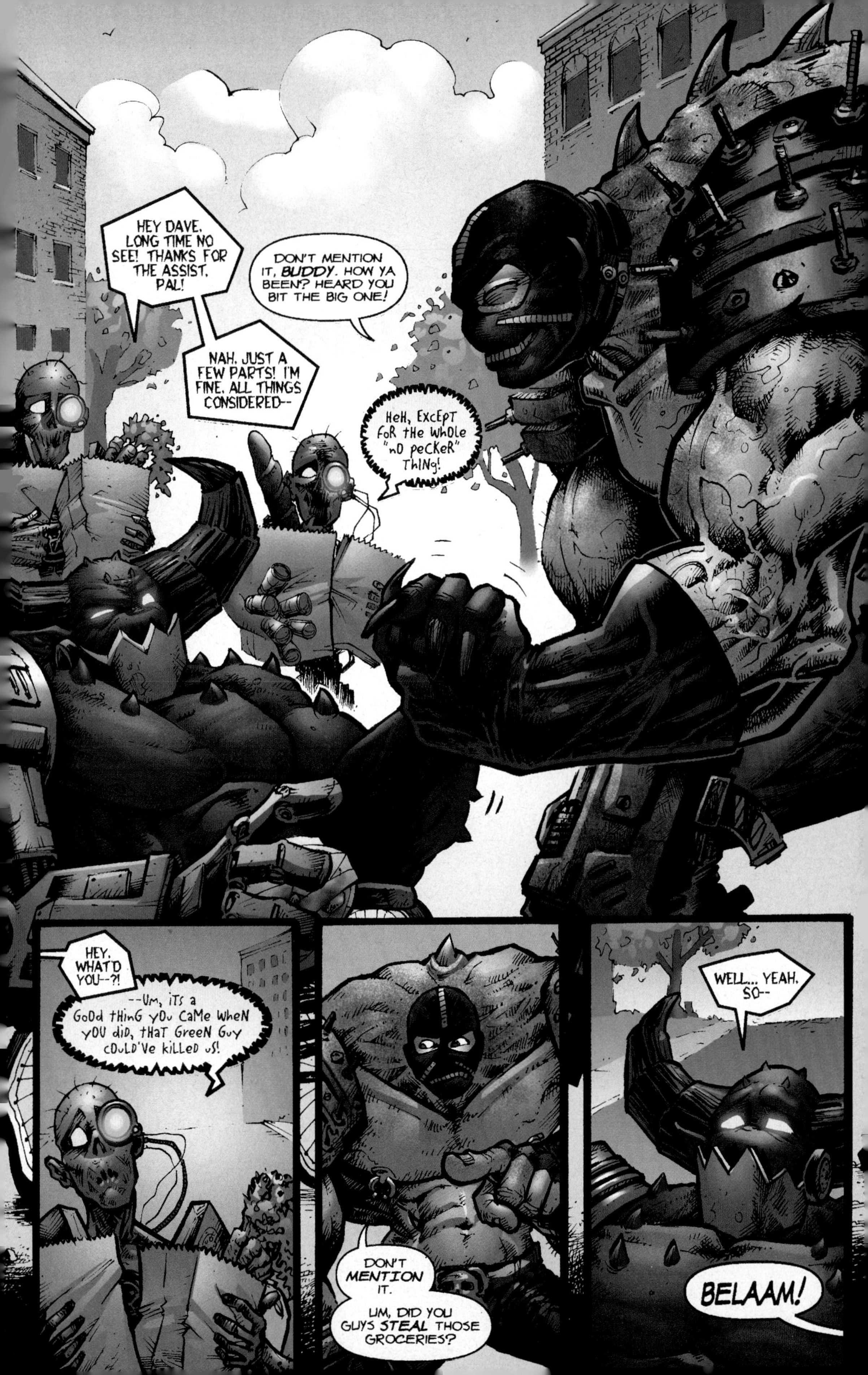
HEY DAVE, LONG TIME NO SEE! THANKS FOR THE ASSIST, PAL!
DON'T MENTION IT, BUDDY. HOW YA BEEN? HEARD YOU BIT THE BIG ONE!
NAH, JUST A FEW PARTS! I'M FINE, ALL THINGS CONSIDERED--
HEH, EXCEPT FOR THE WHOLE "NO PECKER" THING!
HEY, WHAT'D YOU--?!
--UM, ITS A GOOD THING YOU CAME WHEN YOU DID, THAT GREEN GUY COULD'VE KILLED US!
DON'T MENTION IT.
UM, DID YOU GUYS STEAL THOSE GROCERIES?
WELL... YEAH, SO--
BELAAM!

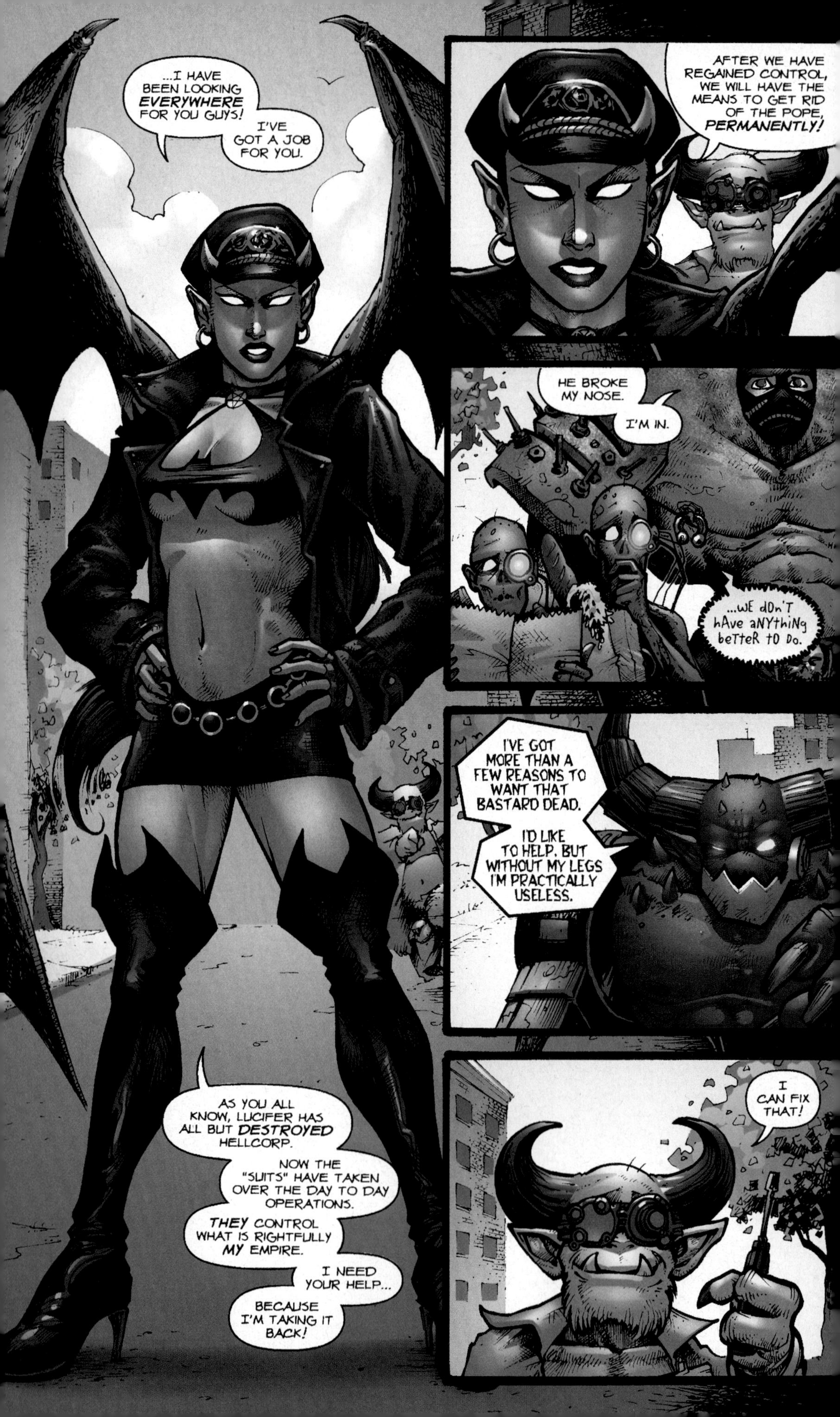
...I HAVE BEEN LOOKING EVERYWHERE FOR YOU GUYS!
I'VE GOT A JOB FOR YOU.
AS YOU ALL KNOW, LUCIFER HAS ALL BUT DESTROYED HELLCORP.
NOW THE "SUITS" HAVE TAKEN OVER THE DAY TO DAY OPERATIONS.
THEY CONTROL WHAT IS RIGHTFULLY MY EMPIRE.
I NEED YOUR HELP...
BECAUSE I'M TAKING IT BACK!
AFTER WE HAVE REGAINED CONTROL, WE WILL HAVE THE MEANS TO GET RID OF THE POPE, PERMANENTLY!
HE BROKE MY NOSE.
I'M IN.
...WE DON'T HAVE ANYTHING BETTER TO DO.
I'VE GOT MORE THAN A FEW REASONS TO WANT THAT BASTARD DEAD.
I'D LIKE TO HELP. BUT WITHOUT MY LEGS I'M PRACTICALLY USELESS.
I CAN FIX THAT!

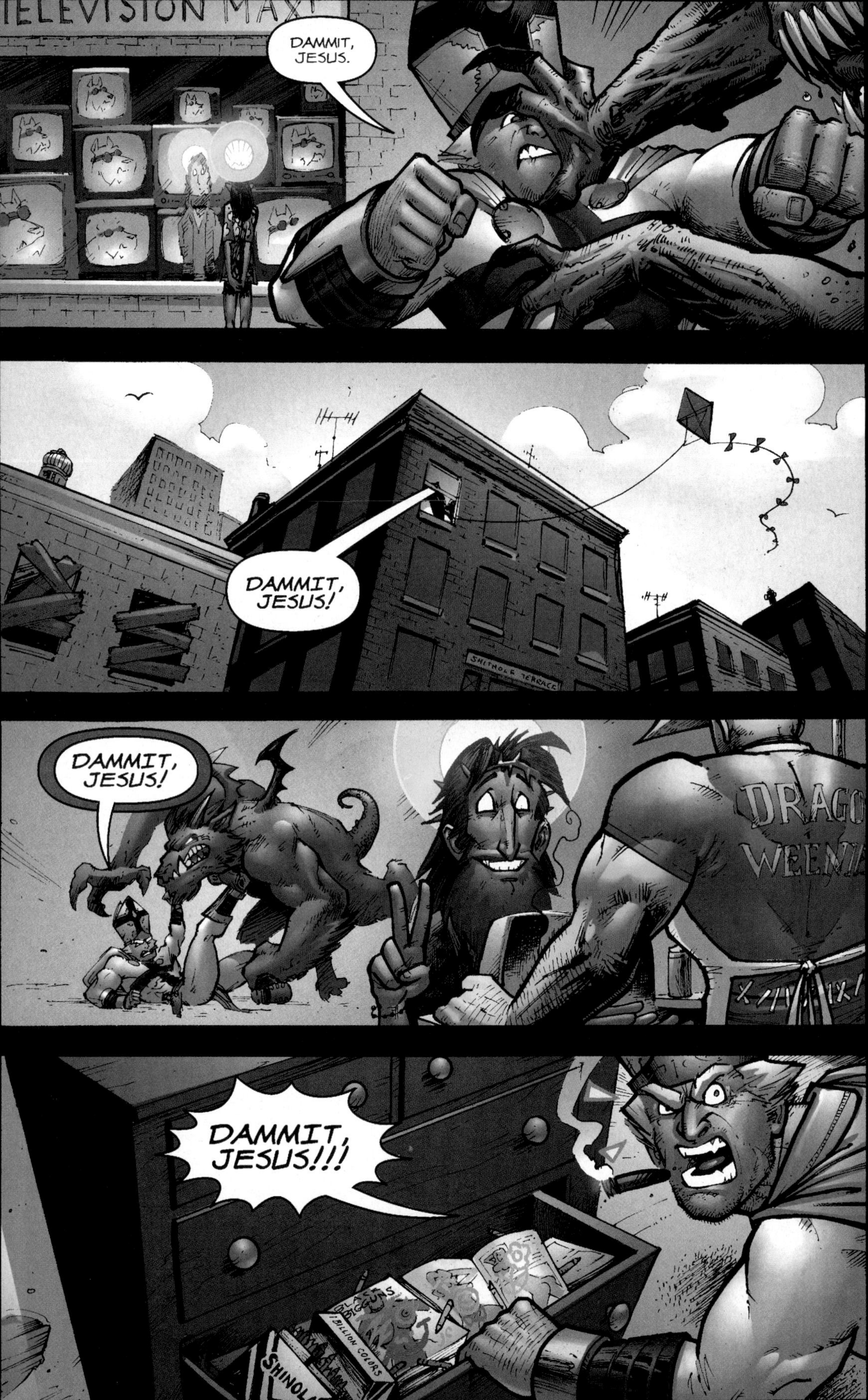
TELEVISION MAX
DAMMIT, JESUS.
DAMMIT, JESUS!
SHITHOLE TERRACE
DAMMIT, JESUS!
DRAGO WEENI
DAMMIT, JESUS!!!
1 BILLION COLORS
SHINOLA

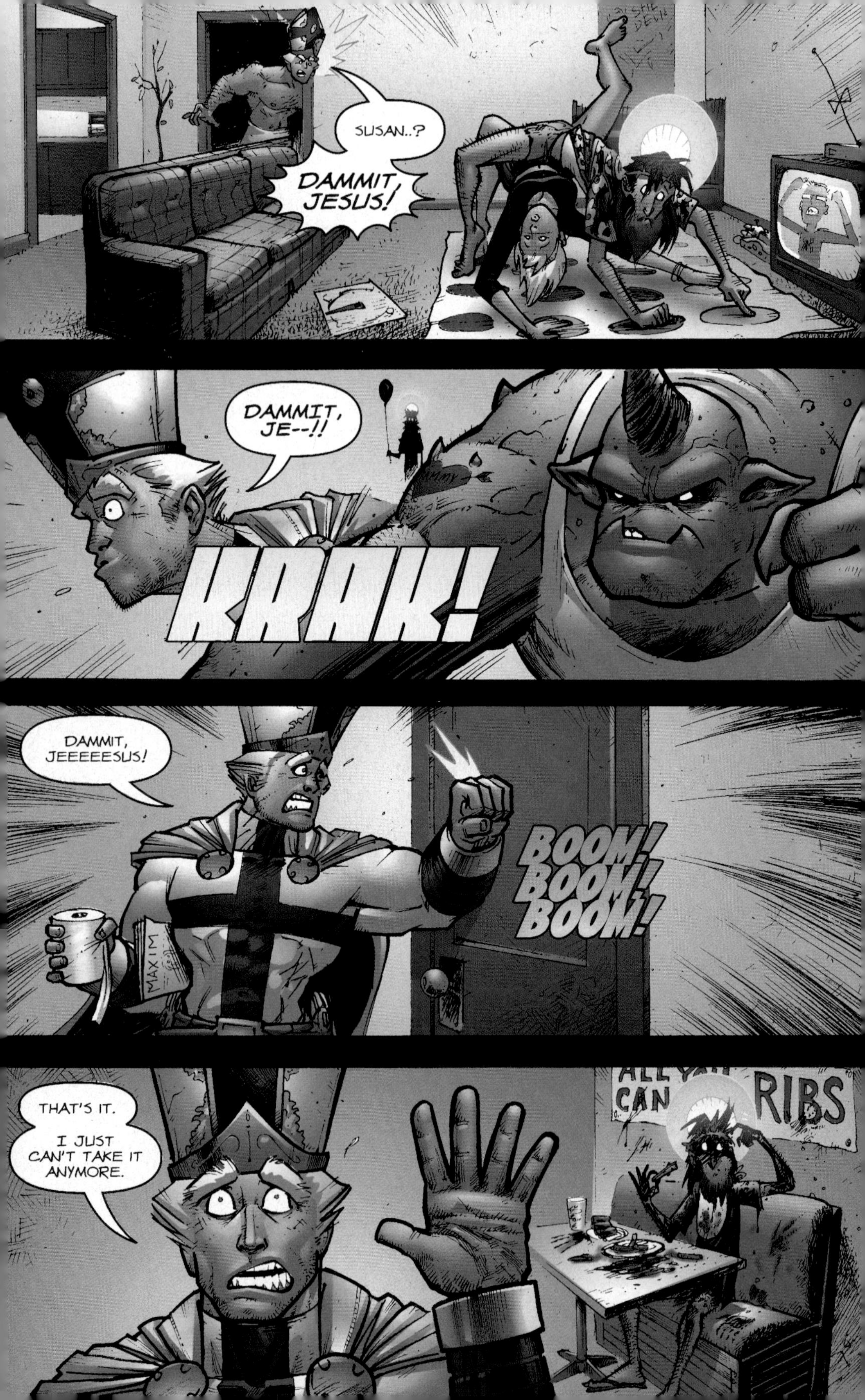
SUSAN..?
DAMMIT, JESUS!
DAMMIT, JE--!!
KRAK!
DAMMIT, JEEEEEESUS!
BOOM! BOOM! BOOM!
MAXIM
THAT'S IT.
I JUST CAN'T TAKE IT ANYMORE.
RIBS

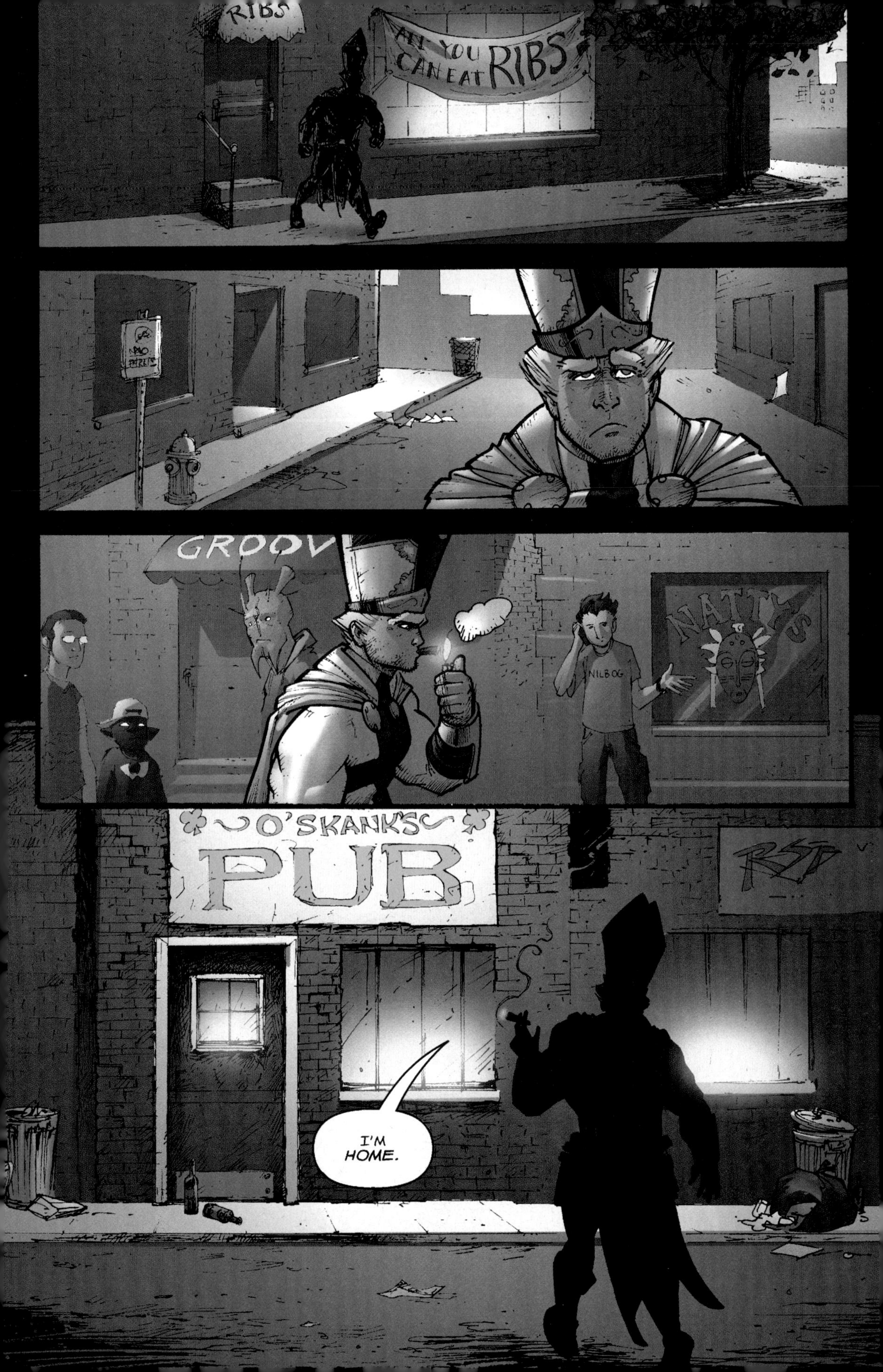
RIBS
ALL YOU CAN EAT RIBS
GROOV
NATTY'S
NILBOG
O'SKANK'S PUB
I'M HOME.

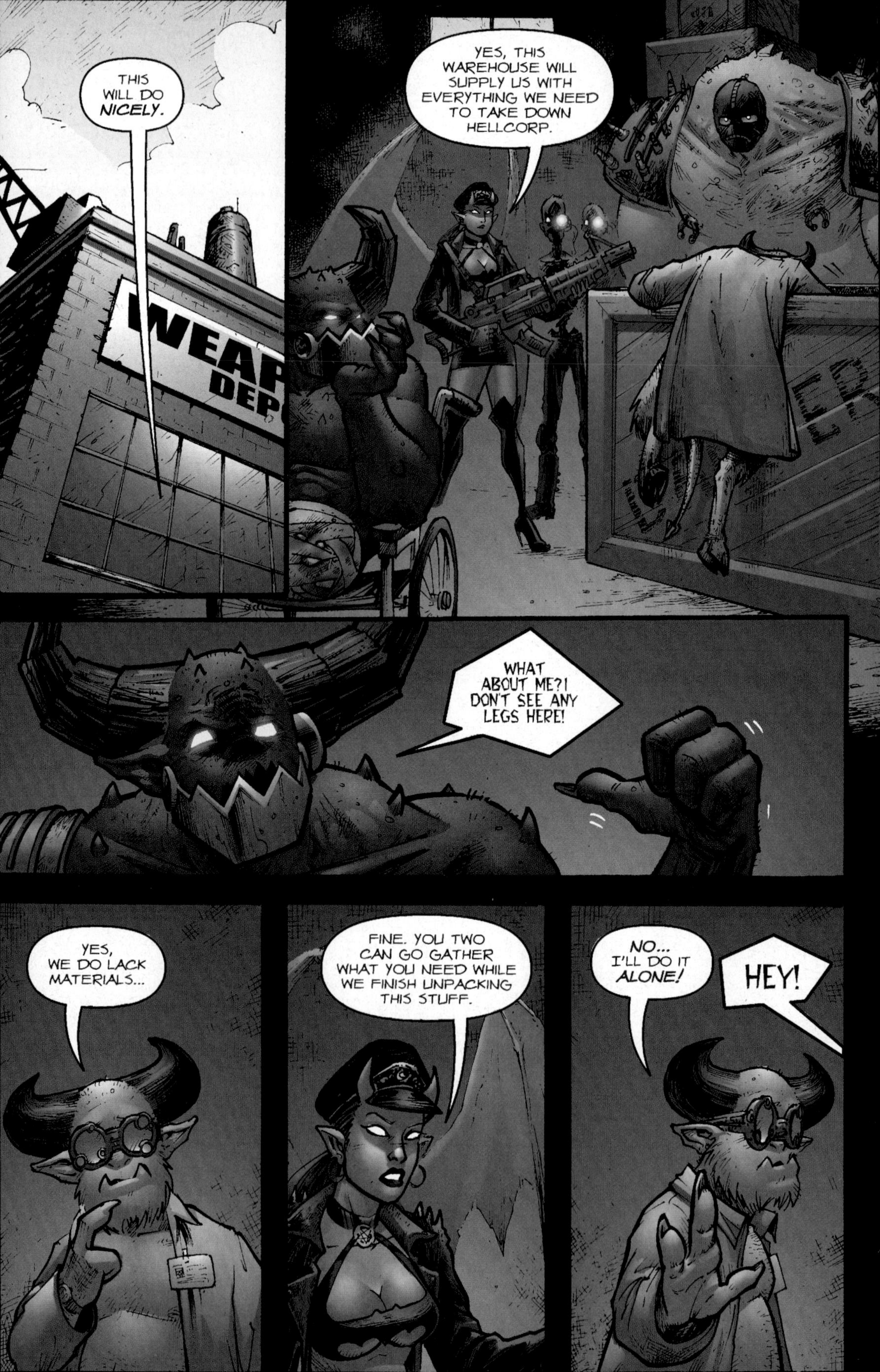
THIS WILL DO NICELY.
WEAP DEP
YES, THIS WAREHOUSE WILL SUPPLY US WITH EVERYTHING WE NEED TO TAKE DOWN HELLCORP.
WHAT ABOUT ME?! DON'T SEE ANY LEGS HERE!
YES, WE DO LACK MATERIALS...
FINE. YOU TWO CAN GO GATHER WHAT YOU NEED WHILE WE FINISH UNPACKING THIS STUFF.
NO... I'LL DO IT ALONE!
HEY!

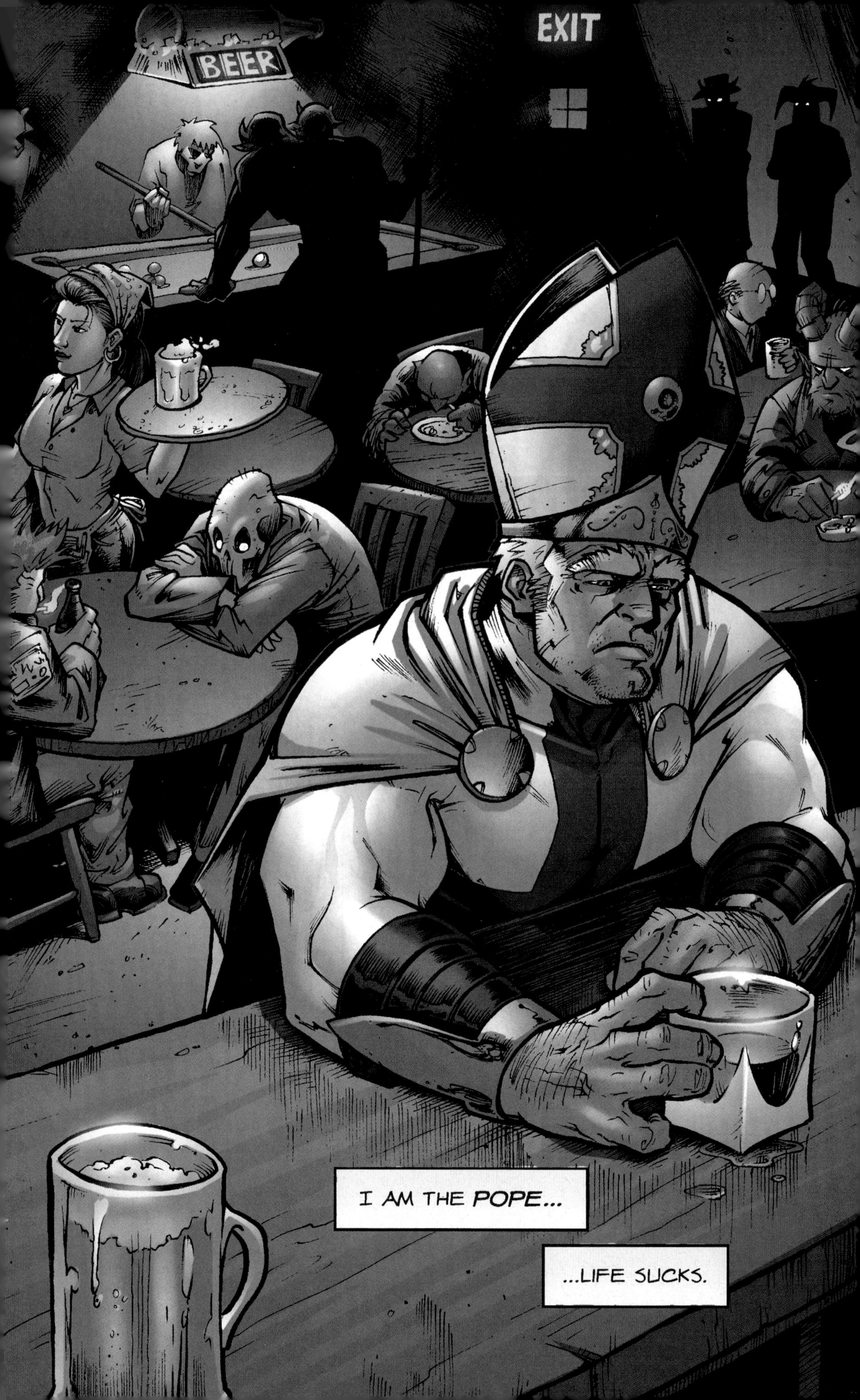
BEER
EXIT
I AM THE POPE...
...LIFE SUCKS.

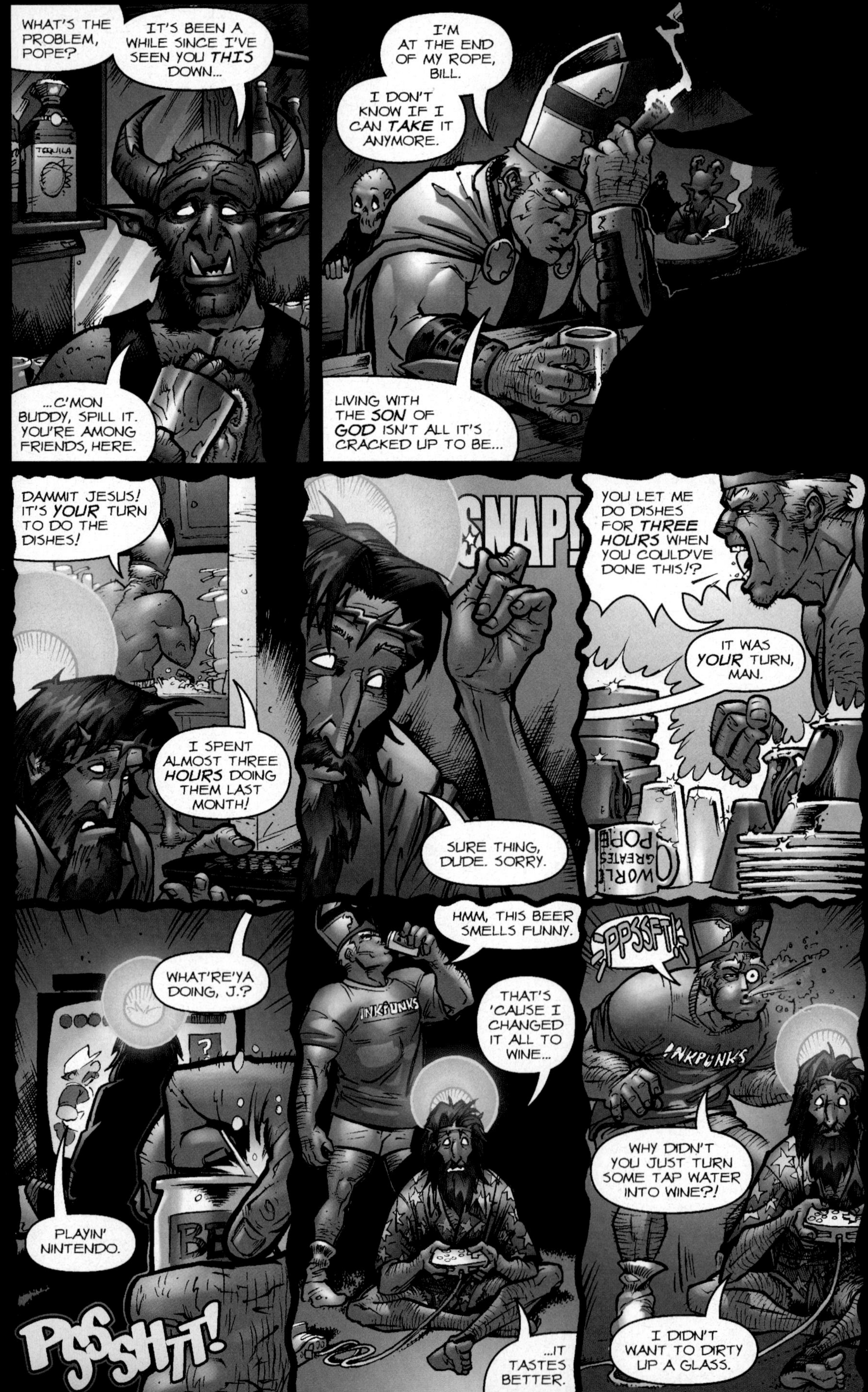
WHAT'S THE PROBLEM, POPE?
IT'S BEEN A WHILE SINCE I'VE SEEN YOU THIS DOWN...
...C'MON BUDDY, SPILL IT. YOU'RE AMONG FRIENDS, HERE.
I'M AT THE END OF MY ROPE, BILL.
I DON'T KNOW IF I CAN TAKE IT ANYMORE.
LIVING WITH THE SON OF GOD ISN'T ALL IT'S CRACKED UP TO BE...
TEQUILA
DAMMIT JESUS! IT'S YOUR TURN TO DO THE DISHES!
I SPENT ALMOST THREE HOURS DOING THEM LAST MONTH!
SNAP!
SURE THING, DUDE. SORRY.
YOU LET ME DO DISHES FOR THREE HOURS WHEN YOU COULD'VE DONE THIS!?
IT WAS YOUR TURN, MAN.
WORLD GREATEST POPE
WHAT'RE'YA DOING, J.?
PLAYIN' NINTENDO.
PSSSHTT!
HMM, THIS BEER SMELLS FUNNY.
THAT'S 'CAUSE I CHANGED IT ALL TO WINE...
...IT TASTES BETTER.
INKPUNKS
PPSSFT!
WHY DIDN'T YOU JUST TURN SOME TAP WATER INTO WINE?!
I DIDN'T WANT TO DIRTY UP A GLASS.

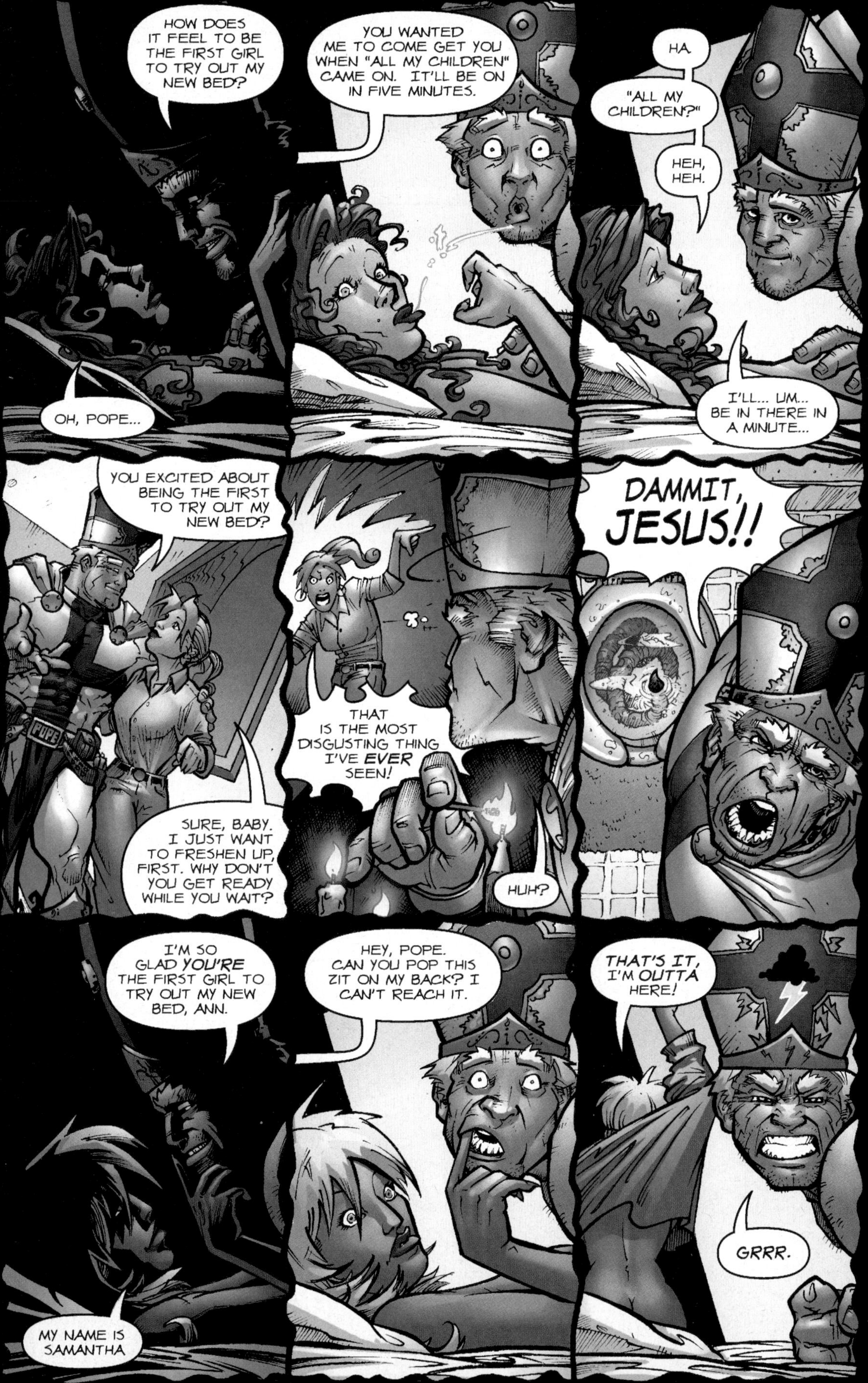
HOW DOES IT FEEL TO BE THE FIRST GIRL TO TRY OUT MY NEW BED?
OH, POPE...
YOU WANTED ME TO COME GET YOU WHEN "ALL MY CHILDREN" CAME ON. IT'LL BE ON IN FIVE MINUTES.
HA.
"ALL MY CHILDREN?"
HEH, HEH.
I'LL... UM... BE IN THERE IN A MINUTE...
YOU EXCITED ABOUT BEING THE FIRST TO TRY OUT MY NEW BED?
POPE
SURE, BABY. I JUST WANT TO FRESHEN UP, FIRST. WHY DON'T YOU GET READY WHILE YOU WAIT?
THAT IS THE MOST DISGUSTING THING I'VE EVER SEEN!
HUH?
DAMMIT, JESUS!!
I'M SO GLAD YOU'RE THE FIRST GIRL TO TRY OUT MY NEW BED, ANN.
MY NAME IS SAMANTHA
HEY, POPE. CAN YOU POP THIS ZIT ON MY BACK? I CAN'T REACH IT.
THAT'S IT, I'M OUTTA HERE!
GRRR.

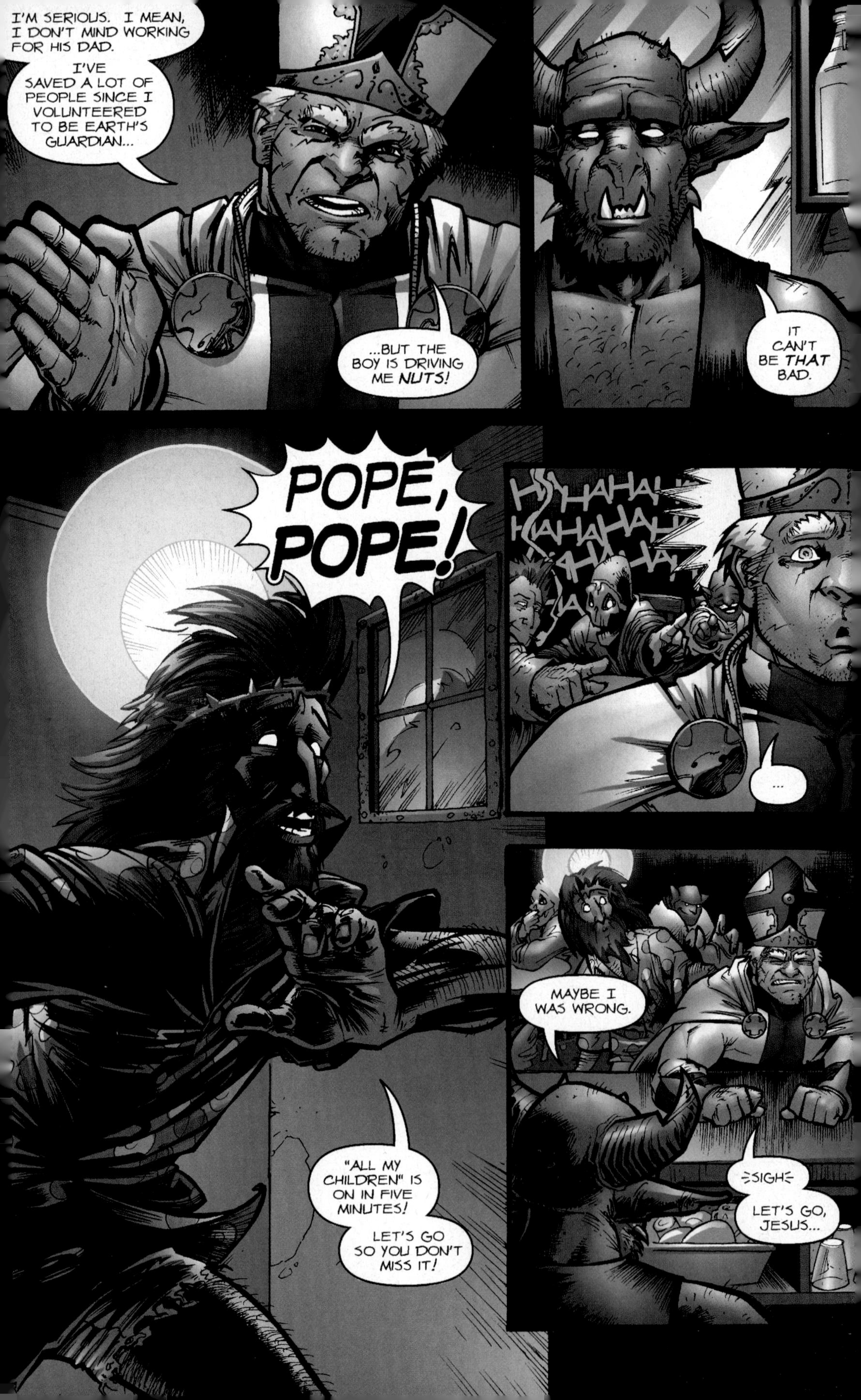
I'M SERIOUS. I MEAN, I DON'T MIND WORKING FOR HIS DAD.
I'VE SAVED A LOT OF PEOPLE SINCE I VOLUNTEERED TO BE EARTH'S GUARDIAN...
...BUT THE BOY IS DRIVING ME NUTS!
IT CAN'T BE THAT BAD.
POPE, POPE!
HAHAHAHAHA
...
"ALL MY CHILDREN" IS ON IN FIVE MINUTES!
LET'S GO SO YOU DON'T MISS IT!
MAYBE I WAS WRONG.
=SIGH=
LET'S GO, JESUS...

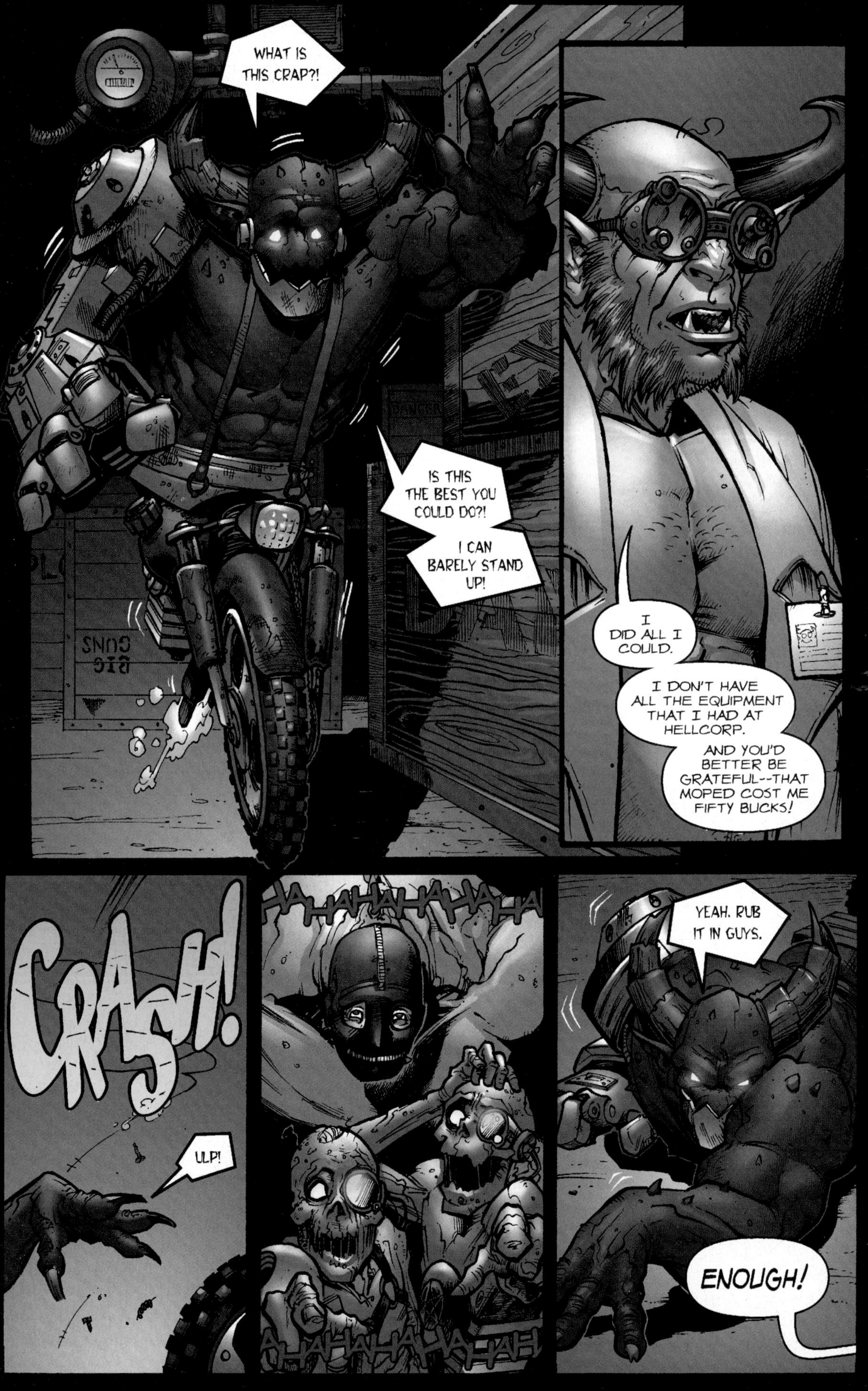
WHAT IS THIS CRAP?!
IS THIS THE BEST YOU COULD DO?!
I CAN BARELY STAND UP!
I DID ALL I COULD.
I DON'T HAVE ALL THE EQUIPMENT THAT I HAD AT HELLCORP.
AND YOU'D BETTER BE GRATEFUL--THAT MOPED COST ME FIFTY BUCKS!
BIG GUNS
CRASH!
ULP!
HAHAHAHAHAHAHA
HAHAHAHAHAHAH
YEAH. RUB IT IN GUYS.
ENOUGH!

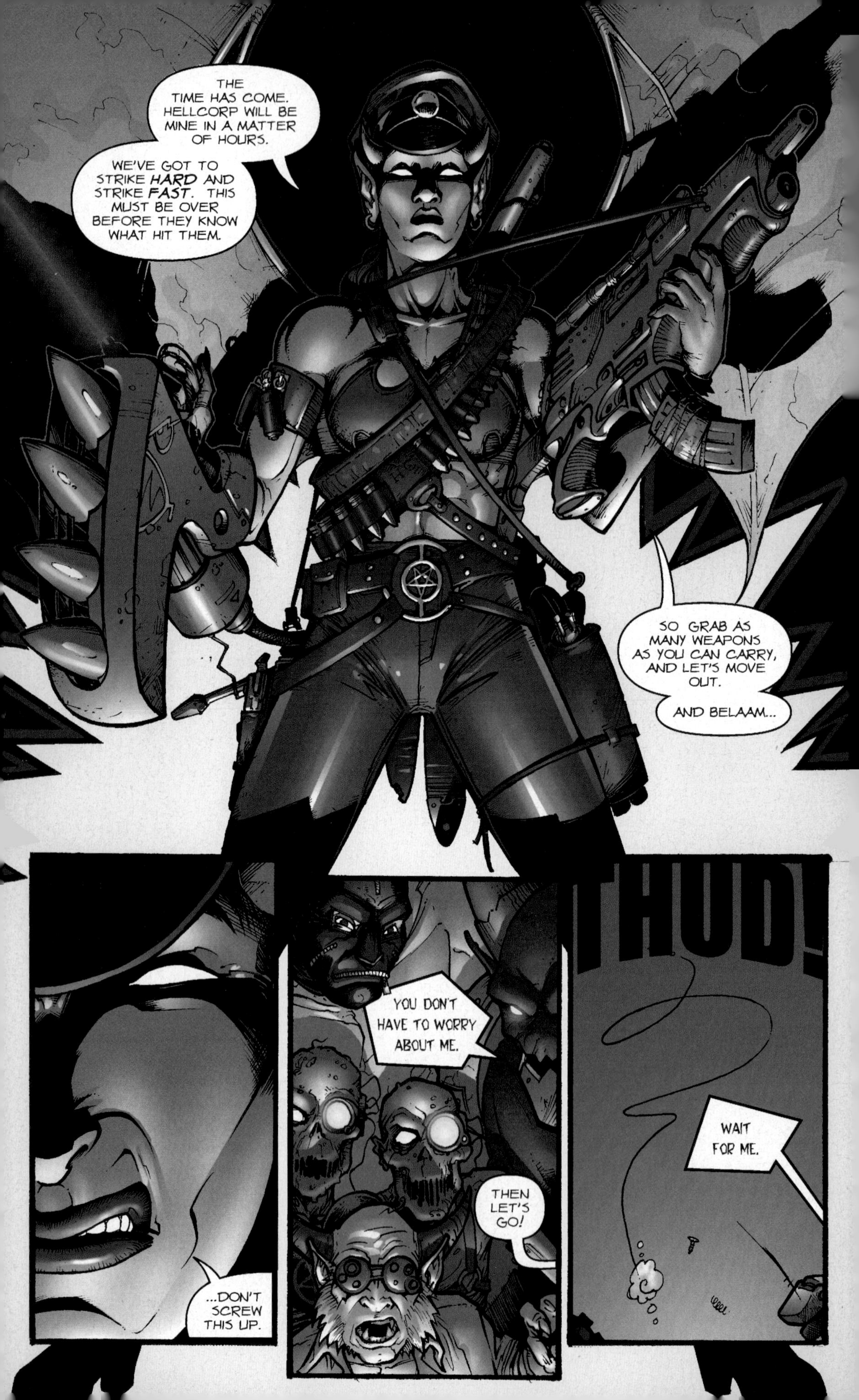
THE TIME HAS COME. HELLCORP WILL BE MINE IN A MATTER OF HOURS.
WE'VE GOT TO STRIKE **HARD** AND STRIKE **FAST**. THIS MUST BE OVER BEFORE THEY KNOW WHAT HIT THEM.
SO GRAB AS MANY WEAPONS AS YOU CAN CARRY, AND LET'S MOVE OUT.
AND BELAAM...
...DON'T SCREW THIS UP.
YOU DON'T HAVE TO WORRY ABOUT ME.
THEN LET'S GO!
THUD!
WAIT FOR ME.

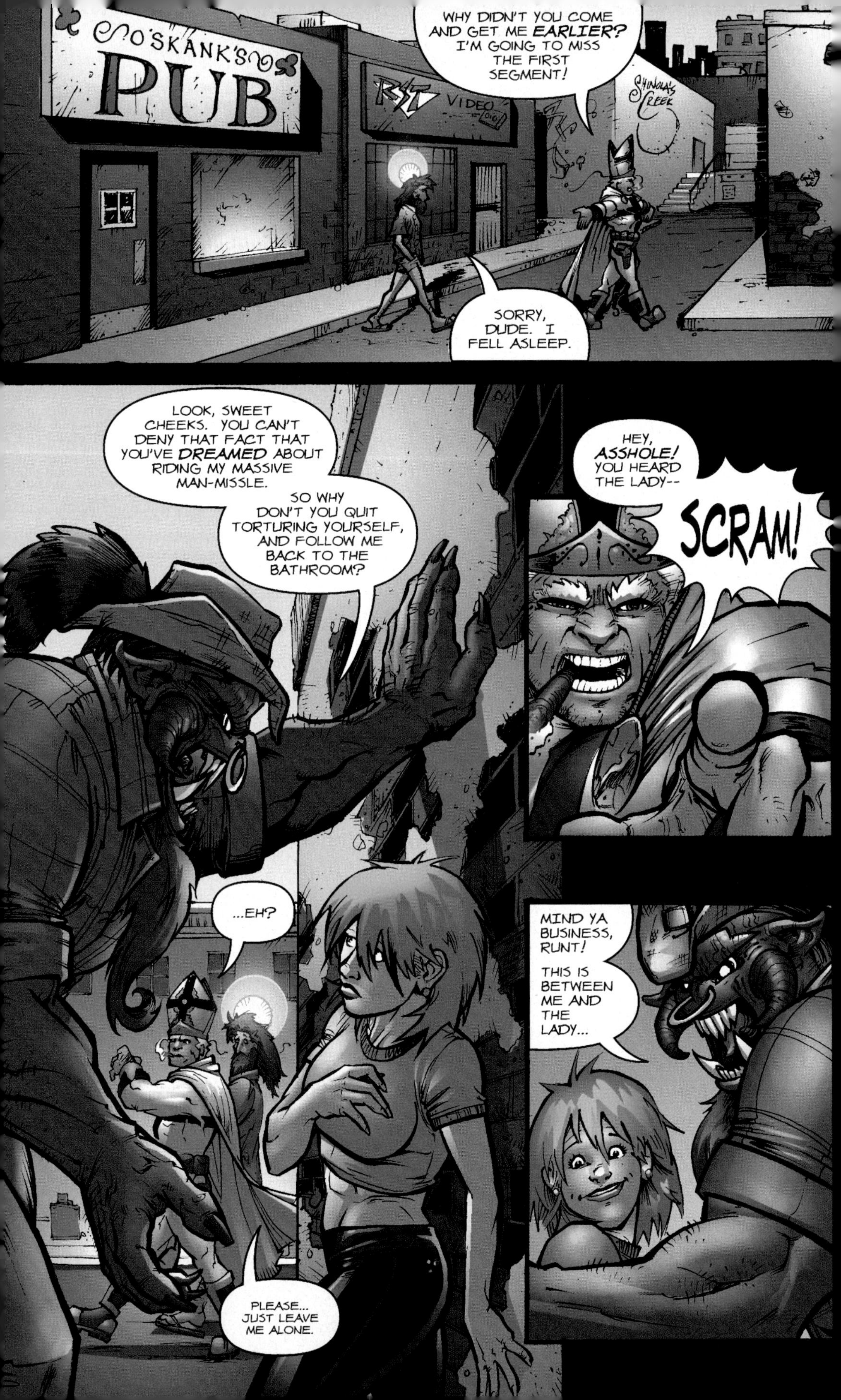
O'SKANK'S PUB
VIDEO
SHINOLA'S CREEK
WHY DIDN'T YOU COME AND GET ME EARLIER? I'M GOING TO MISS THE FIRST SEGMENT!
SORRY, DUDE. I FELL ASLEEP.
LOOK, SWEET CHEEKS. YOU CAN'T DENY THAT FACT THAT YOU'VE DREAMED ABOUT RIDING MY MASSIVE MAN-MISSLE.
SO WHY DON'T YOU QUIT TORTURING YOURSELF, AND FOLLOW ME BACK TO THE BATHROOM?
HEY, ASSHOLE! YOU HEARD THE LADY--
SCRAM!
...EH?
PLEASE... JUST LEAVE ME ALONE.
MIND YA BUSINESS, RUNT!
THIS IS BETWEEN ME AND THE LADY...

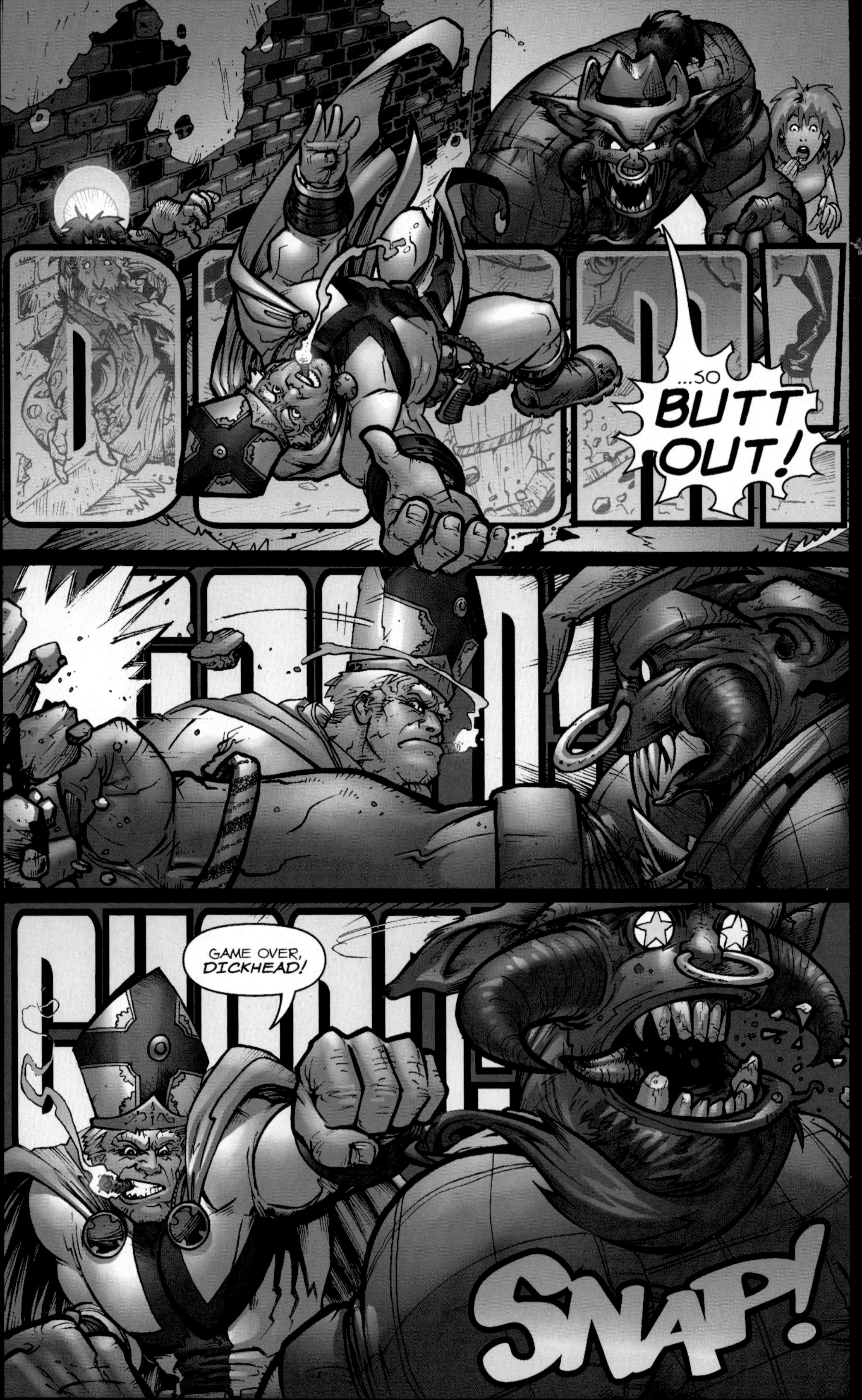
...SO BUTT OUT!
GAME OVER, DICKHEAD!
SNAP!

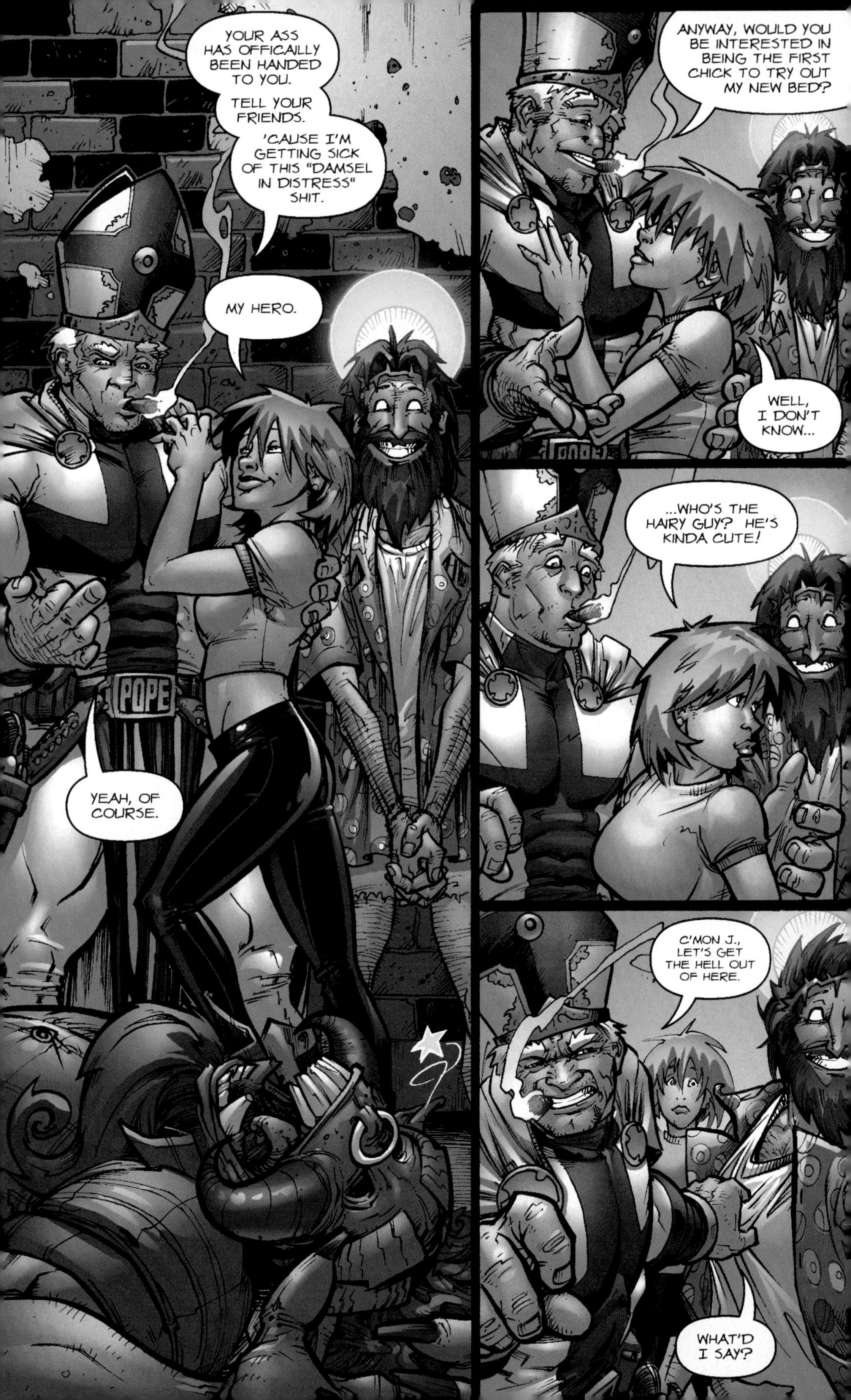
YOUR ASS HAS OFFICAILLY BEEN HANDED TO YOU.
TELL YOUR FRIENDS.
'CAUSE I'M GETTING SICK OF THIS "DAMSEL IN DISTRESS" SHIT.
MY HERO.
YEAH, OF COURSE.
POPE
ANYWAY, WOULD YOU BE INTERESTED IN BEING THE FIRST CHICK TO TRY OUT MY NEW BED?
WELL, I DON'T KNOW...
...WHO'S THE HAIRY GUY? HE'S KINDA CUTE!
C'MON J., LET'S GET THE HELL OUT OF HERE.
WHAT'D I SAY?

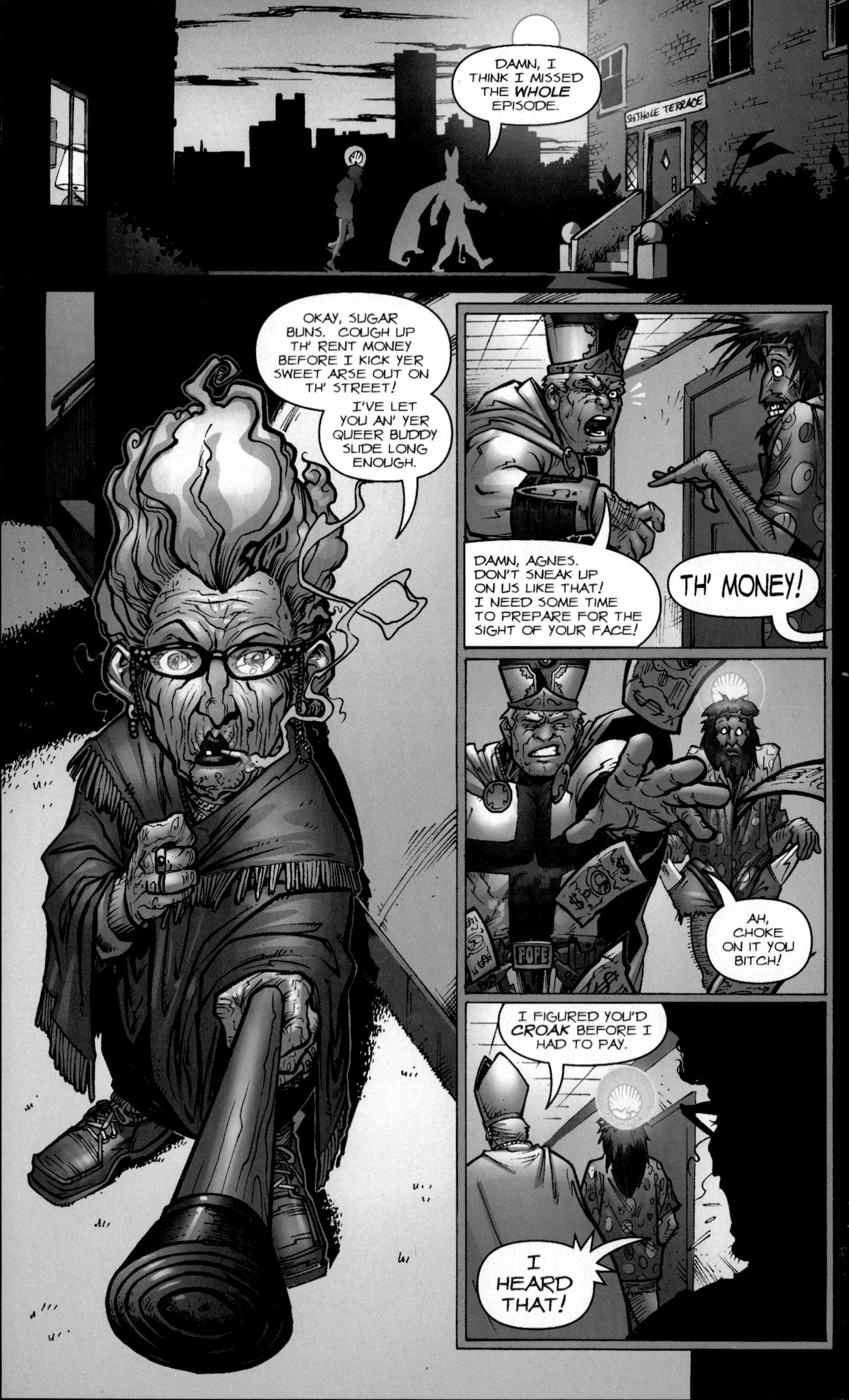
DAMN, I THINK I MISSED THE WHOLE EPISODE.
SHITHOLE TERRACE
OKAY, SUGAR BUNS. COUGH UP TH' RENT MONEY BEFORE I KICK YER SWEET ARSE OUT ON TH' STREET!
I'VE LET YOU AN' YER QUEER BUDDY SLIDE LONG ENOUGH.
DAMN, AGNES. DON'T SNEAK UP ON US LIKE THAT! I NEED SOME TIME TO PREPARE FOR THE SIGHT OF YOUR FACE!
TH' MONEY!
AH, CHOKE ON IT YOU BITCH!
I FIGURED YOU'D CROAK BEFORE I HAD TO PAY.
I HEARD THAT!

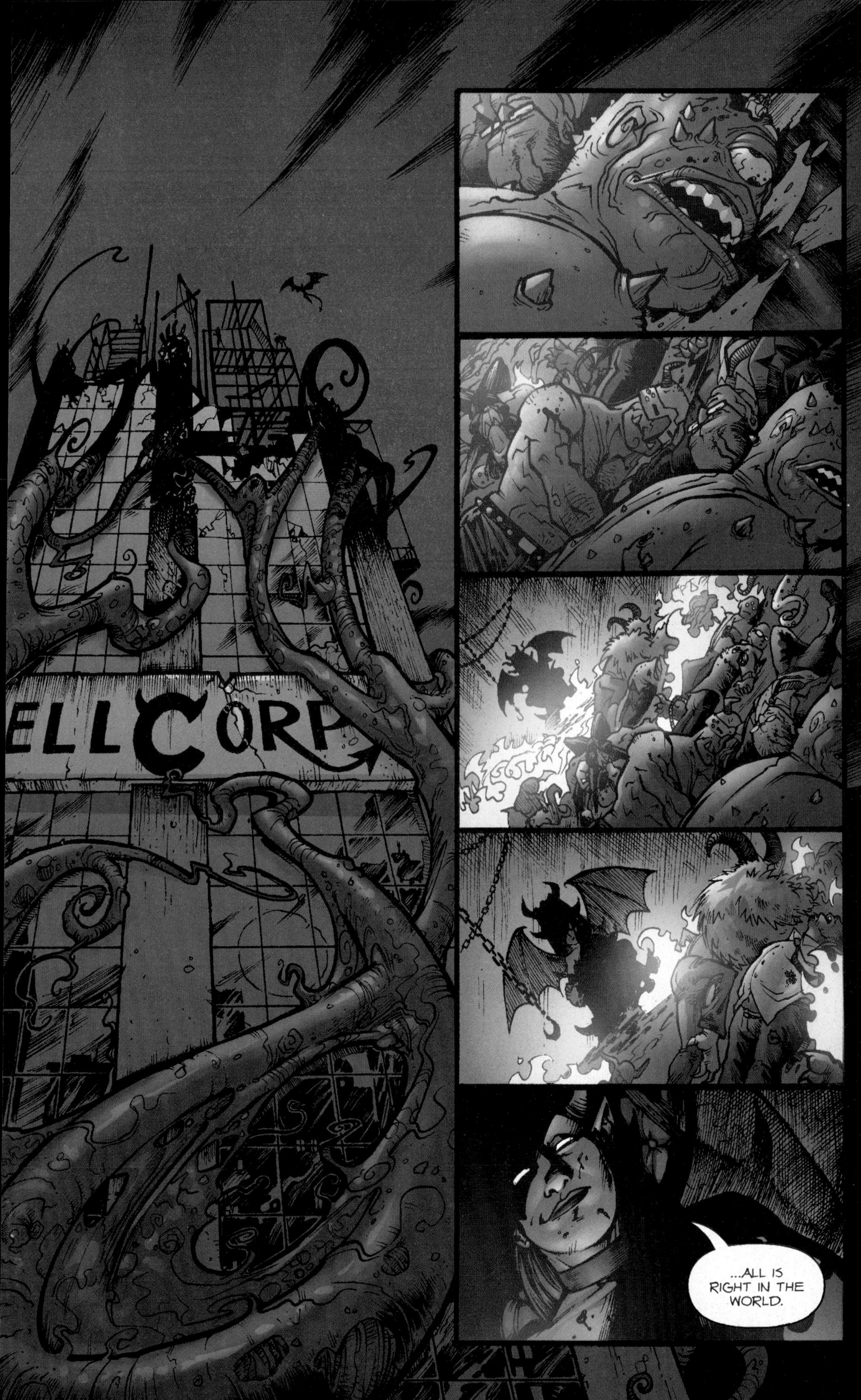
ELL CORP
...ALL IS RIGHT IN THE WORLD.

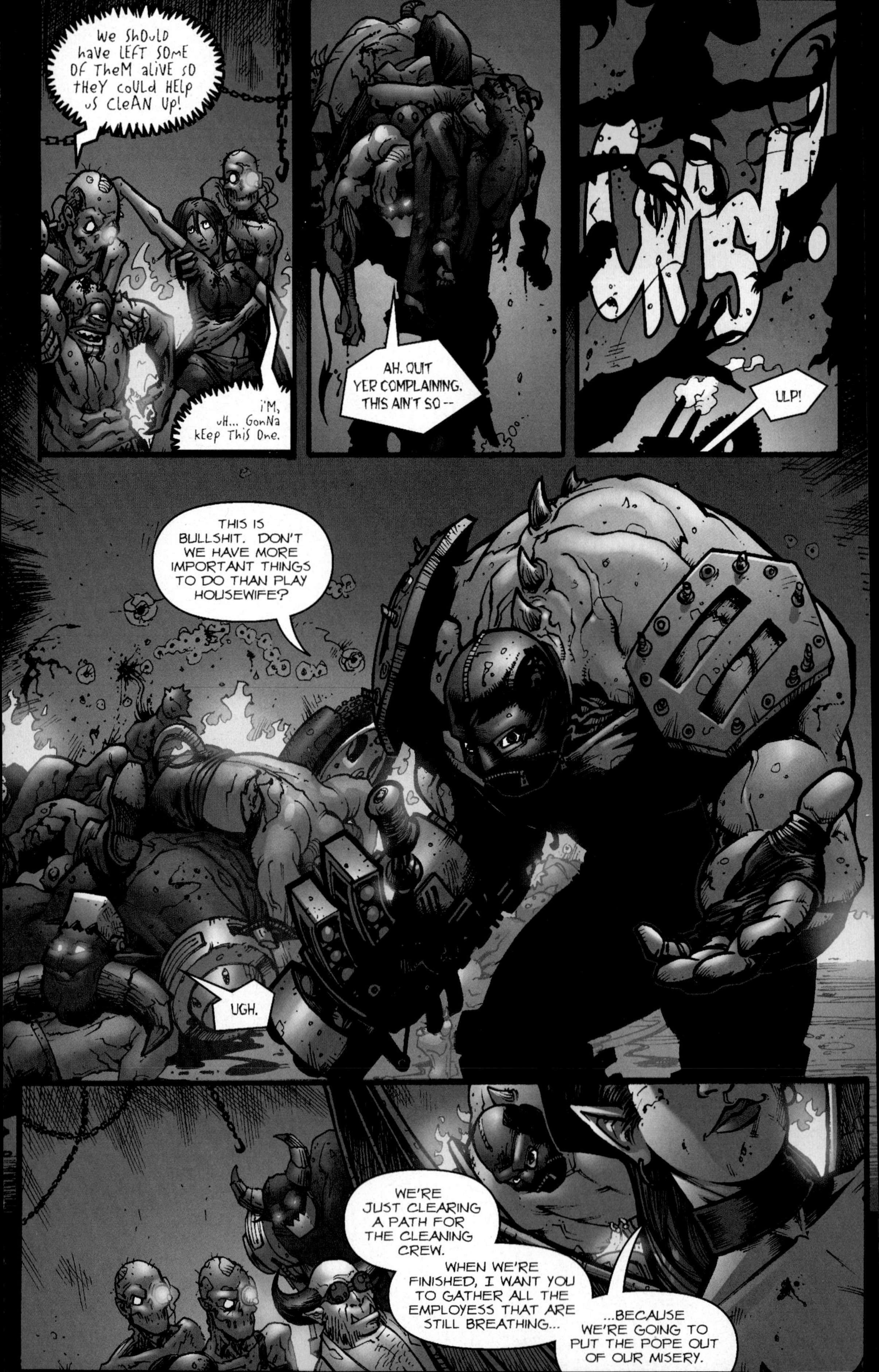
We ShOuLD have LEFT SOME OF TheM aLiVE SO THEY COULd HELp uS CLeAN Up!
i'M, uH... GonNa kEep ThiS One.
AH, QUIT YER COMPLAINING. THIS AIN'T SO --
ULP!
THIS IS BULLSHIT. DON'T WE HAVE MORE IMPORTANT THINGS TO DO THAN PLAY HOUSEWIFE?
UGH.
WE'RE JUST CLEARING A PATH FOR THE CLEANING CREW.
WHEN WE'RE FINISHED, I WANT YOU TO GATHER ALL THE EMPLOYESS THAT ARE STILL BREATHING...
...BECAUSE WE'RE GOING TO PUT THE POPE OUT OF OUR MISERY.

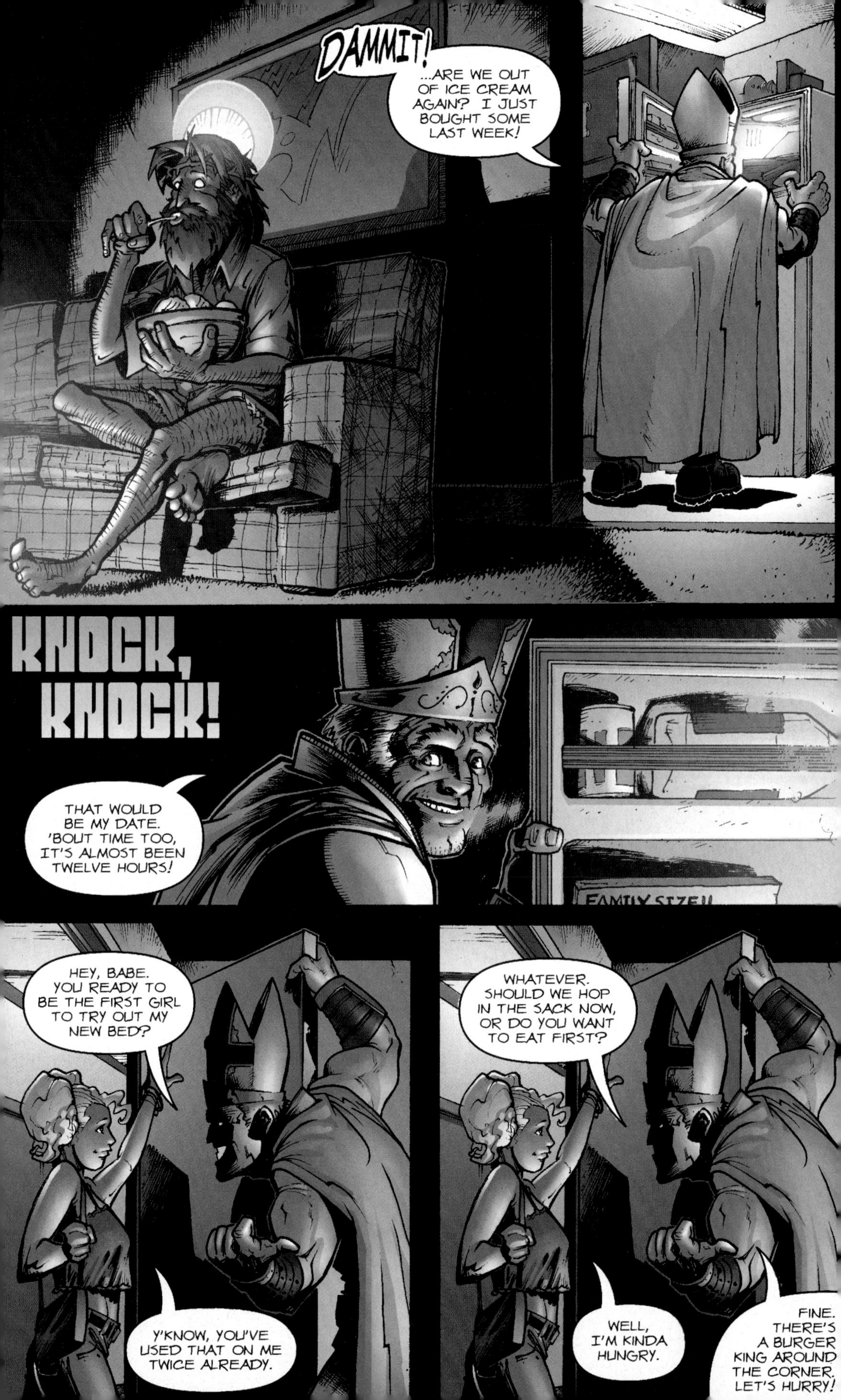
DAMMIT!
...ARE WE OUT OF ICE CREAM AGAIN? I JUST BOUGHT SOME LAST WEEK!
KNOCK, KNOCK!
THAT WOULD BE MY DATE. 'BOUT TIME TOO, IT'S ALMOST BEEN TWELVE HOURS!
FAMILY SIZE!!
HEY, BABE. YOU READY TO BE THE FIRST GIRL TO TRY OUT MY NEW BED?
Y'KNOW, YOU'VE USED THAT ON ME TWICE ALREADY.
WHATEVER. SHOULD WE HOP IN THE SACK NOW, OR DO YOU WANT TO EAT FIRST?
WELL, I'M KINDA HUNGRY.
FINE. THERE'S A BURGER KING AROUND THE CORNER. LET'S HURRY!

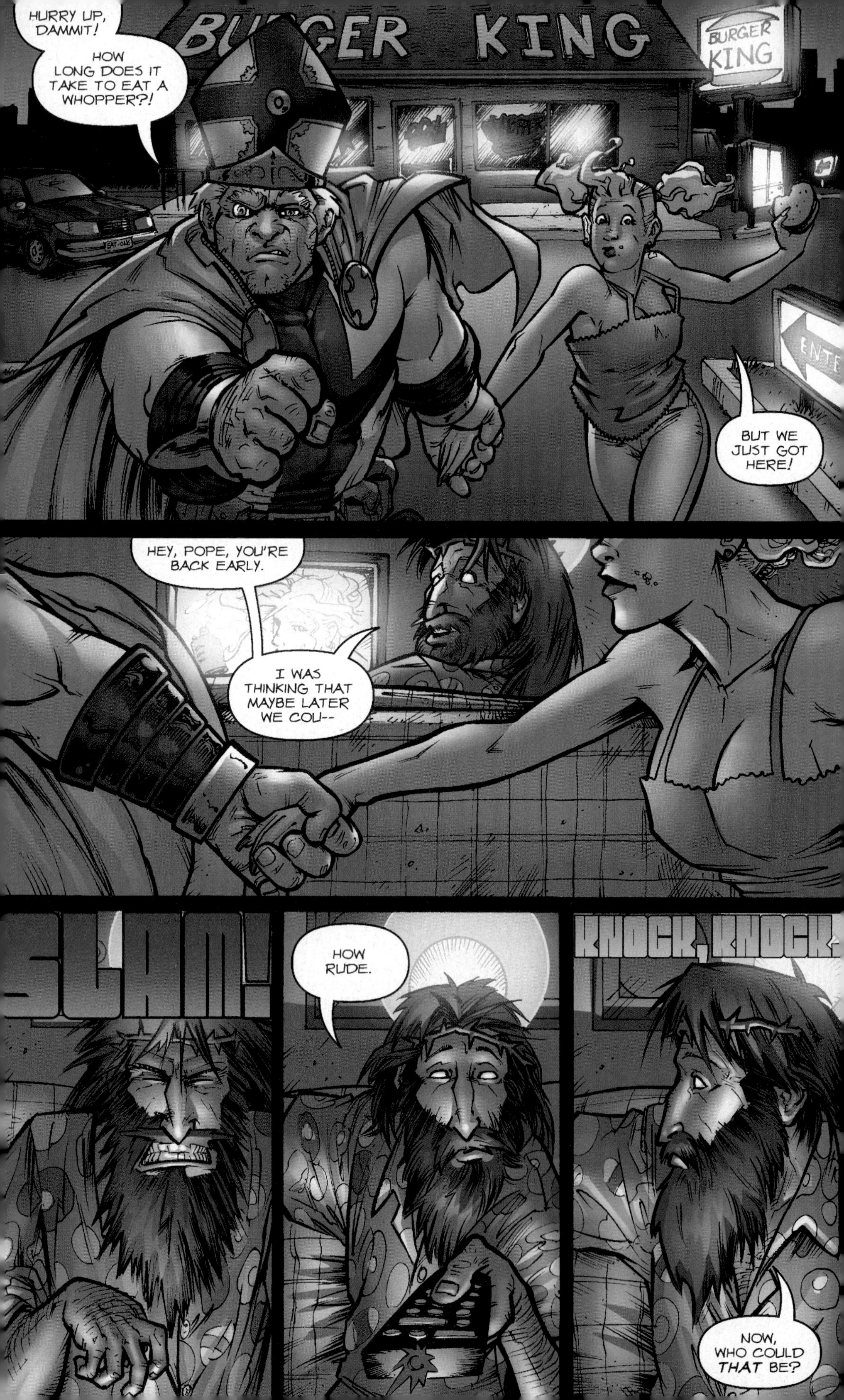
BURGER KING
BURGER KING
HURRY UP, DAMMIT!
HOW LONG DOES IT TAKE TO EAT A WHOPPER?!
BUT WE JUST GOT HERE!
HEY, POPE, YOU'RE BACK EARLY.
I WAS THINKING THAT MAYBE LATER WE COU--
SLAM!
HOW RUDE.
KNOCK, KNOCK
NOW, WHO COULD THAT BE?

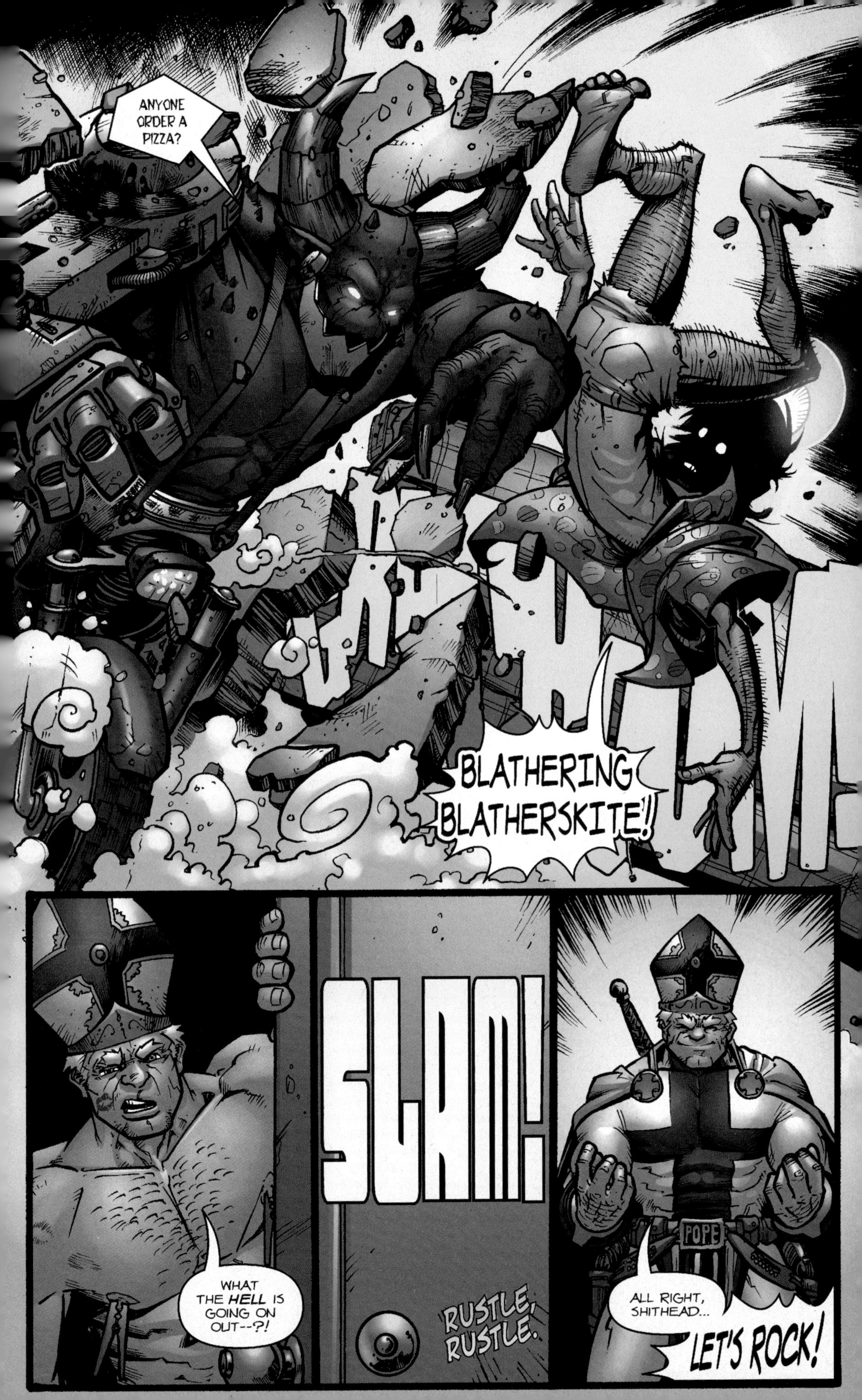
ANYONE ORDER A PIZZA?
BLATHERING BLATHERSKITE!
WHAT THE HELL IS GOING ON OUT--?!
SLAM!
RUSTLE, RUSTLE.
ALL RIGHT, SHITHEAD...
LET'S ROCK!
POPE

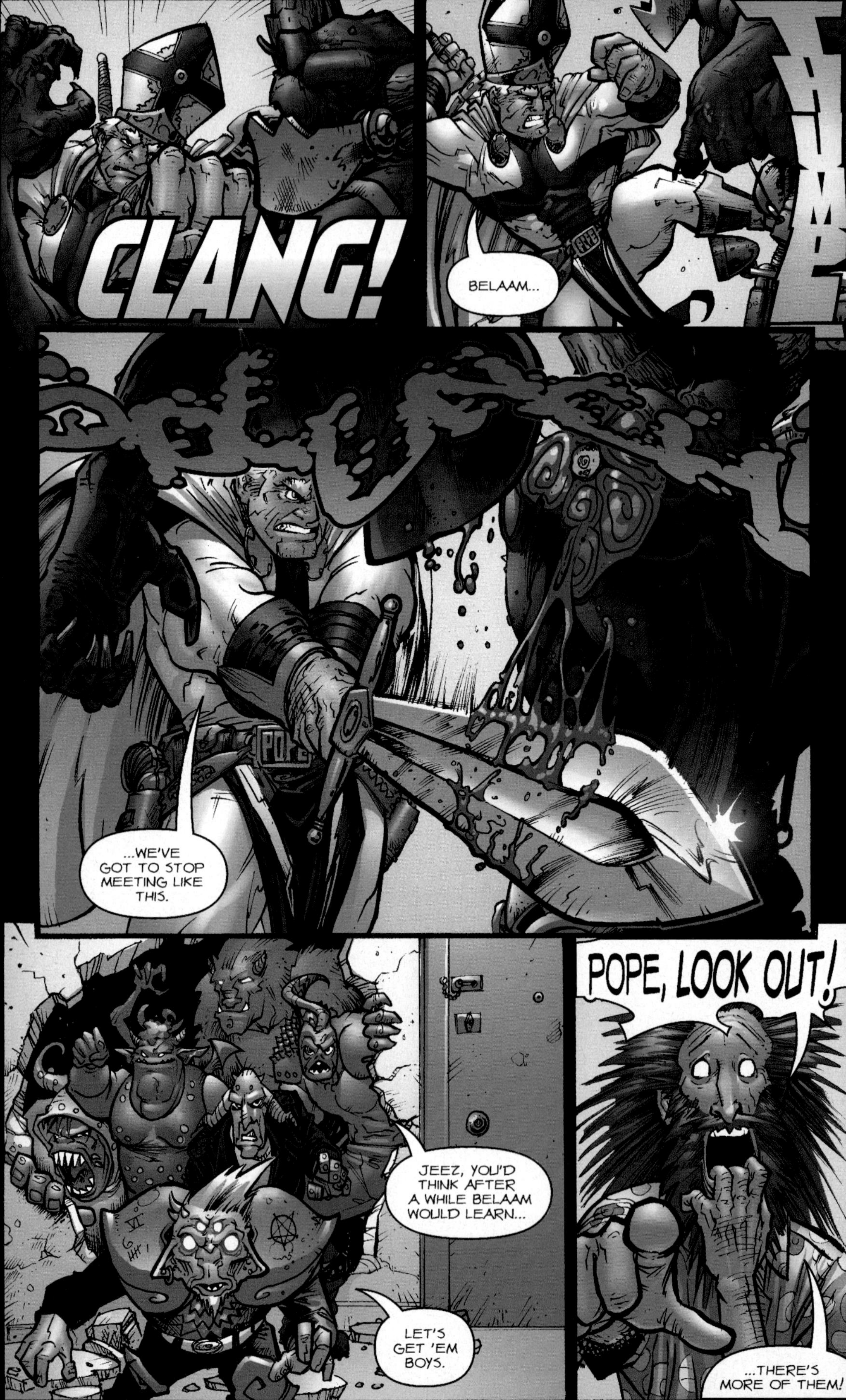
CLANG!
BELAAM...
...WE'VE GOT TO STOP MEETING LIKE THIS.
JEEZ, YOU'D THINK AFTER A WHILE BELAAM WOULD LEARN...
LET'S GET 'EM BOYS.
POPE, LOOK OUT!
...THERE'S MORE OF THEM!

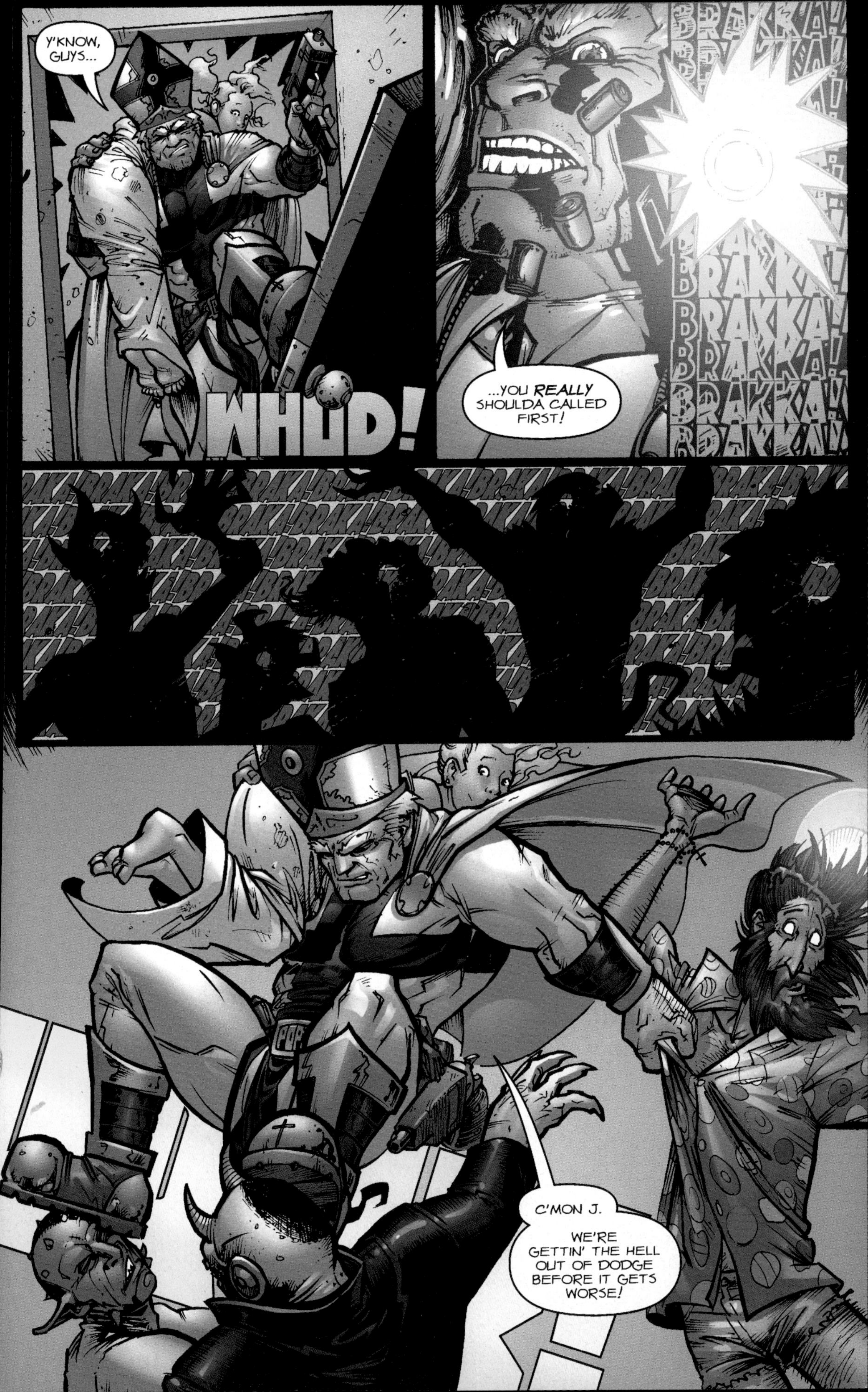
Y'KNOW, GUYS...
WHUD!
...YOU REALLY SHOULDA CALLED FIRST!
BRAKKA! BRAKKA! BRAKKA!
C'MON J.
WE'RE GETTIN' THE HELL OUT OF DODGE BEFORE IT GETS WORSE!

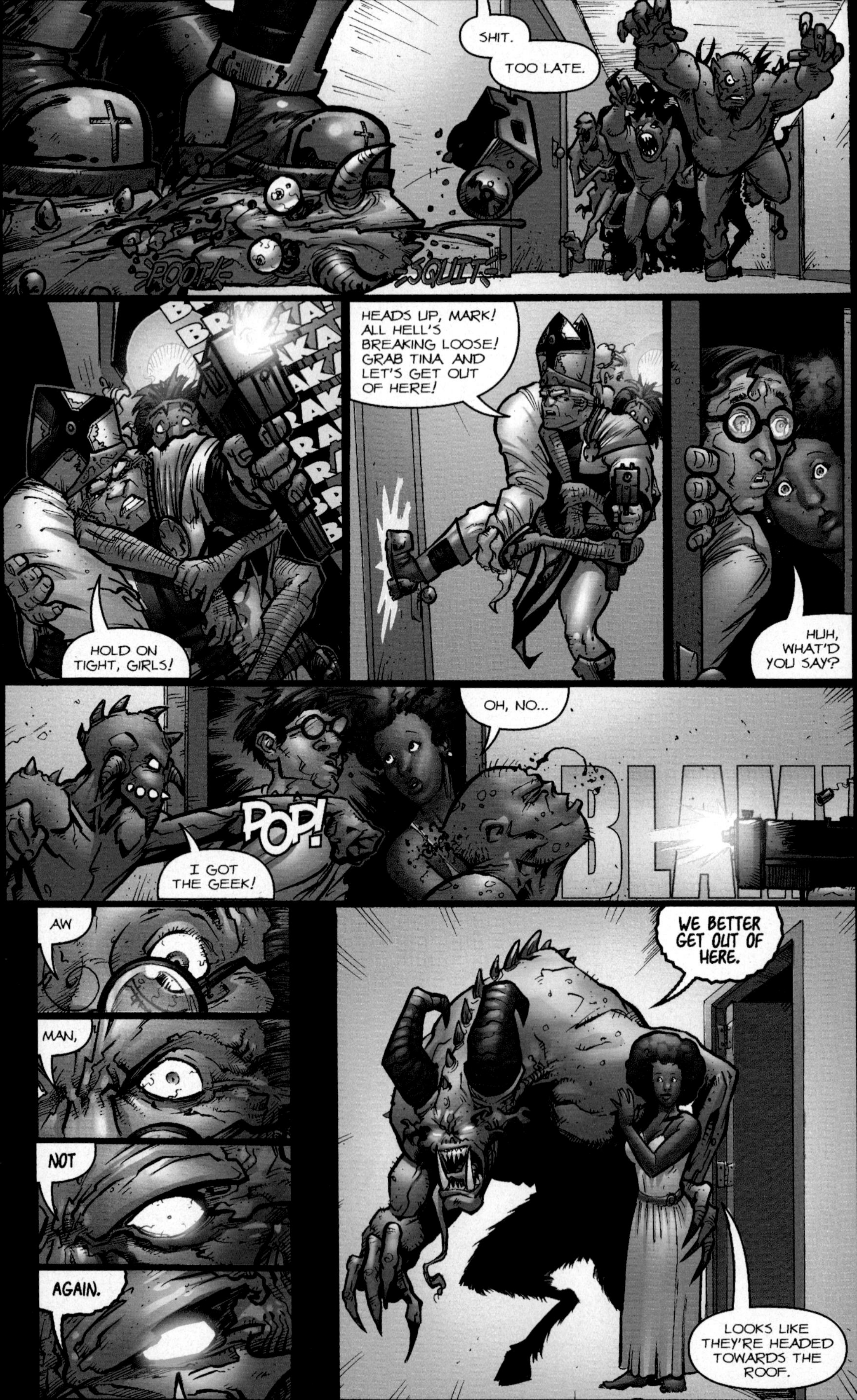

SHIT.
TOO LATE.
POOT!
SQUIT!
HEADS UP, MARK! ALL HELL'S BREAKING LOOSE! GRAB TINA AND LET'S GET OUT OF HERE!
HOLD ON TIGHT, GIRLS!
HUH, WHAT'D YOU SAY?
OH, NO...
I GOT THE GEEK!
POP!
AW
MAN,
NOT
AGAIN.
WE BETTER GET OUT OF HERE.
LOOKS LIKE THEY'RE HEADED TOWARDS THE ROOF.

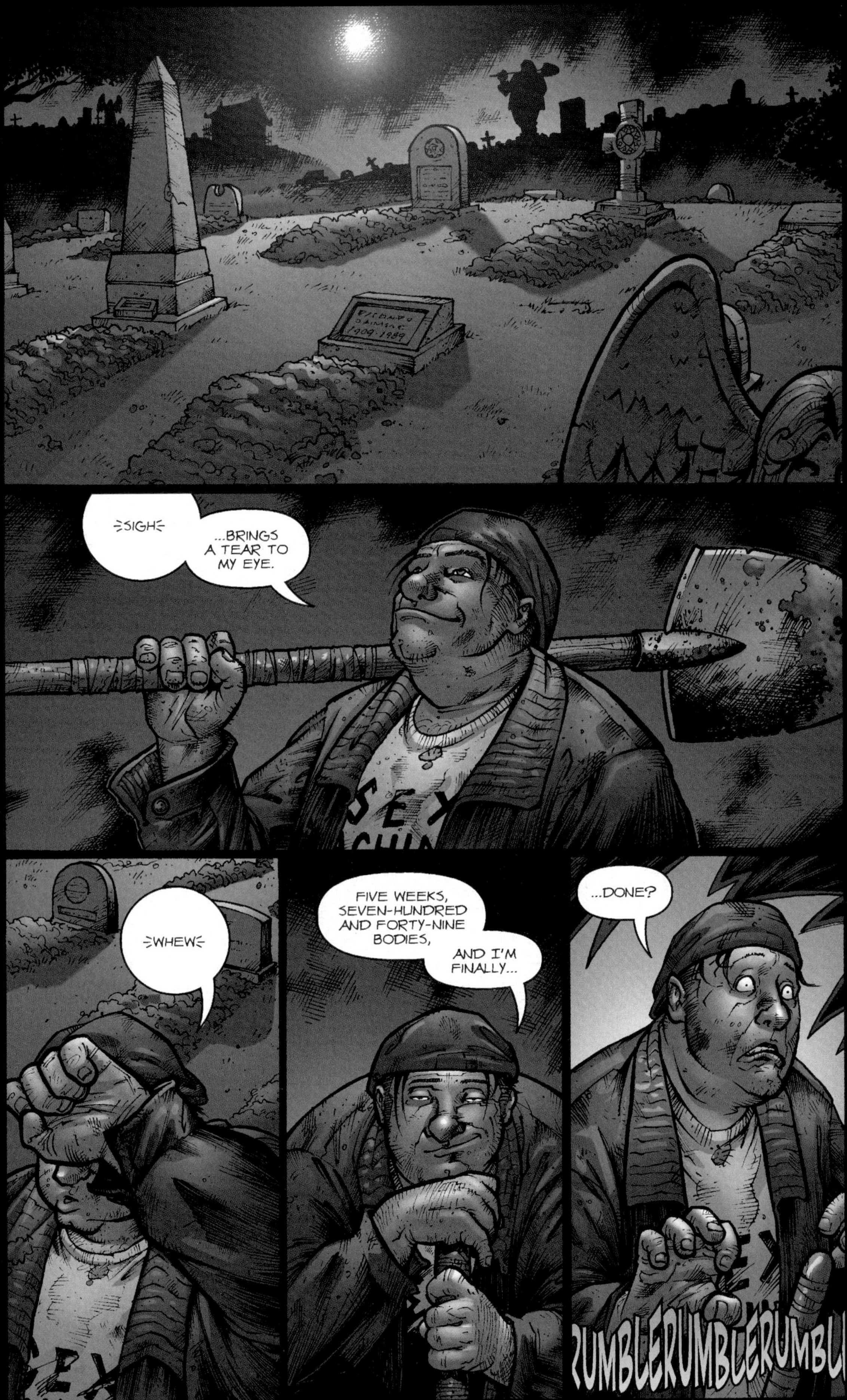

=SIGH=
...BRINGS A TEAR TO MY EYE.
=WHEW=
FIVE WEEKS, SEVEN-HUNDRED AND FORTY-NINE BODIES,
AND I'M FINALLY...
...DONE?
RUMBLERUMBLERUMBL

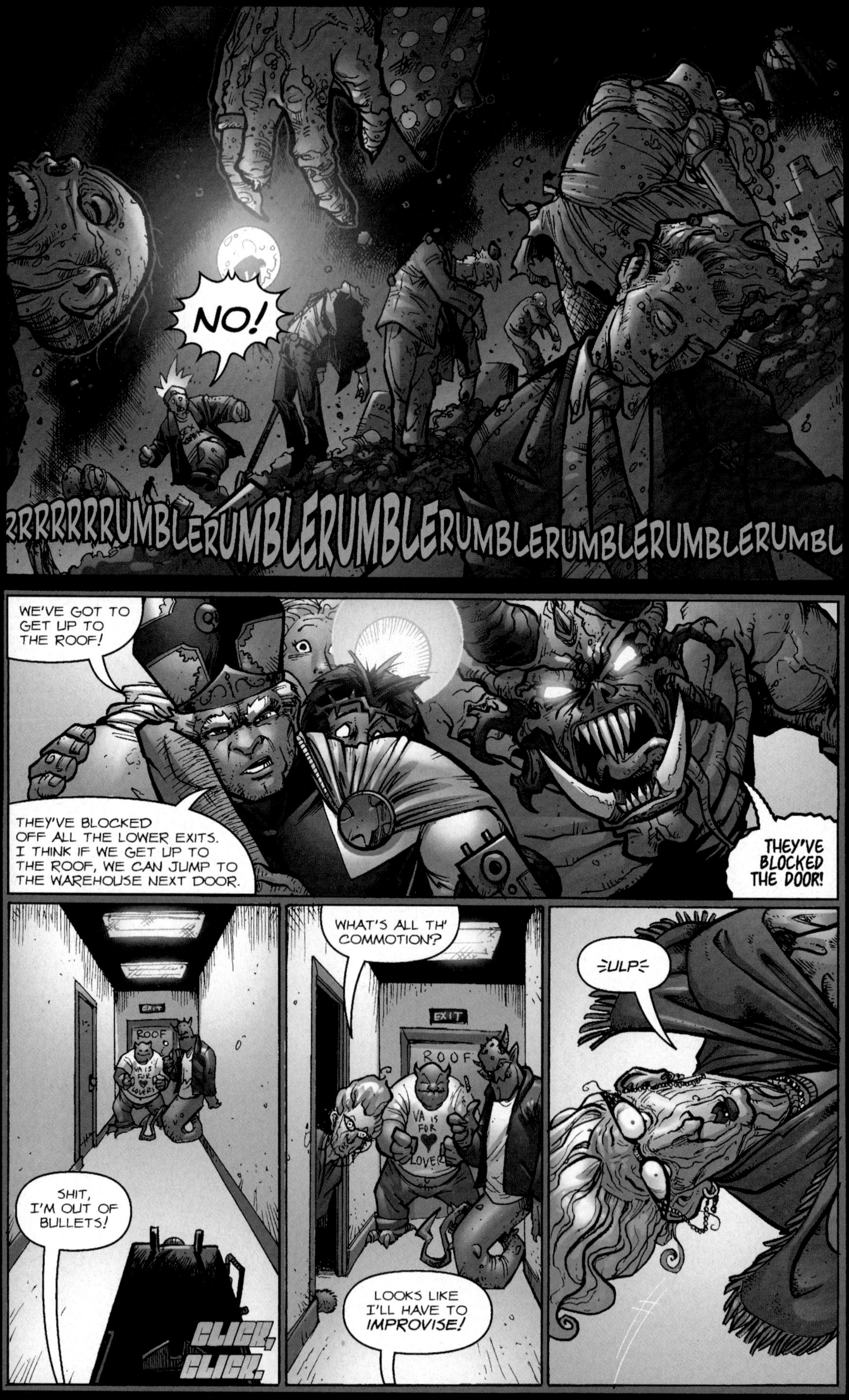
NO!
RRRRRRRUMBLERUMBLERUMBLERUMBLERUMBLERUMBLERUMBL
WE'VE GOT TO GET UP TO THE ROOF!
THEY'VE BLOCKED OFF ALL THE LOWER EXITS. I THINK IF WE GET UP TO THE ROOF, WE CAN JUMP TO THE WAREHOUSE NEXT DOOR.
THEY'VE BLOCKED THE DOOR!
EXIT
ROOF
SHIT, I'M OUT OF BULLETS!
CLICK, CLICK.
WHAT'S ALL TH' COMMOTION?
EXIT
ROOF
LOOKS LIKE I'LL HAVE TO IMPROVISE!
ULP

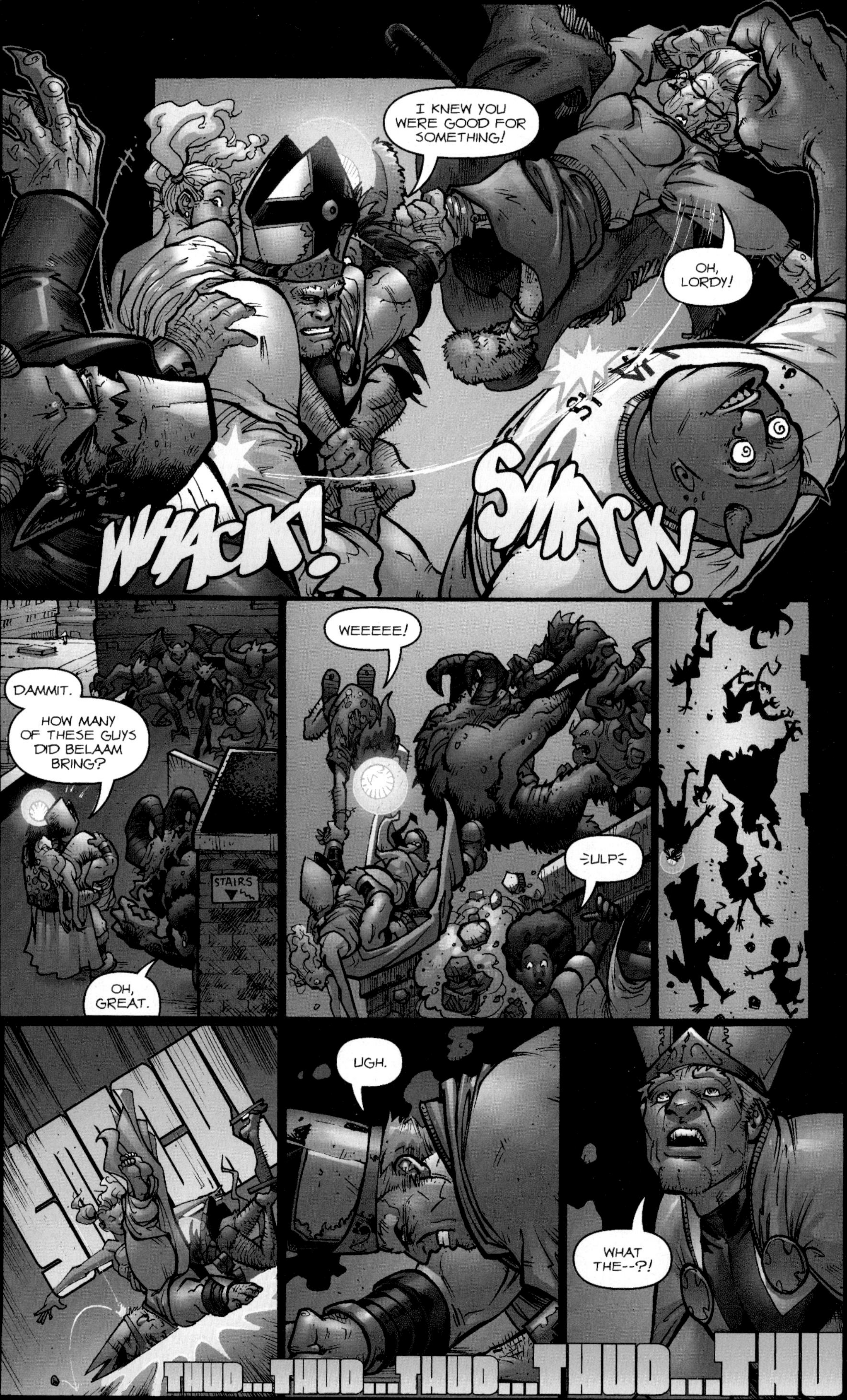
I KNEW YOU WERE GOOD FOR SOMETHING!
OH, LORDY!
WHACK!
SMACK!
DAMMIT.
HOW MANY OF THESE GUYS DID BELAAM BRING?
STAIRS
OH, GREAT.
WEEEEE!
ULP
UGH.
WHAT THE--?!
THUD...THUD...THUD...THUD...THU

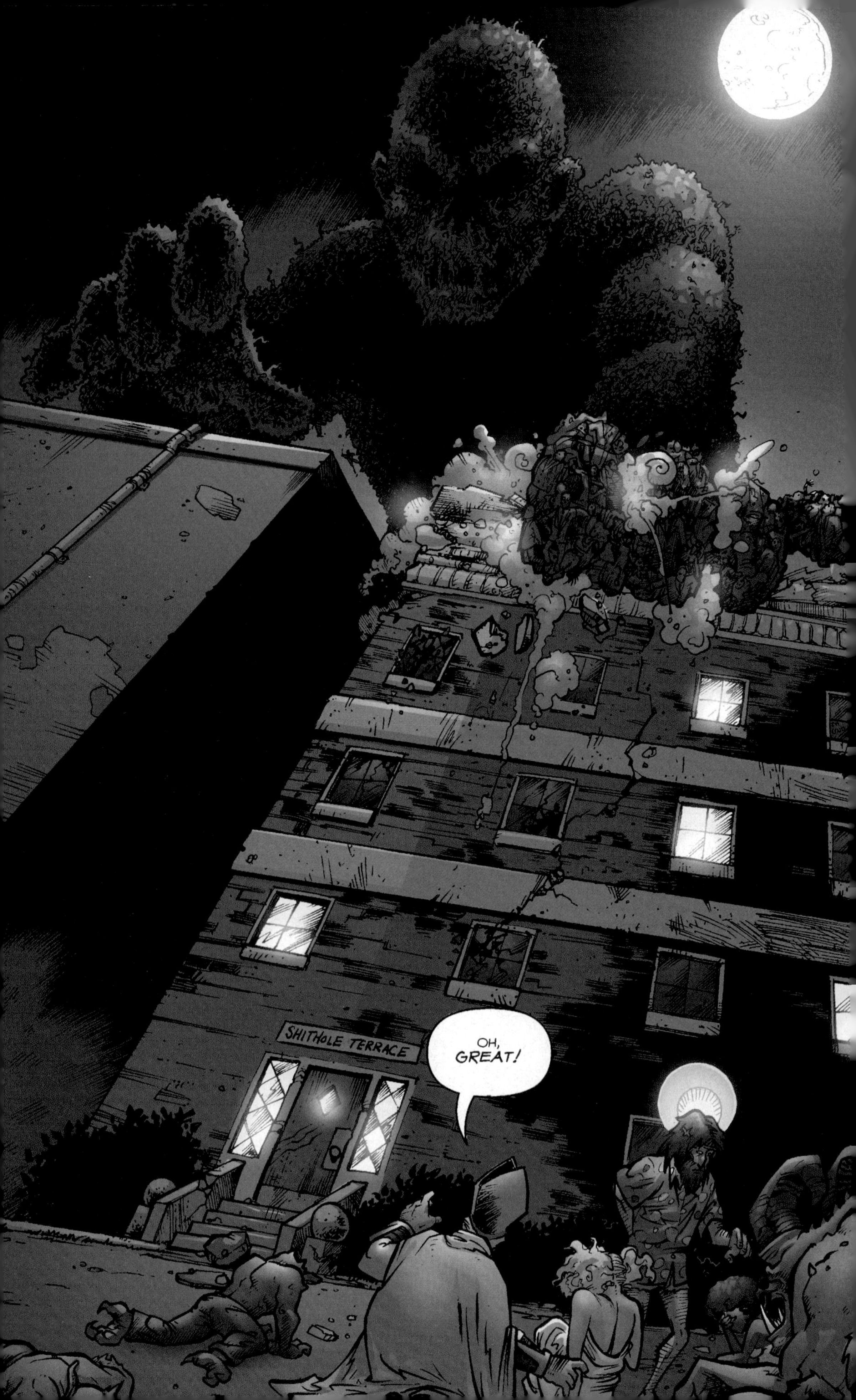
SHITHOLE TERRACE
OH, GREAT!

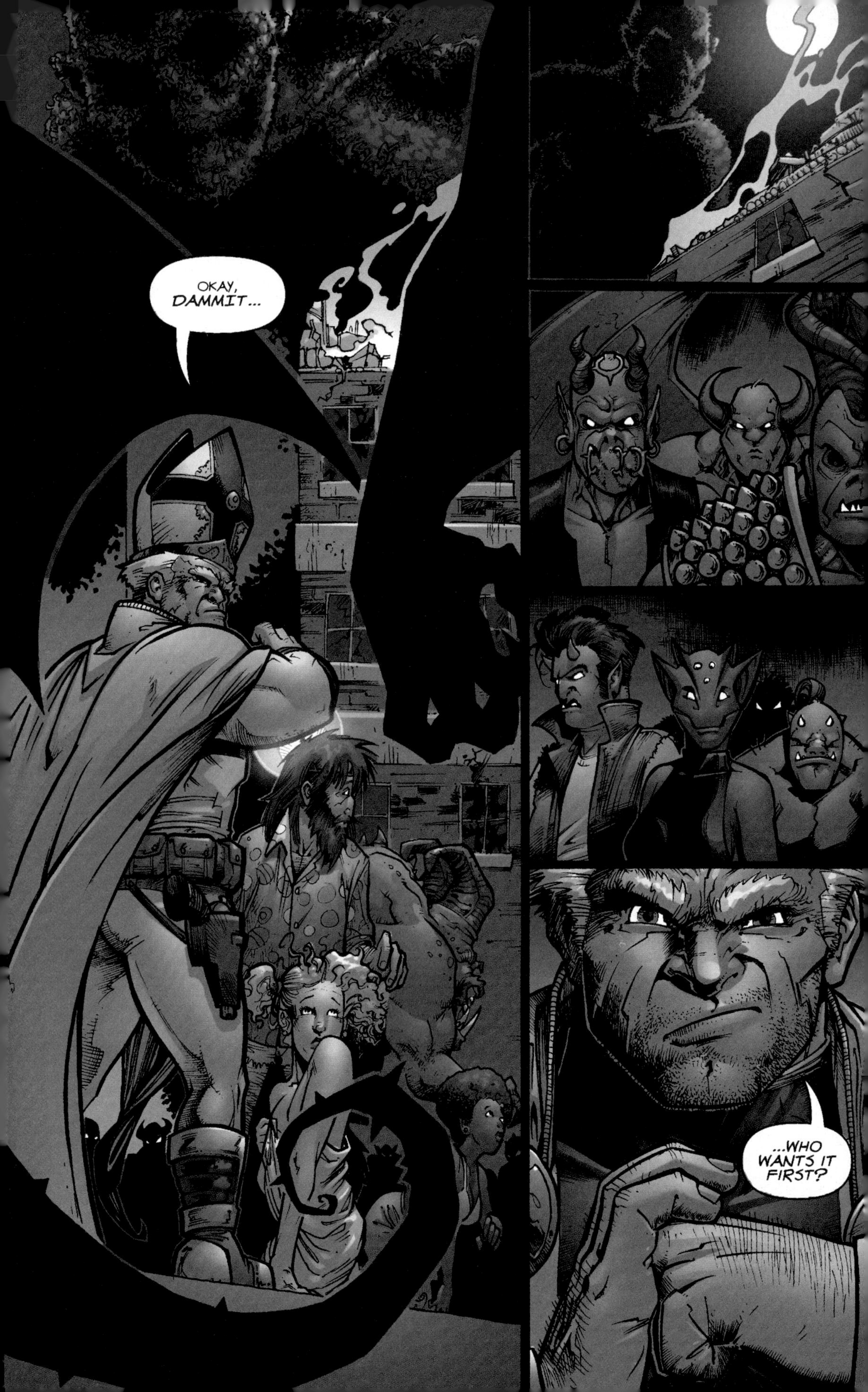
OKAY, DAMMIT...
...WHO WANTS IT FIRST?

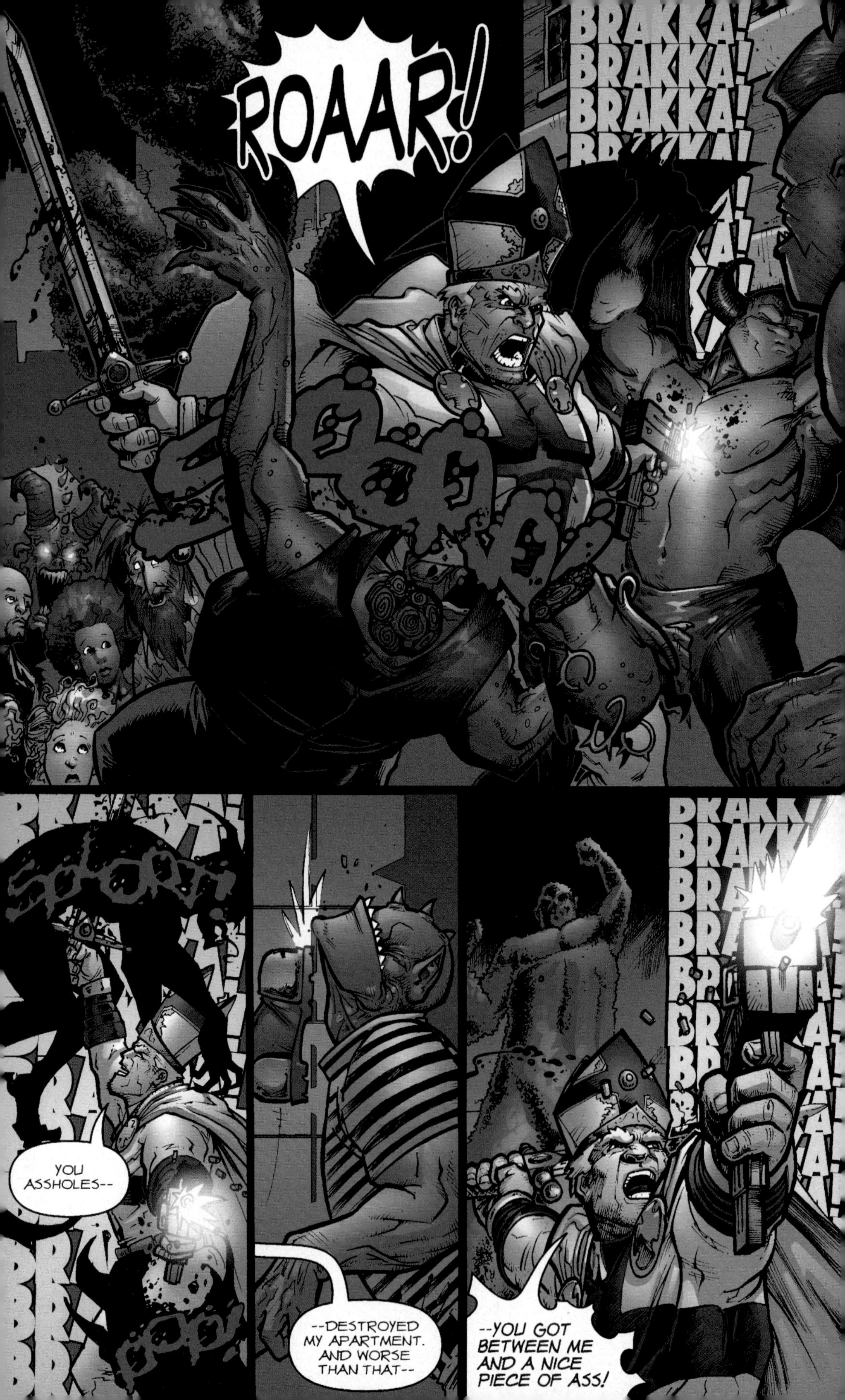
ROAAR!
BRAKKA!
BRAKKA!
BRAKKA!
YOU ASSHOLES--
--DESTROYED MY APARTMENT. AND WORSE THAN THAT--
--YOU GOT BETWEEN ME AND A NICE PIECE OF ASS!

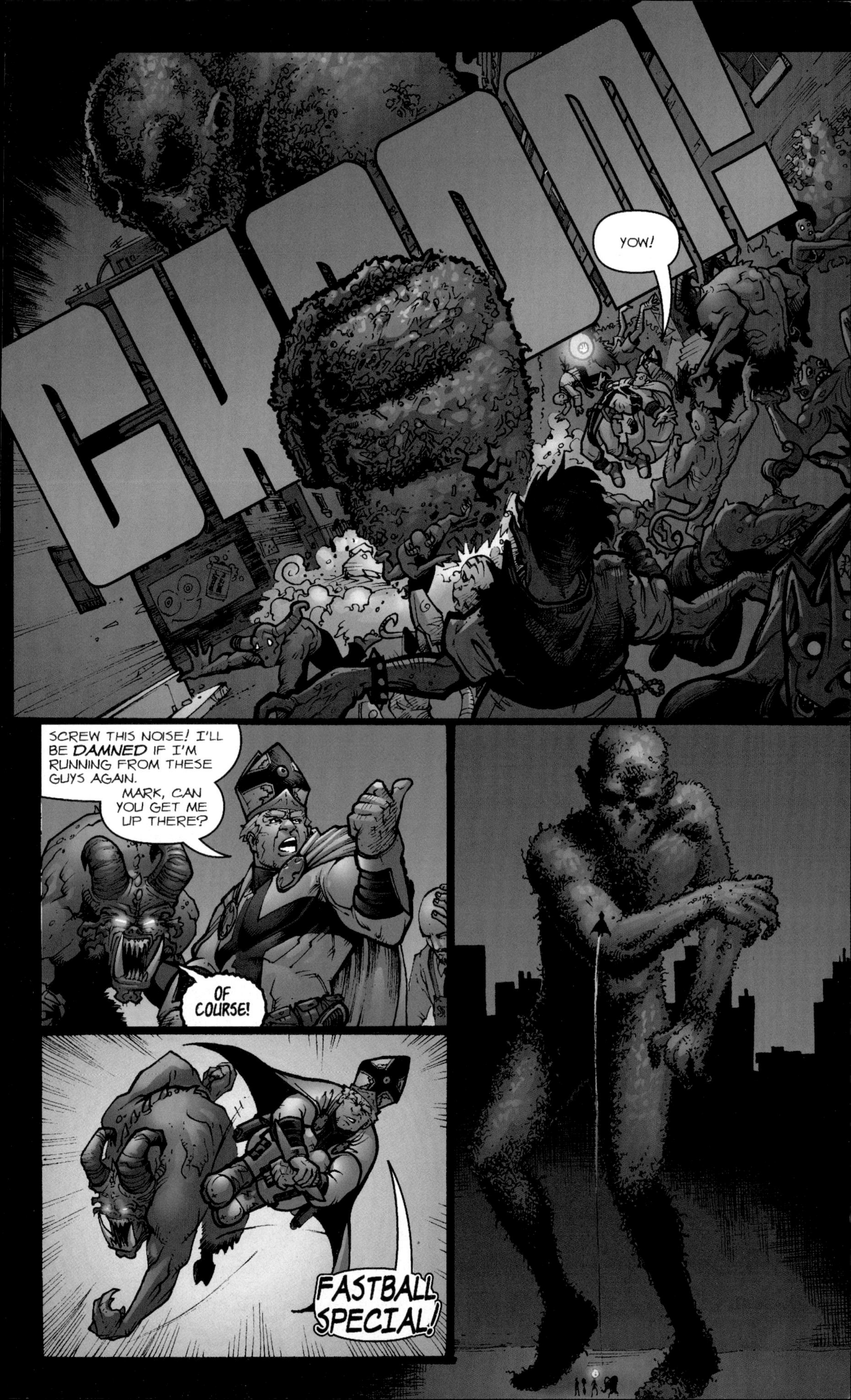
CHOOM!
YOW!
SCREW THIS NOISE! I'LL BE DAMNED IF I'M RUNNING FROM THESE GUYS AGAIN.
MARK, CAN YOU GET ME UP THERE?
OF COURSE!
FASTBALL SPECIAL!

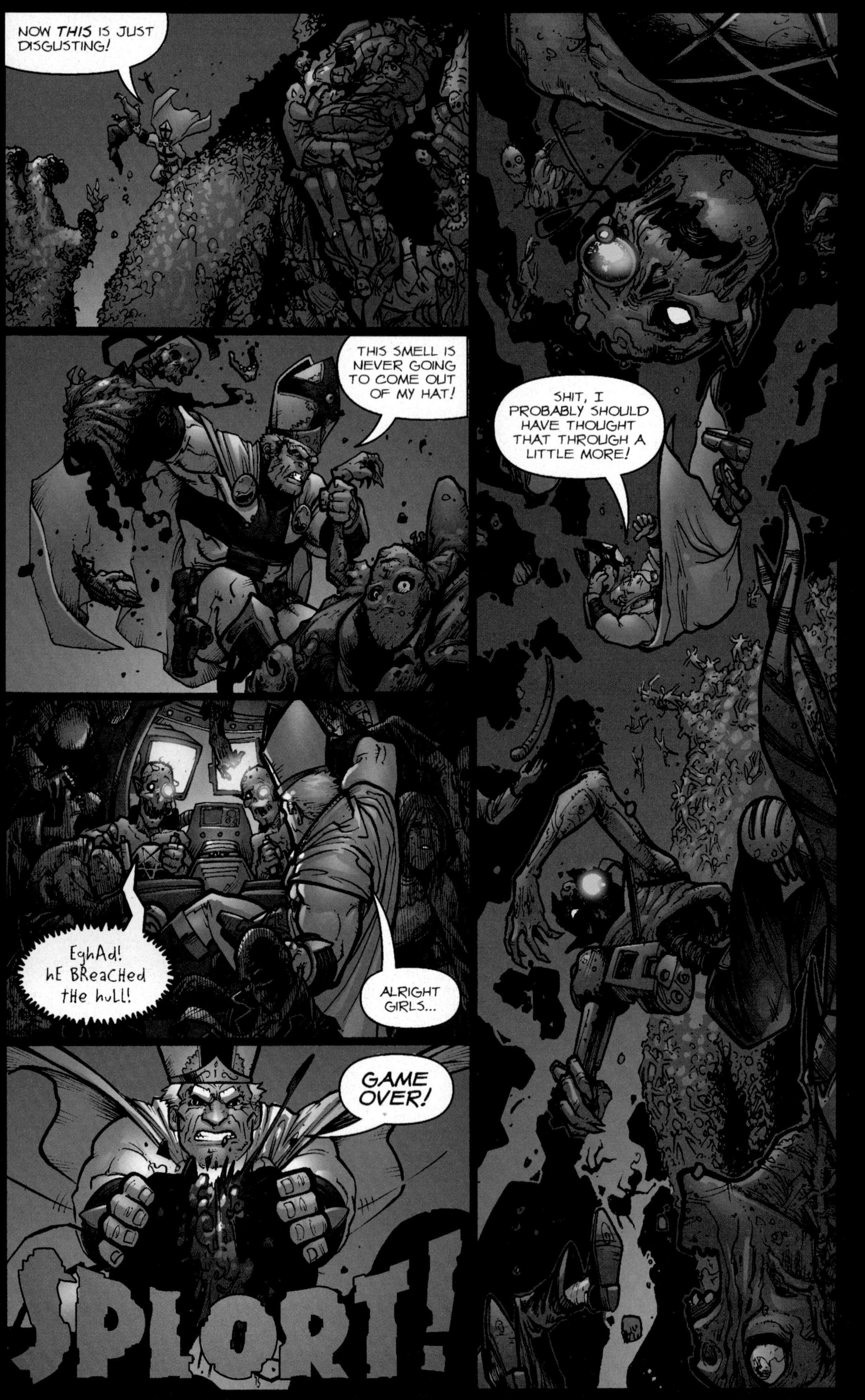
NOW *THIS* IS JUST DISGUSTING!
THIS SMELL IS NEVER GOING TO COME OUT OF MY HAT!
EghAd! hE BReacHed tHe hull!
ALRIGHT GIRLS...
GAME OVER!
SPLORT!
SHIT, I PROBABLY SHOULD HAVE THOUGHT THAT THROUGH A LITTLE MORE!

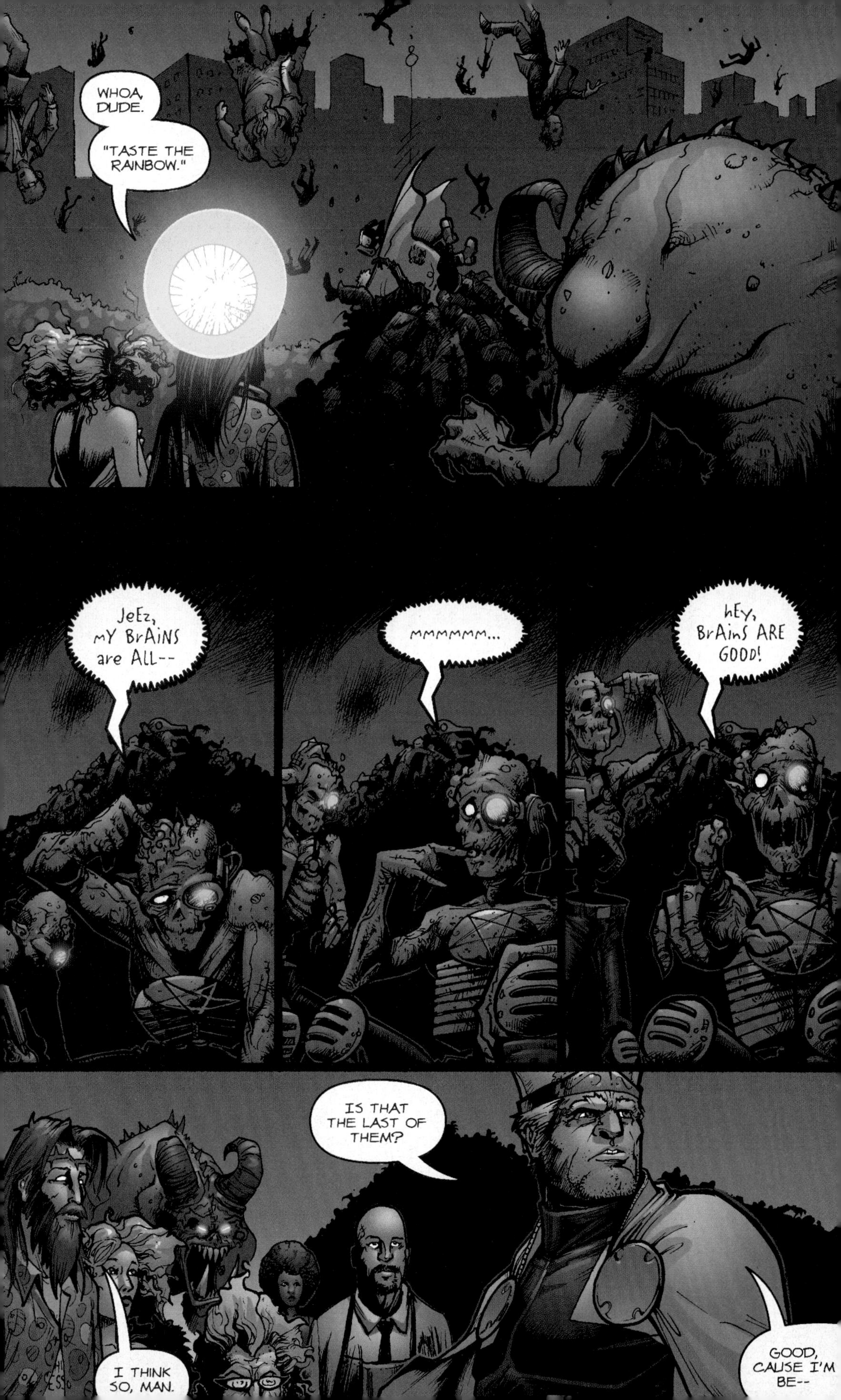

WHOA, DUDE.
"TASTE THE RAINBOW."
JeEz, MY BrAiNS are ALL--
MMMMMM...
hEy, BrAinS ARE GOOD!
IS THAT THE LAST OF THEM?
I THINK SO, MAN.
GOOD, CAUSE I'M BE--

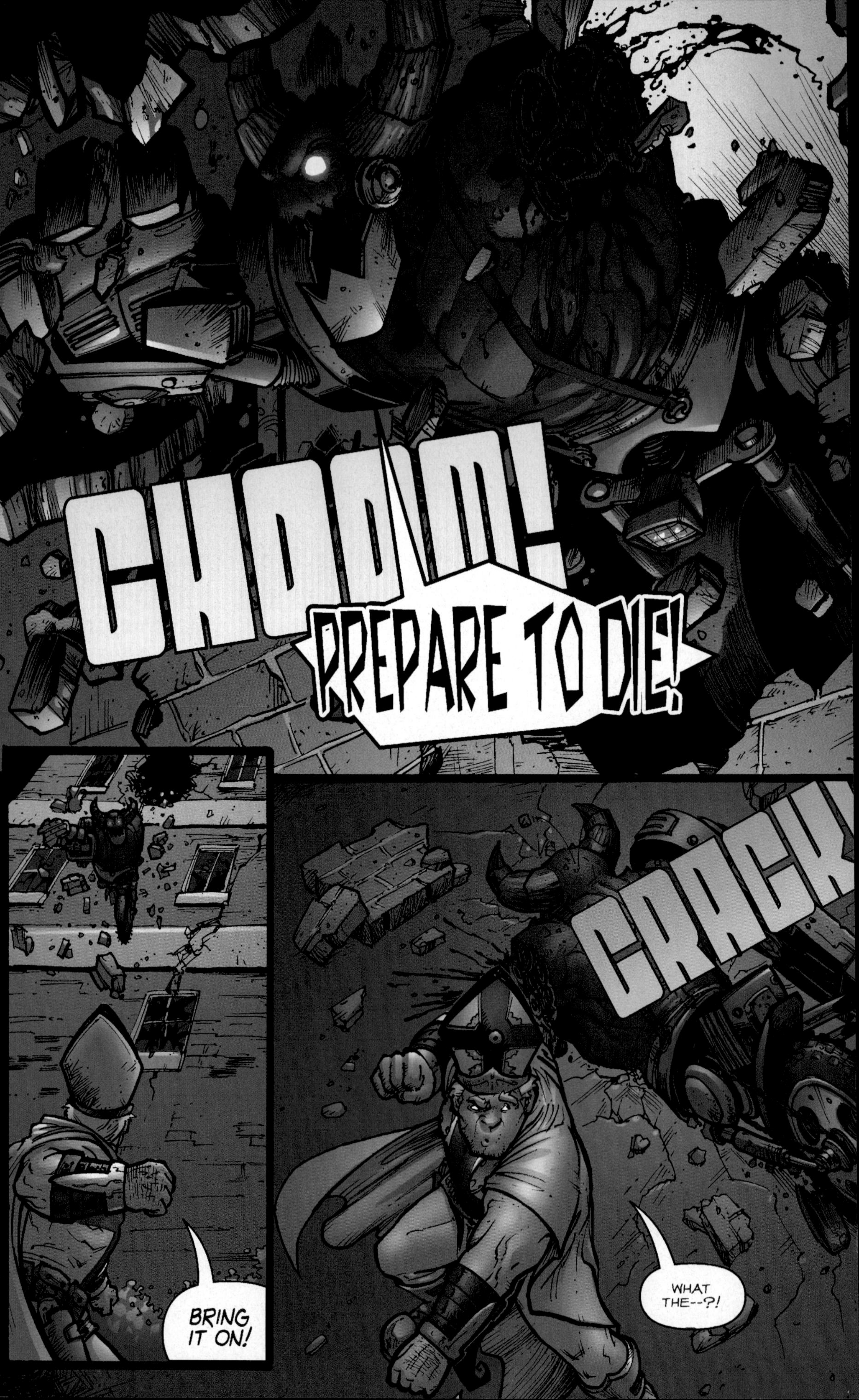
CHOOM!
PREPARE TO DIE!
BRING IT ON!
CRACK
WHAT THE--?!

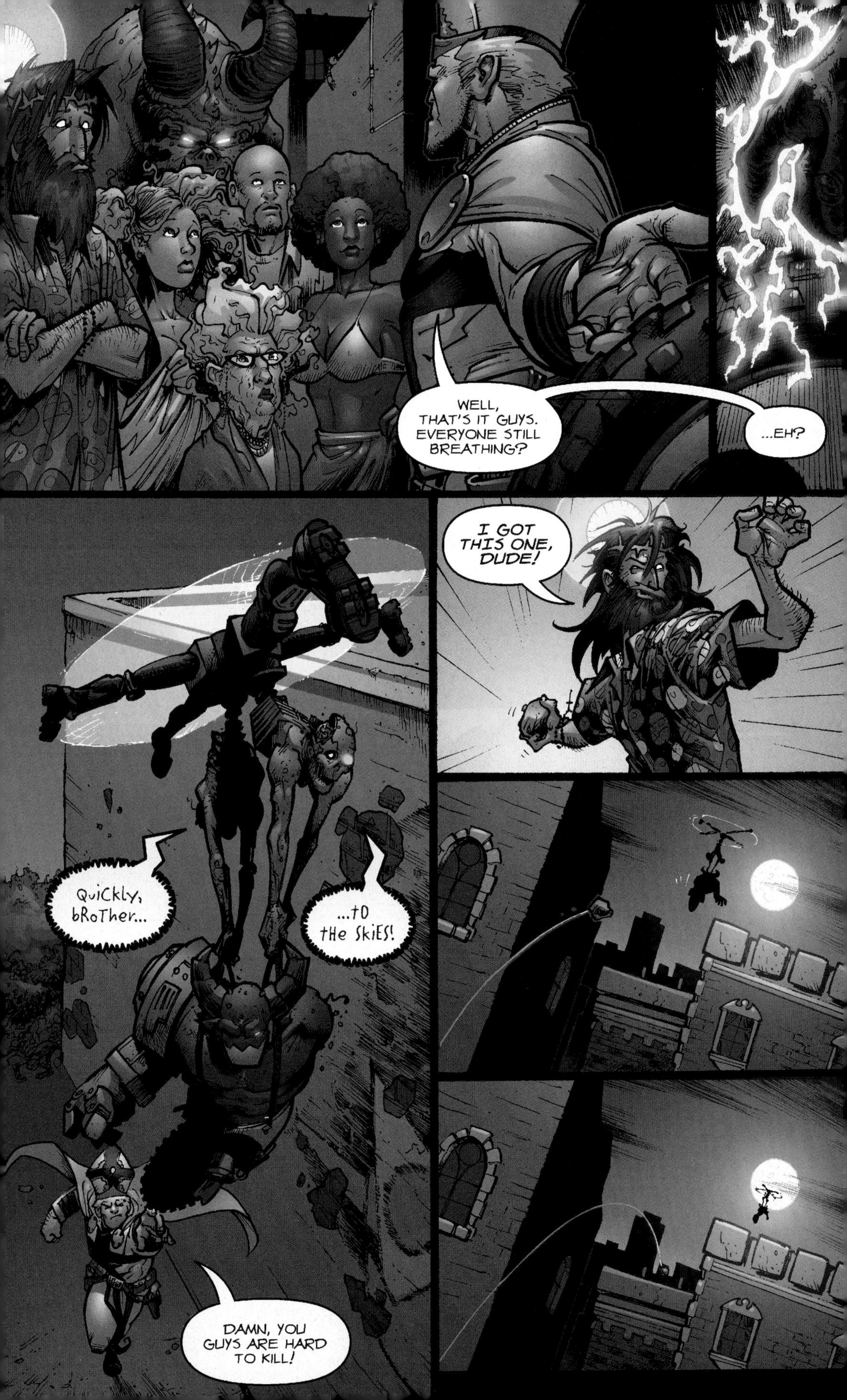
WELL, THAT'S IT GUYS. EVERYONE STILL BREATHING?
...EH?
QUICKLY, BROTHER...
...TO THE SKIES!
DAMN, YOU GUYS ARE HARD TO KILL!
I GOT THIS ONE, DUDE!

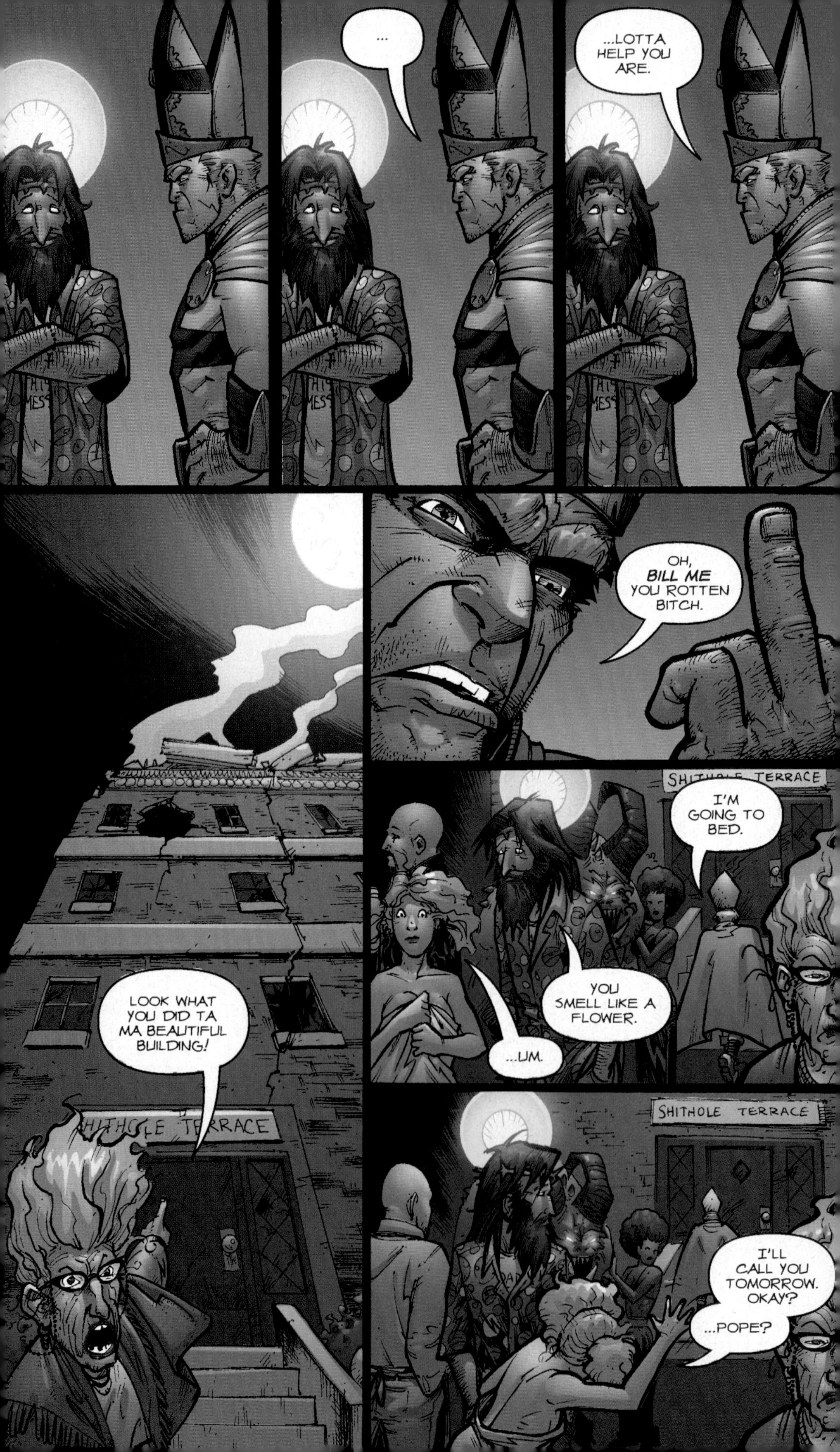
...
...LOTTA HELP YOU ARE.
LOOK WHAT YOU DID TA MA BEAUTIFUL BUILDING!
OH, BILL ME YOU ROTTEN BITCH.
SHITHOLE TERRACE
I'M GOING TO BED.
YOU SMELL LIKE A FLOWER.
...UM.
SHITHOLE TERRACE
I'LL CALL YOU TOMORROW. OKAY?
...POPE?

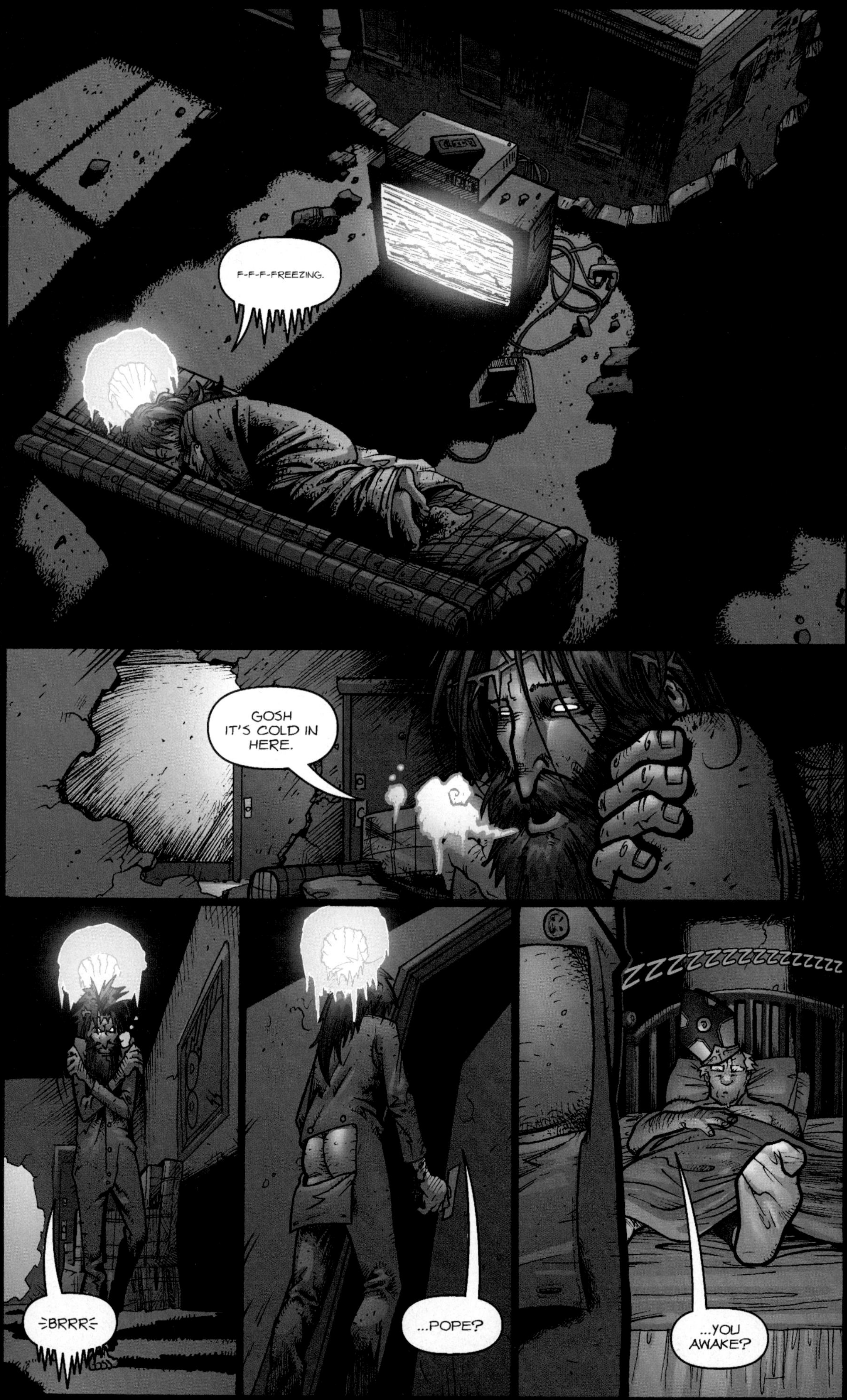
F-F-F-FREEZING.
GOSH IT'S COLD IN HERE.
BRRR
...POPE?
ZZZZZZZZZZZZZZZZZZ
...YOU AWAKE?

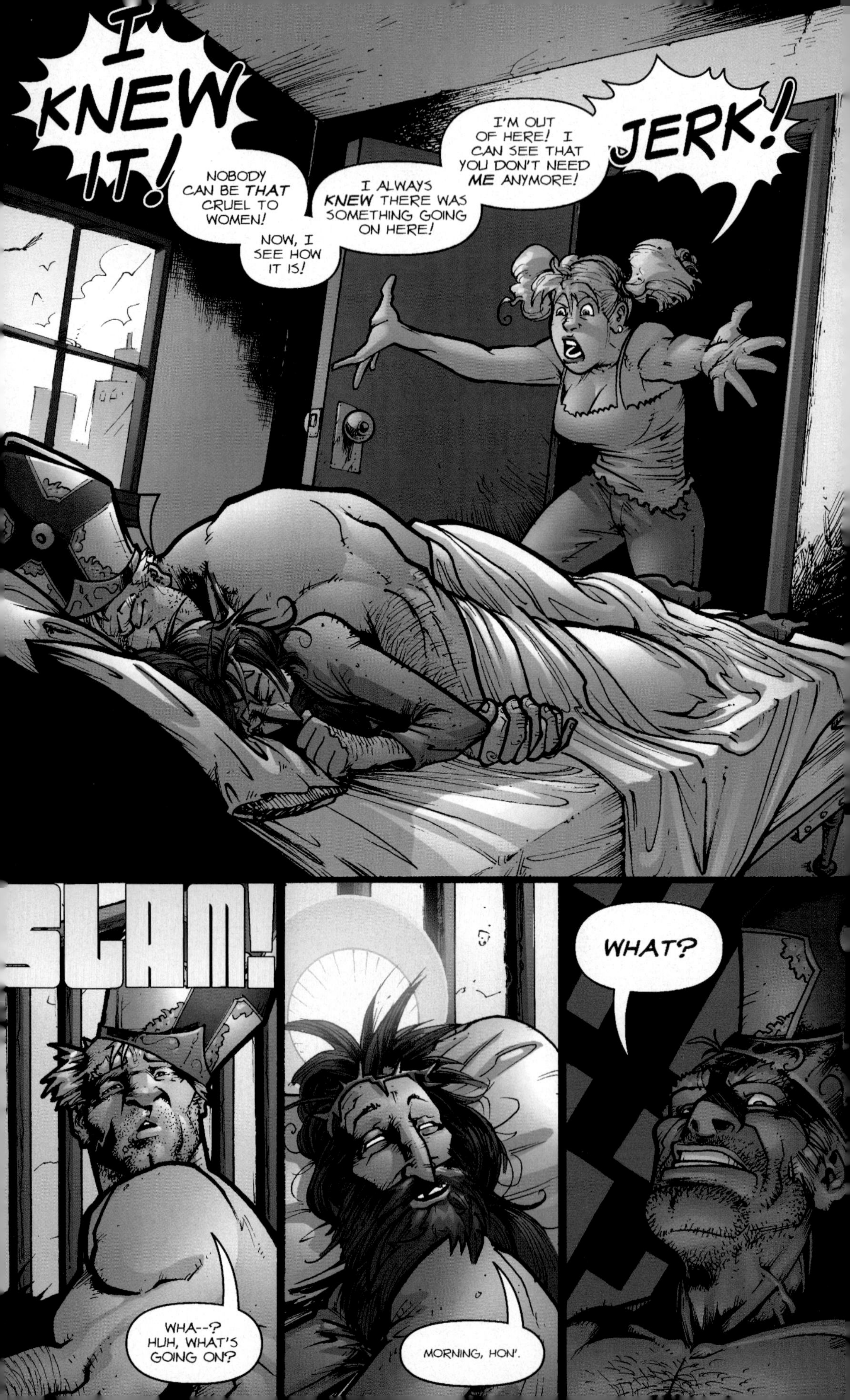
I KNEW IT!
NOBODY CAN BE THAT CRUEL TO WOMEN!
NOW, I SEE HOW IT IS!
I ALWAYS KNEW THERE WAS SOMETHING GOING ON HERE!
I'M OUT OF HERE! I CAN SEE THAT YOU DON'T NEED ME ANYMORE!
JERK!
SLAM!
WHA--? HUH, WHAT'S GOING ON?
MORNING, HON'.
WHAT?

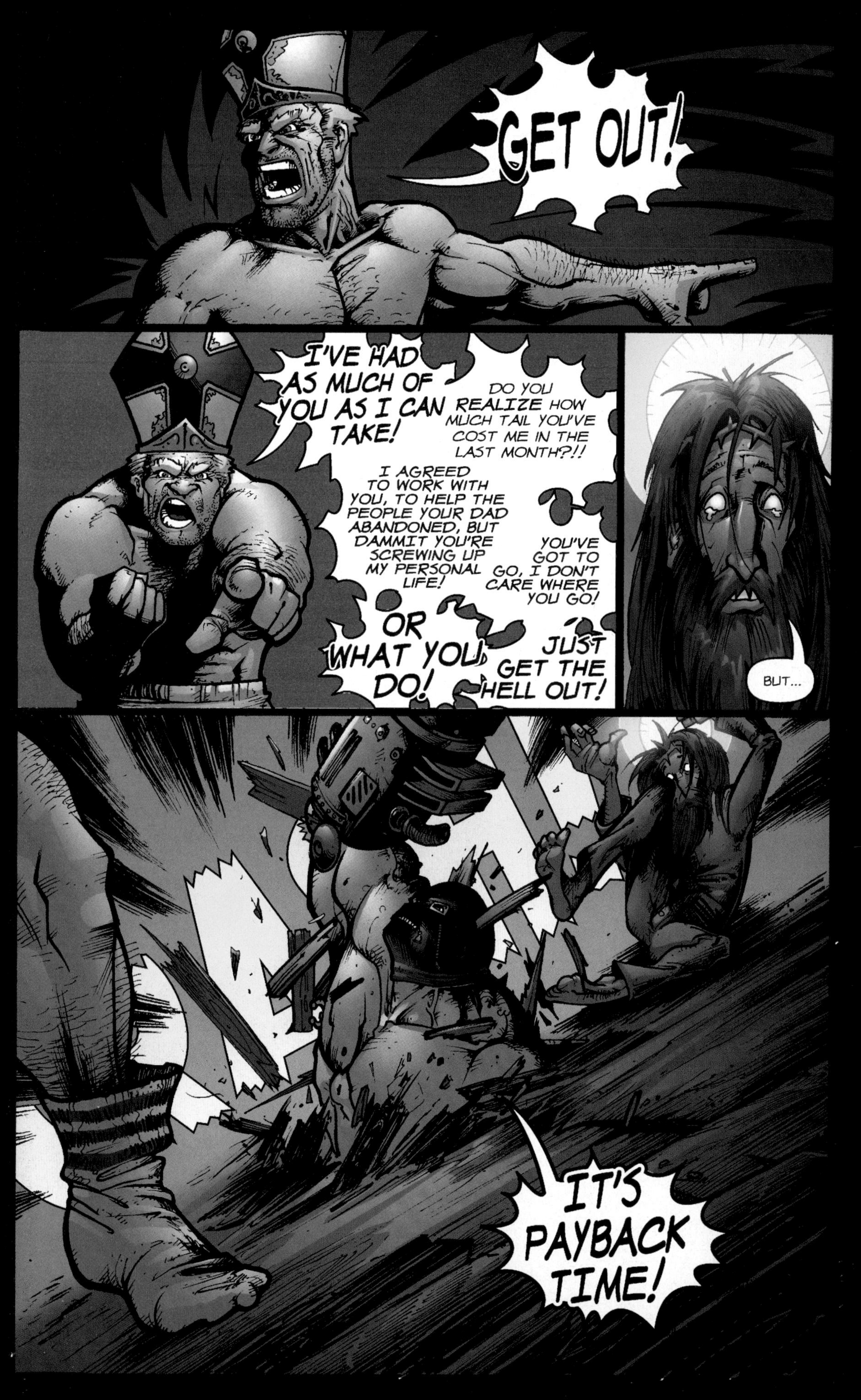
GET OUT!
I'VE HAD AS MUCH OF YOU AS I CAN TAKE!
DO YOU REALIZE HOW MUCH TAIL YOU'VE COST ME IN THE LAST MONTH?!!
I AGREED TO WORK WITH YOU, TO HELP THE PEOPLE YOUR DAD ABANDONED, BUT DAMMIT YOU'RE SCREWING UP MY PERSONAL LIFE!
YOU'VE GOT TO GO, I DON'T CARE WHERE YOU GO!
OR WHAT YOU DO!
JUST GET THE HELL OUT!
BUT...
IT'S PAYBACK TIME!

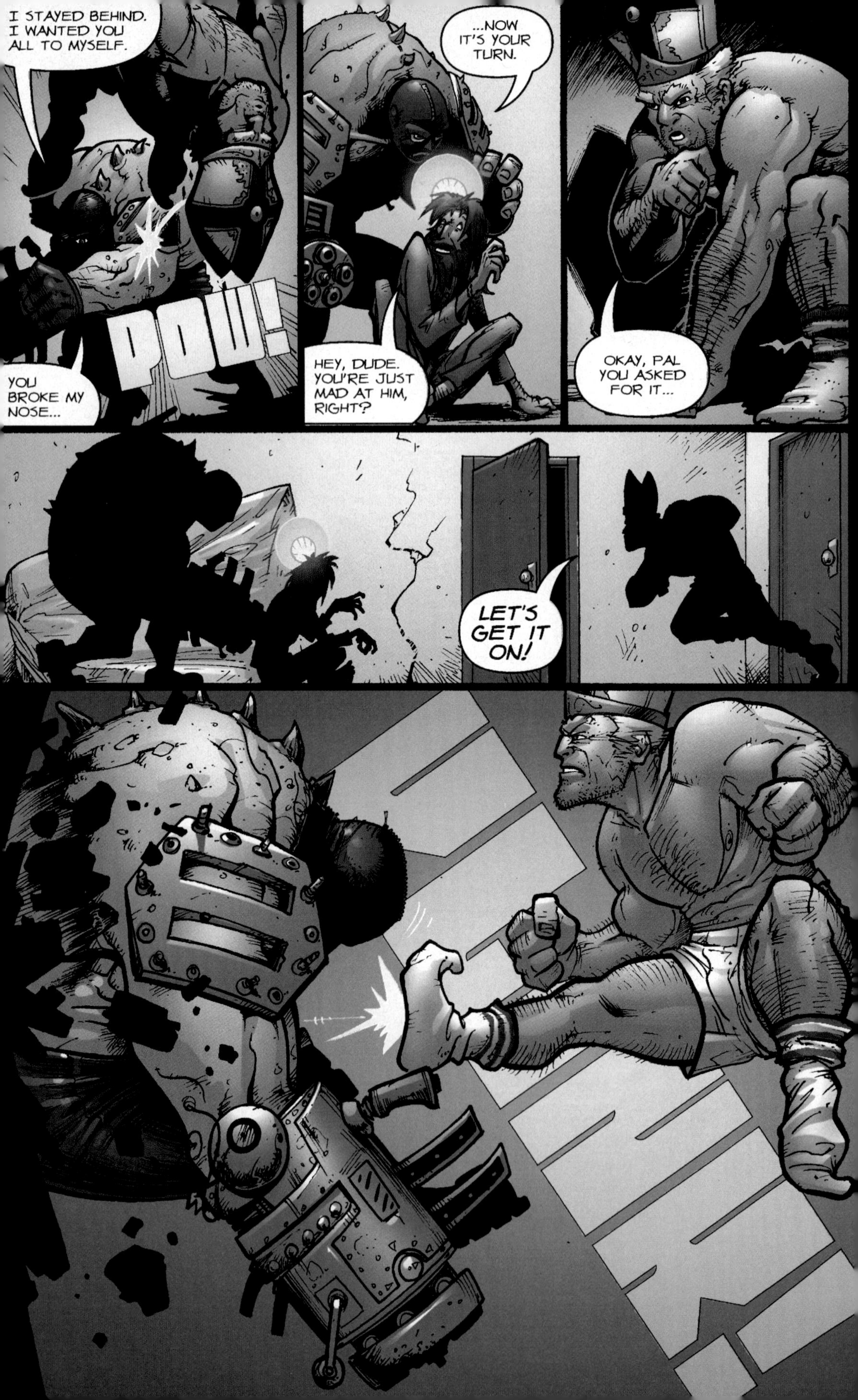
I STAYED BEHIND. I WANTED YOU ALL TO MYSELF.
POW!
YOU BROKE MY NOSE...
...NOW IT'S YOUR TURN.
HEY, DUDE. YOU'RE JUST MAD AT HIM, RIGHT?
OKAY, PAL YOU ASKED FOR IT...
LET'S GET IT ON!

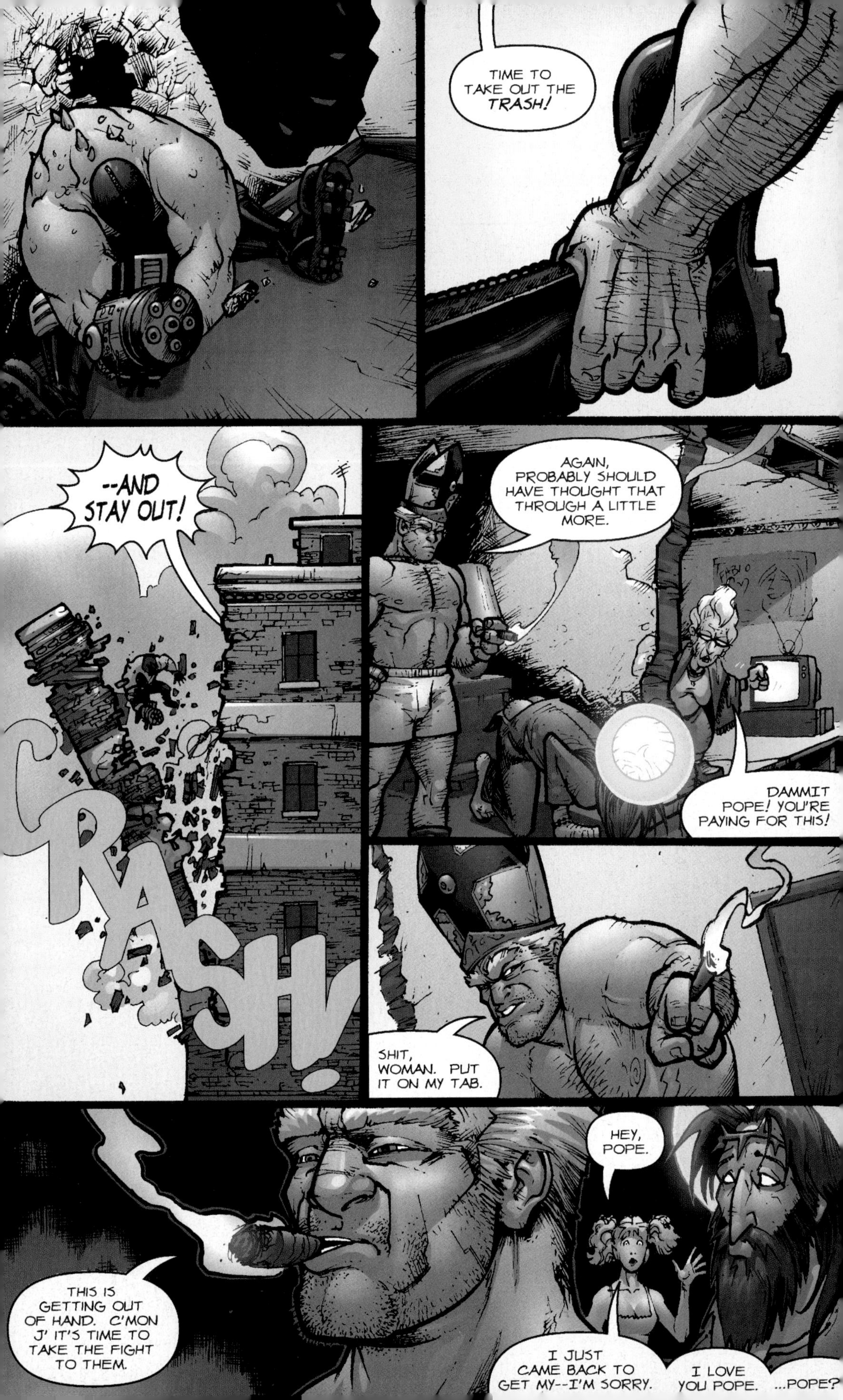
TIME TO TAKE OUT THE TRASH!
--AND STAY OUT!
CRASH!
AGAIN, PROBABLY SHOULD HAVE THOUGHT THAT THROUGH A LITTLE MORE.
DAMMIT POPE! YOU'RE PAYING FOR THIS!
SHIT, WOMAN. PUT IT ON MY TAB.
THIS IS GETTING OUT OF HAND. C'MON J' IT'S TIME TO TAKE THE FIGHT TO THEM.
HEY, POPE.
I JUST CAME BACK TO GET MY--I'M SORRY.
I LOVE YOU POPE.
...POPE?

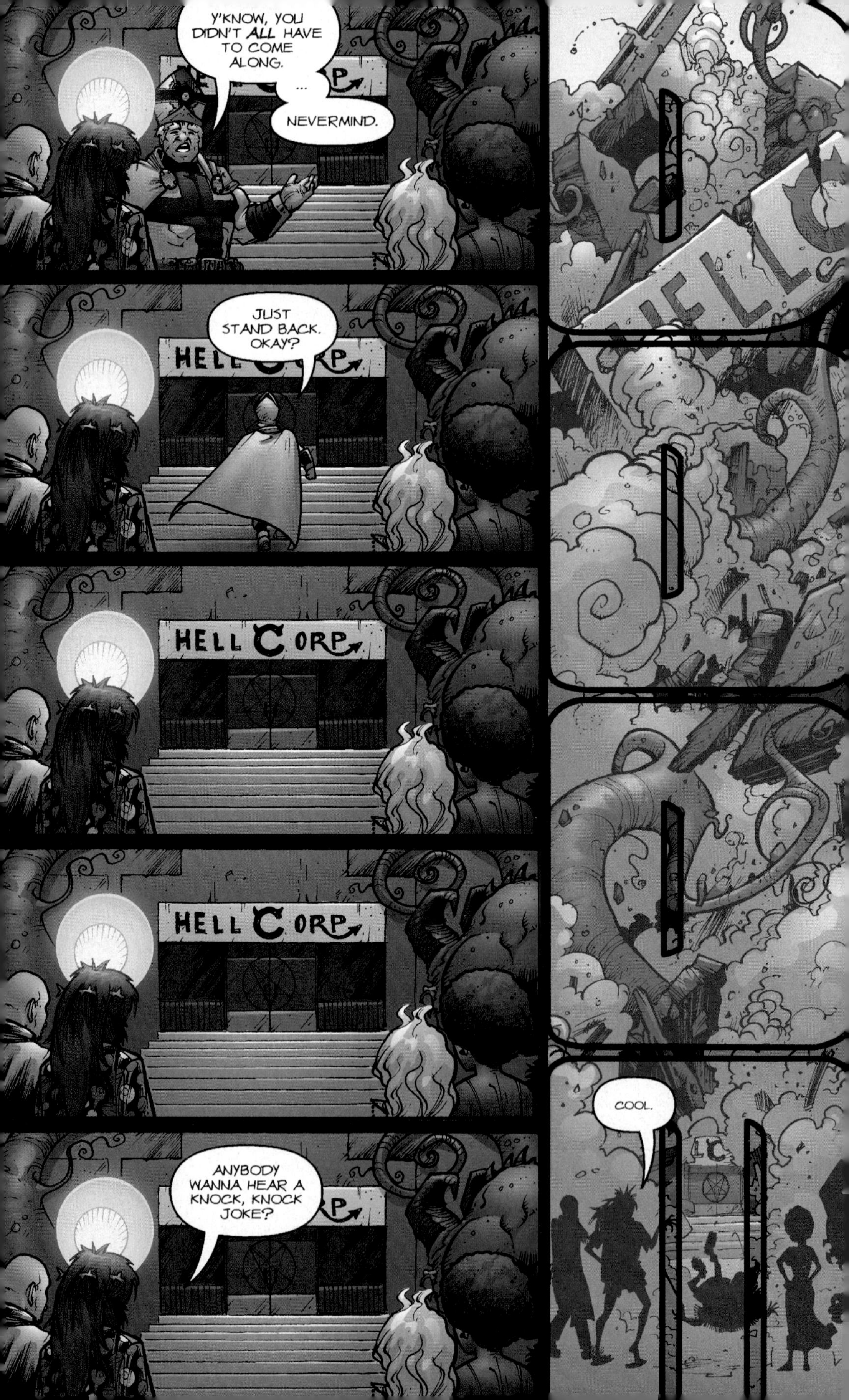
Y'KNOW, YOU DIDN'T ALL HAVE TO COME ALONG.
...
NEVERMIND.
JUST STAND BACK. OKAY?
HELL CORP
HELL CORP
HELL CORP
ANYBODY WANNA HEAR A KNOCK, KNOCK JOKE?
COOL.

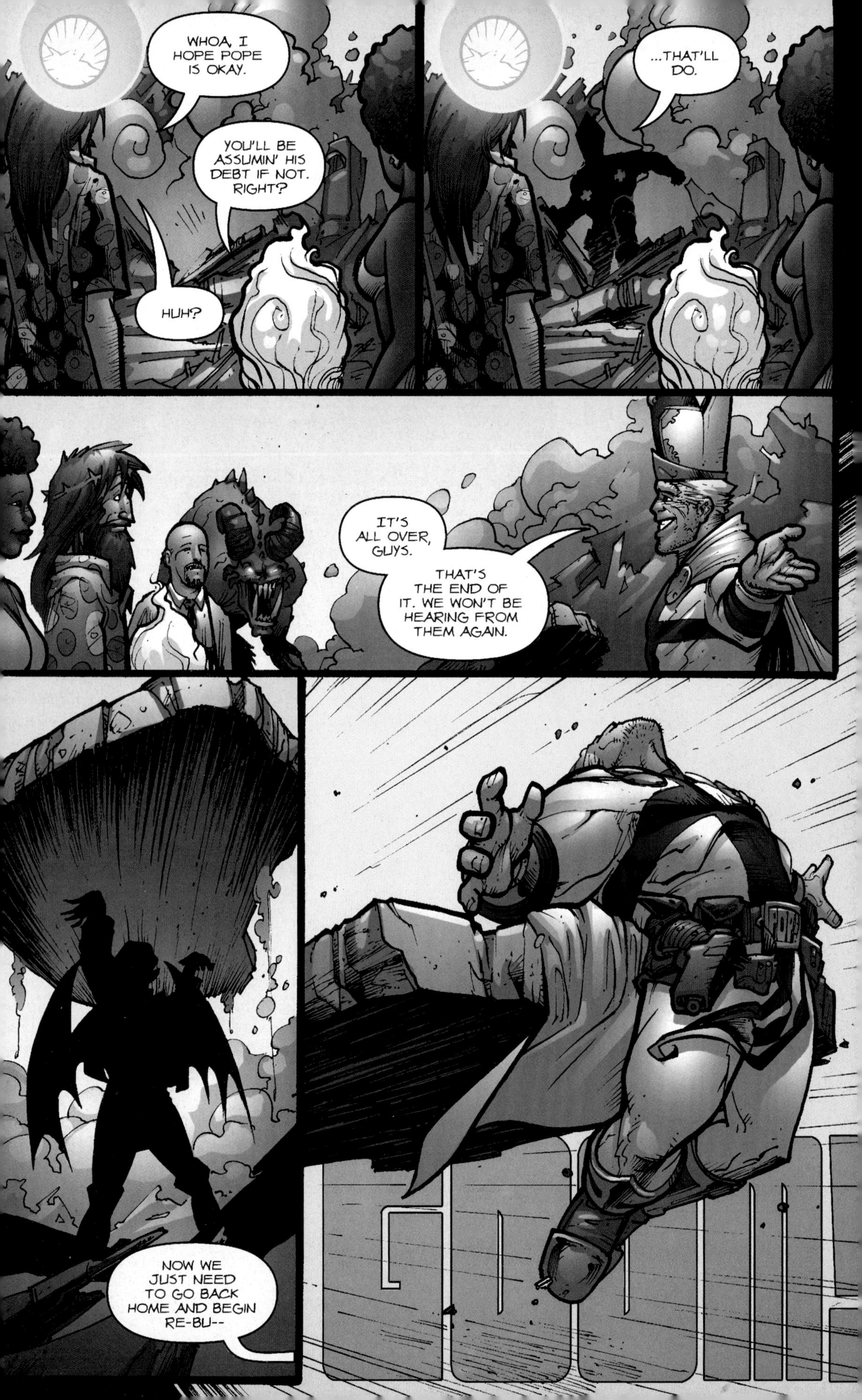
WHOA, I HOPE POPE IS OKAY.
YOU'LL BE ASSUMIN' HIS DEBT IF NOT. RIGHT?
HUH?
...THAT'LL DO.
IT'S ALL OVER, GUYS.
THAT'S THE END OF IT. WE WON'T BE HEARING FROM THEM AGAIN.
NOW WE JUST NEED TO GO BACK HOME AND BEGIN RE-BU--

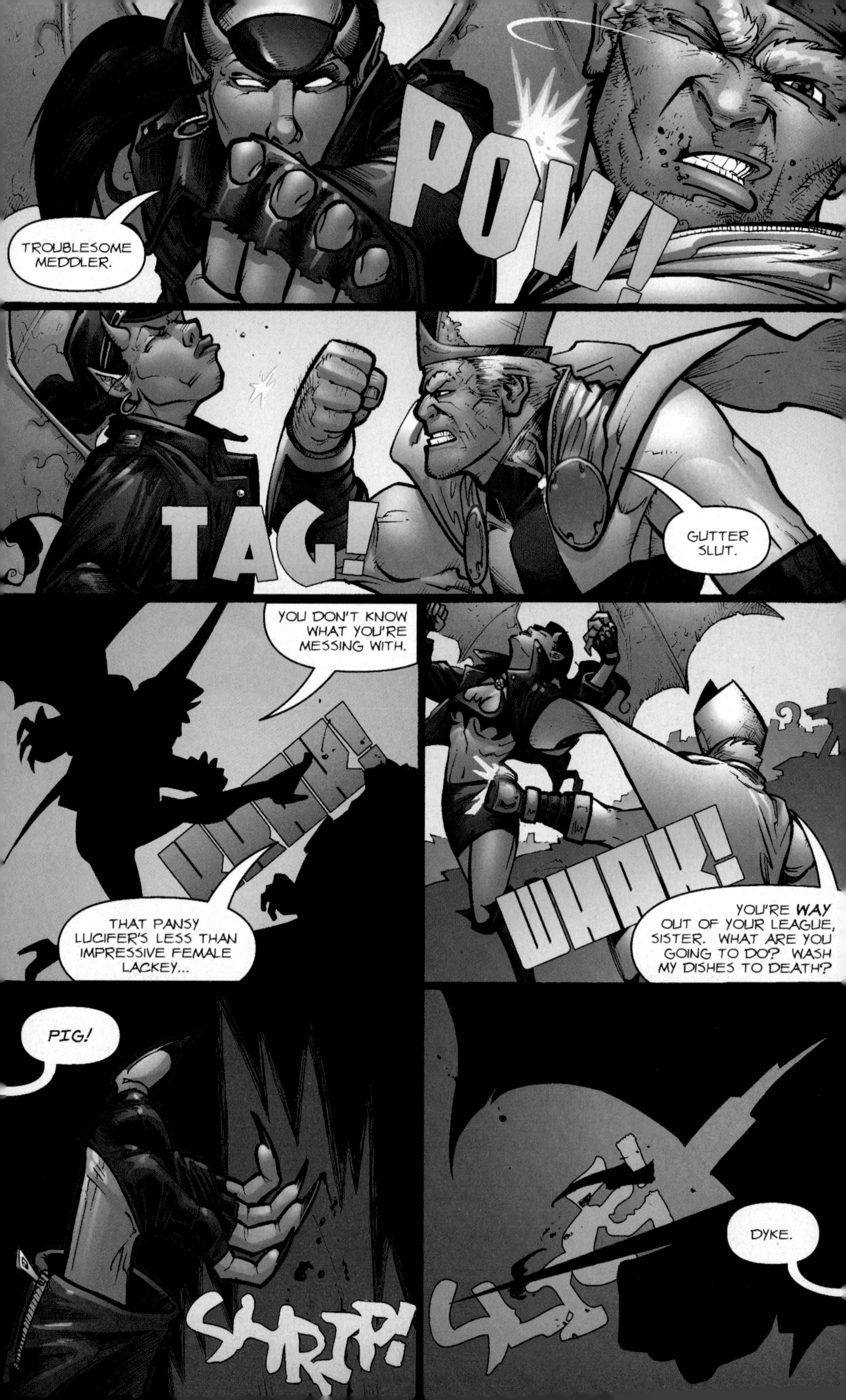
TROUBLESOME MEDDLER.
POW!
TAG!
GUTTER SLUT.
YOU DON'T KNOW WHAT YOU'RE MESSING WITH.
THAT PANSY LUCIFER'S LESS THAN IMPRESSIVE FEMALE LACKEY...
WHAK!
YOU'RE **WAY** OUT OF YOUR LEAGUE, SISTER. WHAT ARE YOU GOING TO DO? WASH MY DISHES TO DEATH?
PIG!
SHRIP!
DYKE.

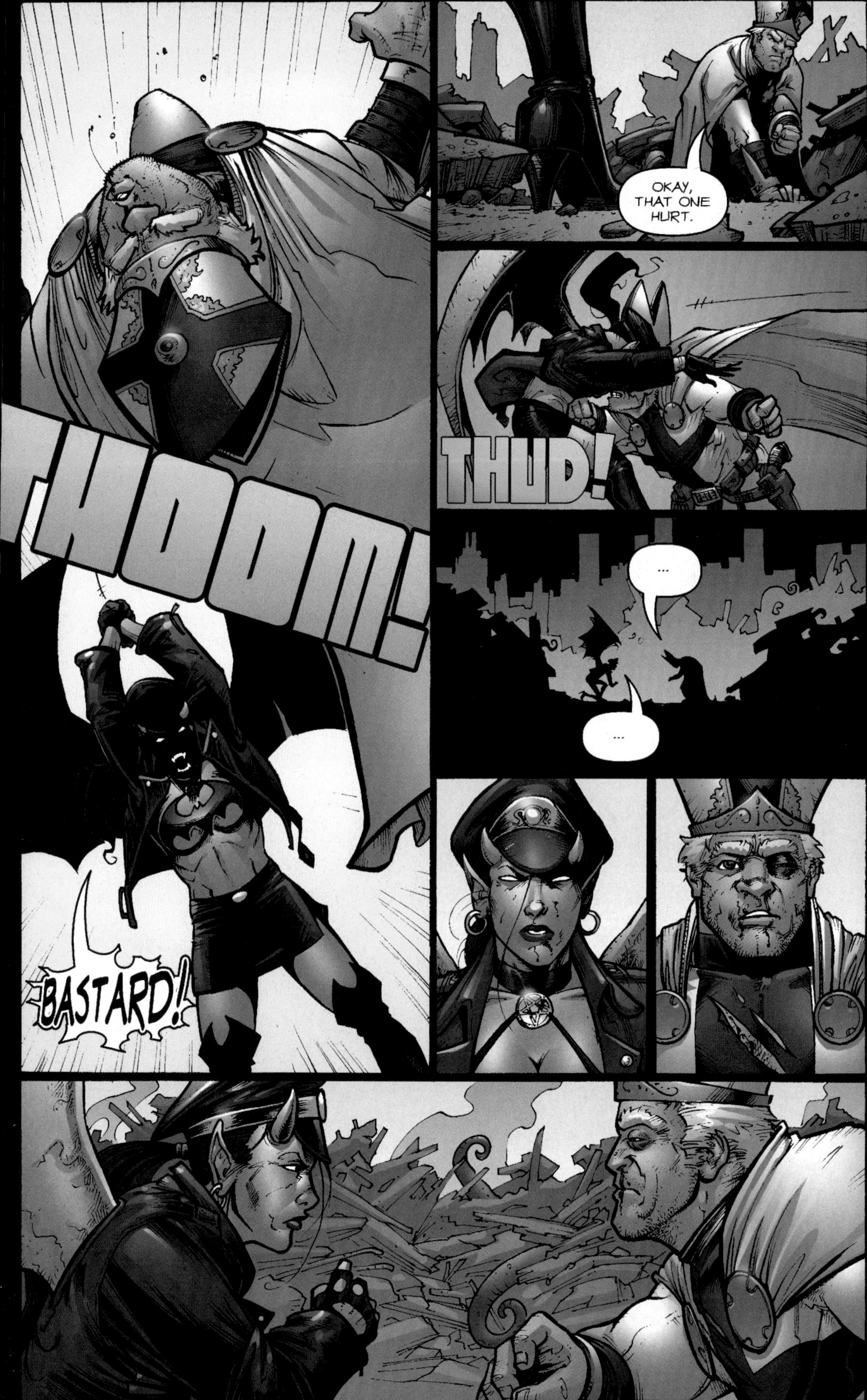

WHOOM!
BASTARD!
OKAY, THAT ONE HURT.
THUD!
...
...

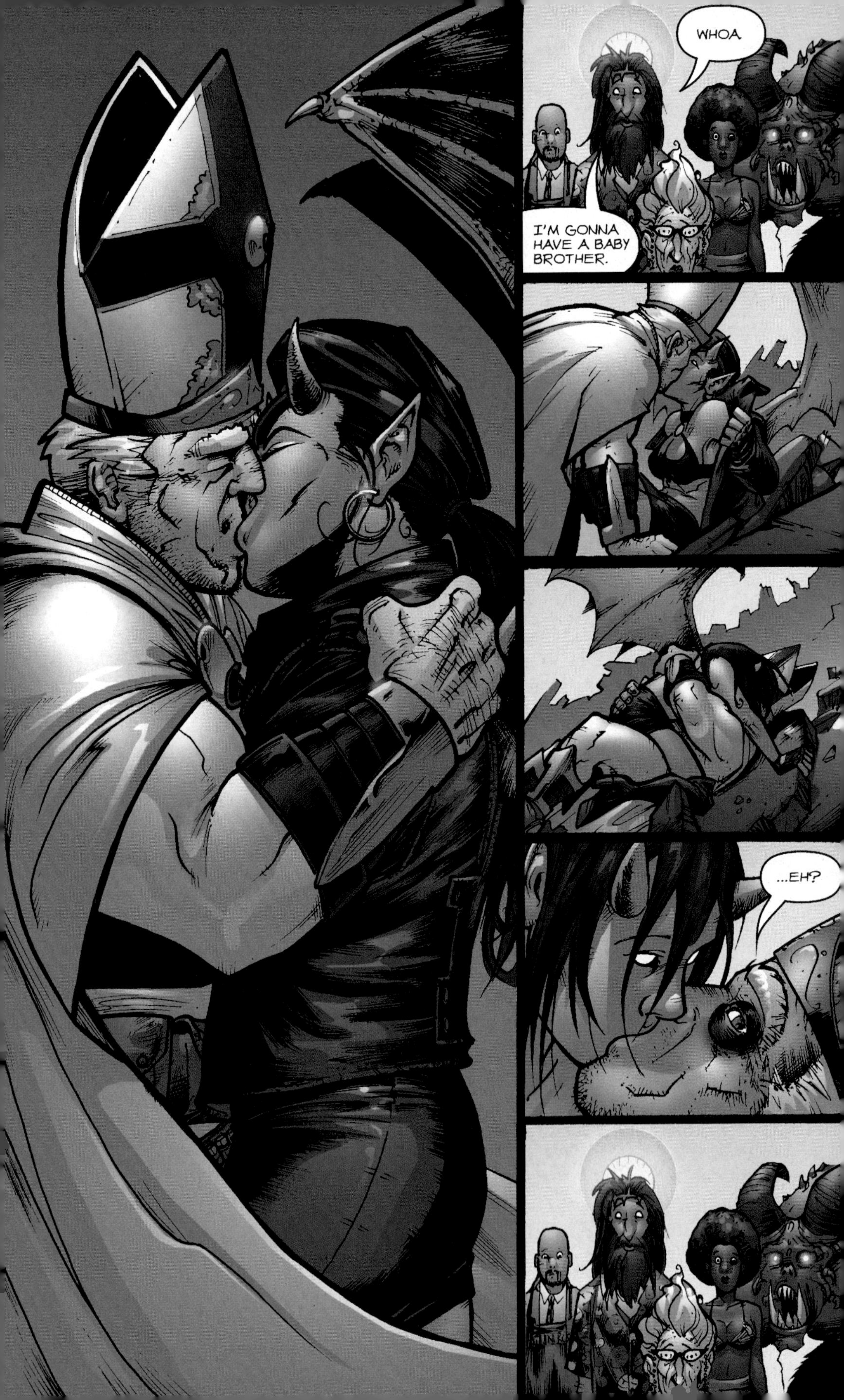
WHOA
I'M GONNA HAVE A BABY BROTHER.
...EH?

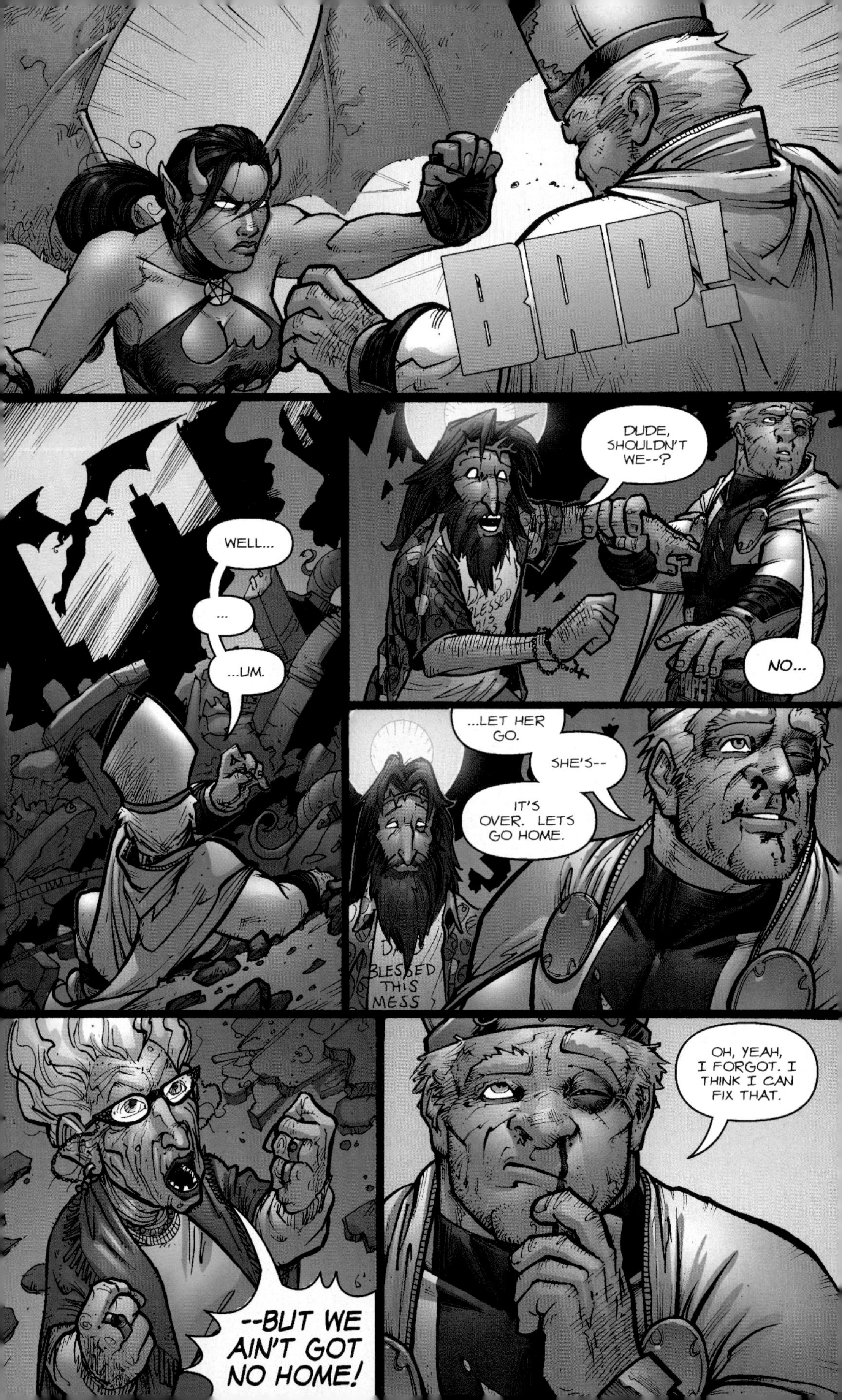
BAP!
WELL...
...
...UM.
DUDE, SHOULDN'T WE--?
NO...
...LET HER GO.
SHE'S--
IT'S OVER. LETS GO HOME.
DAD BLESSED THIS MESS
--BUT WE AIN'T GOT NO HOME!
OH, YEAH, I FORGOT. I THINK I CAN FIX THAT.

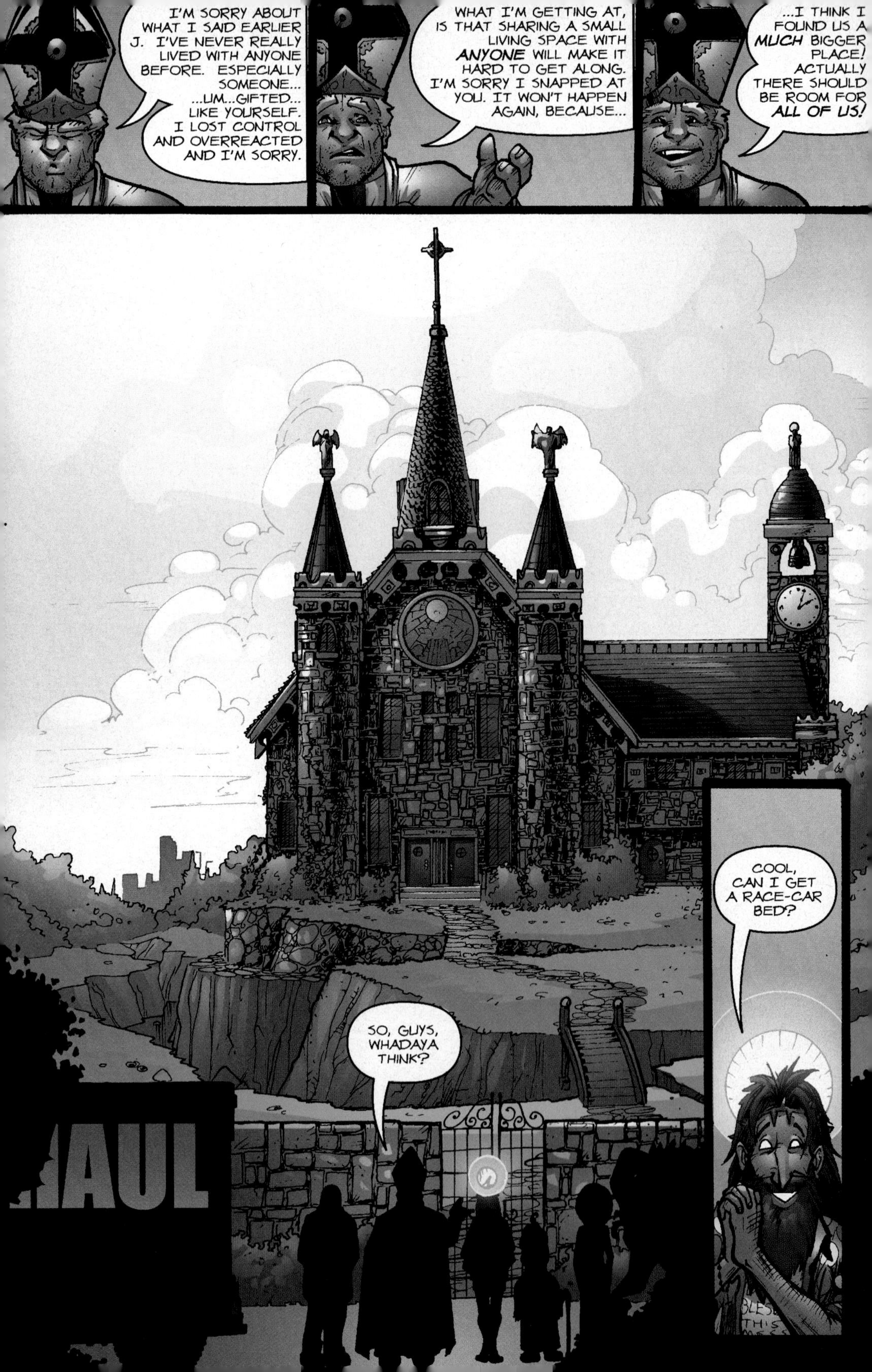

I'M SORRY ABOUT WHAT I SAID EARLIER J. I'VE NEVER REALLY LIVED WITH ANYONE BEFORE. ESPECIALLY SOMEONE... ...UM...GIFTED... LIKE YOURSELF. I LOST CONTROL AND OVERREACTED AND I'M SORRY.
WHAT I'M GETTING AT, IS THAT SHARING A SMALL LIVING SPACE WITH ANYONE WILL MAKE IT HARD TO GET ALONG. I'M SORRY I SNAPPED AT YOU. IT WON'T HAPPEN AGAIN, BECAUSE...
...I THINK I FOUND US A MUCH BIGGER PLACE! ACTUALLY THERE SHOULD BE ROOM FOR ALL OF US!
SO, GUYS, WHADAYA THINK?
COOL, CAN I GET A RACE-CAR BED?
HAUL

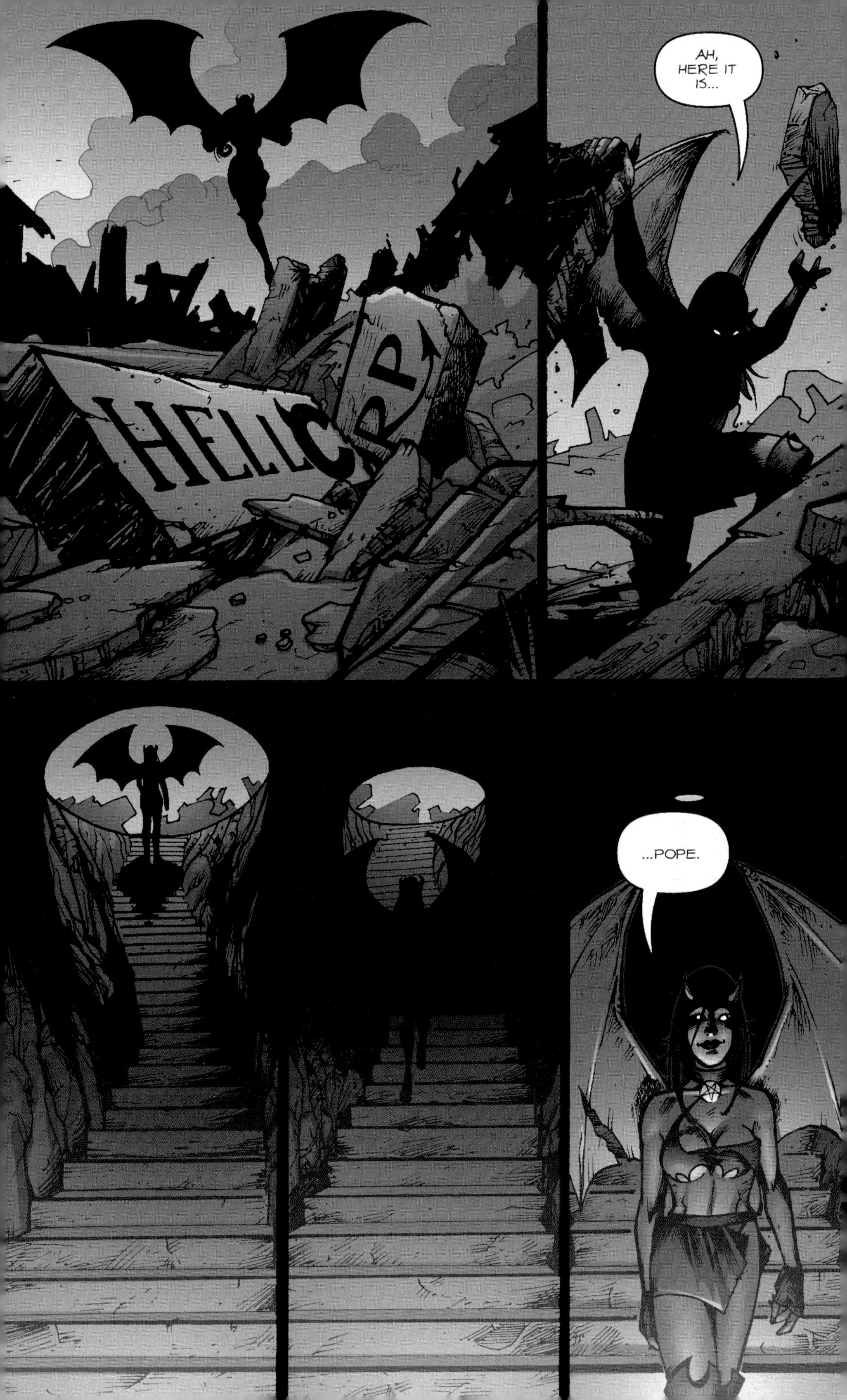
HELL
AH, HERE IT IS...
...POPE.

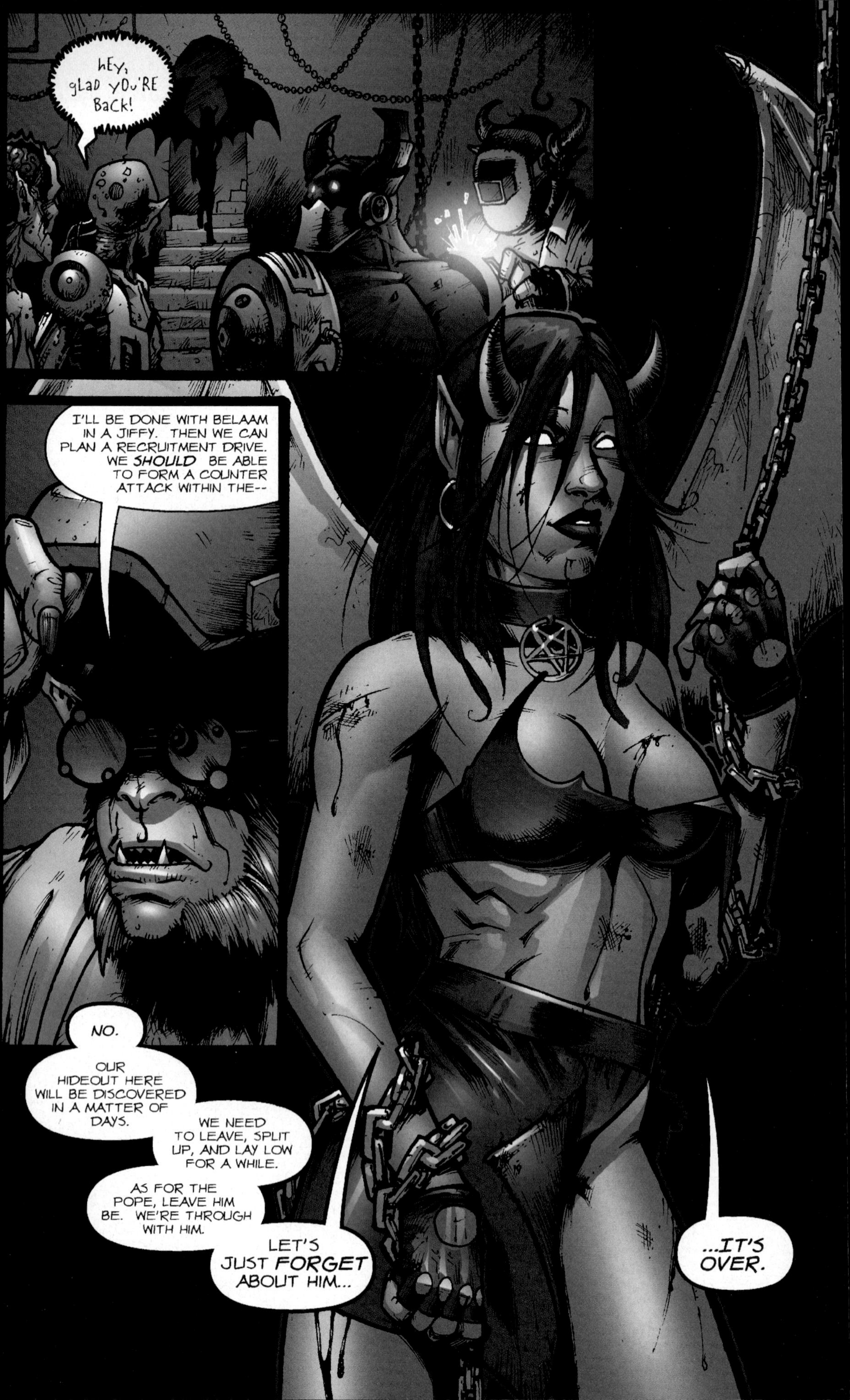
HEY, GLAD YOU'RE BACK!
I'LL BE DONE WITH BELAAM IN A JIFFY. THEN WE CAN PLAN A RECRUITMENT DRIVE. WE SHOULD BE ABLE TO FORM A COUNTER ATTACK WITHIN THE--
NO.
OUR HIDEOUT HERE WILL BE DISCOVERED IN A MATTER OF DAYS.
WE NEED TO LEAVE, SPLIT UP, AND LAY LOW FOR A WHILE.
AS FOR THE POPE, LEAVE HIM BE. WE'RE THROUGH WITH HIM.
LET'S JUST FORGET ABOUT HIM...
...IT'S OVER.

Sketchbook

Welcome to the Battle Pope Volume 2 sketchbook. As I'm sure most of you know this is a color reprint of an old black and white series Tony Moore, Matthew Roberts, some others, and I did way back in the year 2001. We also did a trade paperback then. All the sketches and most of the commentary seen here is from that old volume (I wouldn't have remembered all this stuff).

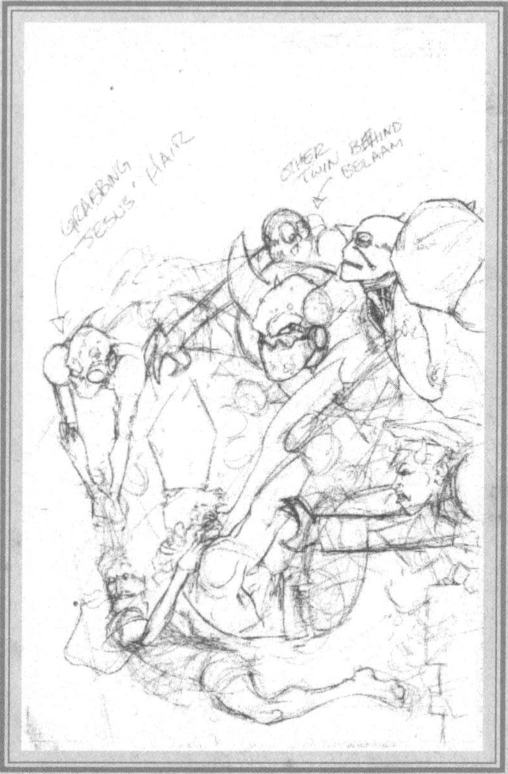
GRABBING JESUS' HAIR
OTHER TWIN BEHIND BELAAM

Matthew Roberts is either REALLY good or REALLY lazy. I know which one, but I'm not going to tell you (he's not lazy). On this page are the ONLY drawings of Pope that Matt has EVER done aside from the pages that saw print; no sketches, no layouts, no character studies... NOTHING. I will say this for him: from what I can see, he didn't need to. The one with Jesus and the bag of nuts was a sort of "fan art" piece Matt posted on the message board at PencilJack.com. It was all I needed to see. After spotting that pic, I immediately contacted Matt, and offered him the Mayhem miniseries (which became issues 7 and 8 of this series). He also ended up doing the 3 pages in Shorts #1 after the original artist bailed on me. I believe they were drawn after the cover for Mayhem one, of which Matt's rough pencils are also shown here. I had sent Matt a layout for that cover and told him to re-sketch it and send it back to me... instead he dove right into the full size drawing and sent me the rough pencils when he was about to finalize them. Without knowing this, I told him that when he drew the final version he needed to rotate it more so Pope would look more like he was falling off of the building. He seemed too horizontal in the "layout" above. Because Matt had sent me the rough pencils and not a layout, he had to break out the light table and redraw the whole thing. I felt bad for him... well, for a little while.

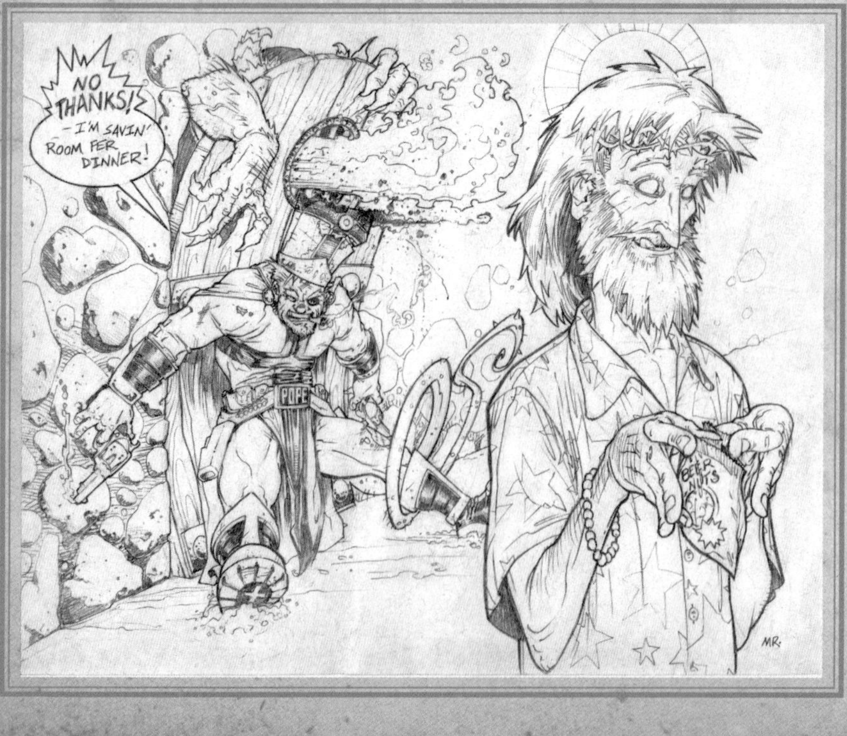
NO THANKS! - I'M SAVIN' ROOM FER DINNER!
POPE
BEER NUTS
MR.

Tony knows what he's doing. He always had... but at this point in his Battle Pope career, little sketching was needed. All the characters were (for the most part, at least) designed in my layouts and any tweaking and finalizing was done by Tony on the actual boards, so there's not a whole lot to show in this TPB... aside from this CHOICE design for "unicycle Belaam." Since Tony wasn't drawing Mayhem, the mini-series where Belaam's new wheels debuted, he had to do the design for Matt. That's not to say that Matt couldn't do it himself, he just asked what it should look like, so I got Tony to do this sketch to make things easier on him. It's not like Tony was doing anything anyway at the time anyway. College? A likely story...

Belaam is meant to be a very pitiful character. Other than making him lose a body part every time we see him, I wanted to do something even worse to the fellow to make him even more useless. I figured having his severed legs be replaced with a unicycle type wheel would make him as useless as ever, while also providing a pretty humorous visual.

"SUSPENDER" TYPE BELTS
TURNIQUET TO HOLD TORSO IN PLACE
GAS CAP
BIKE MOTOR
HUB
COOL SHOCKS
STUDDED MOTOCROSS TIRE

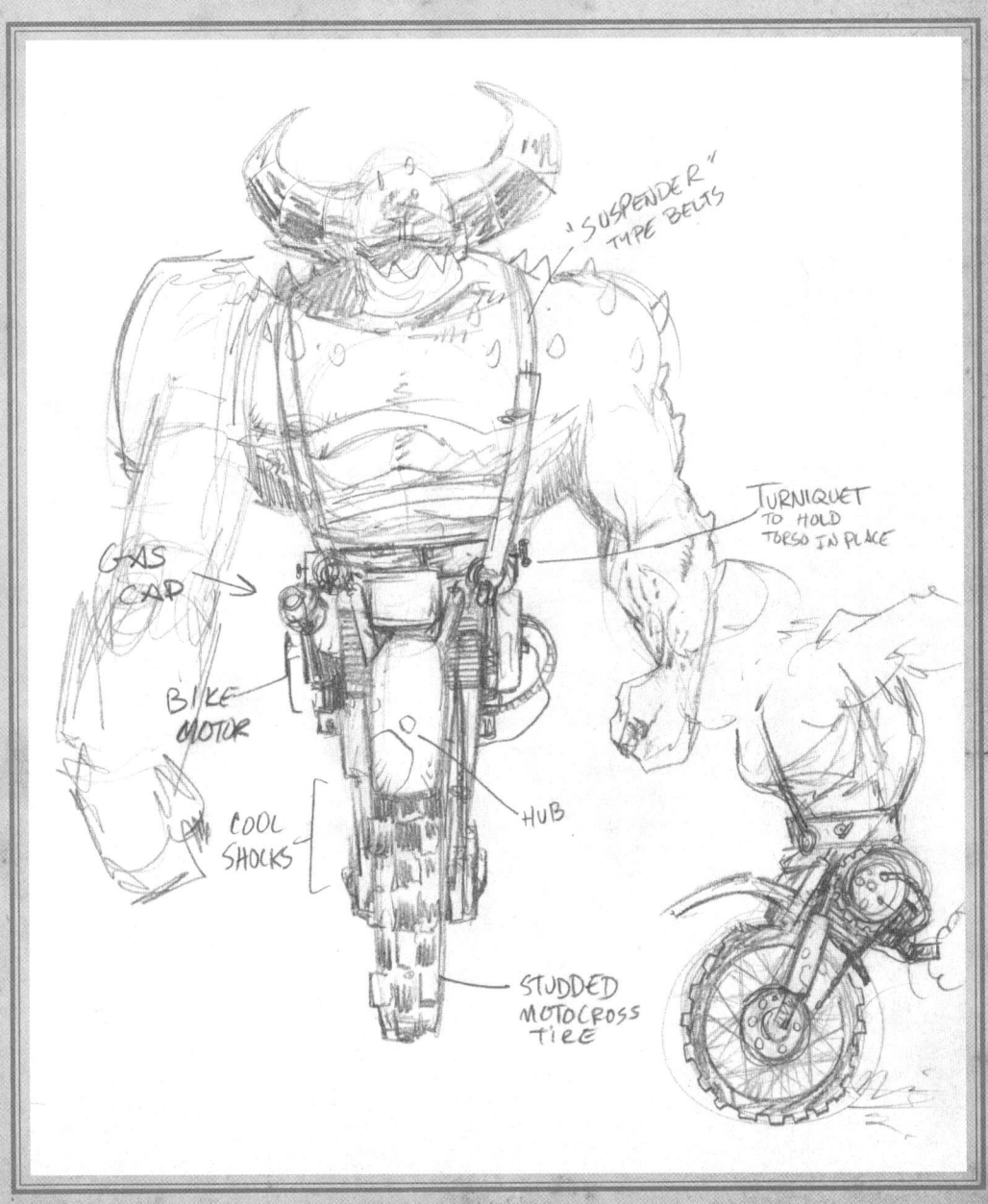

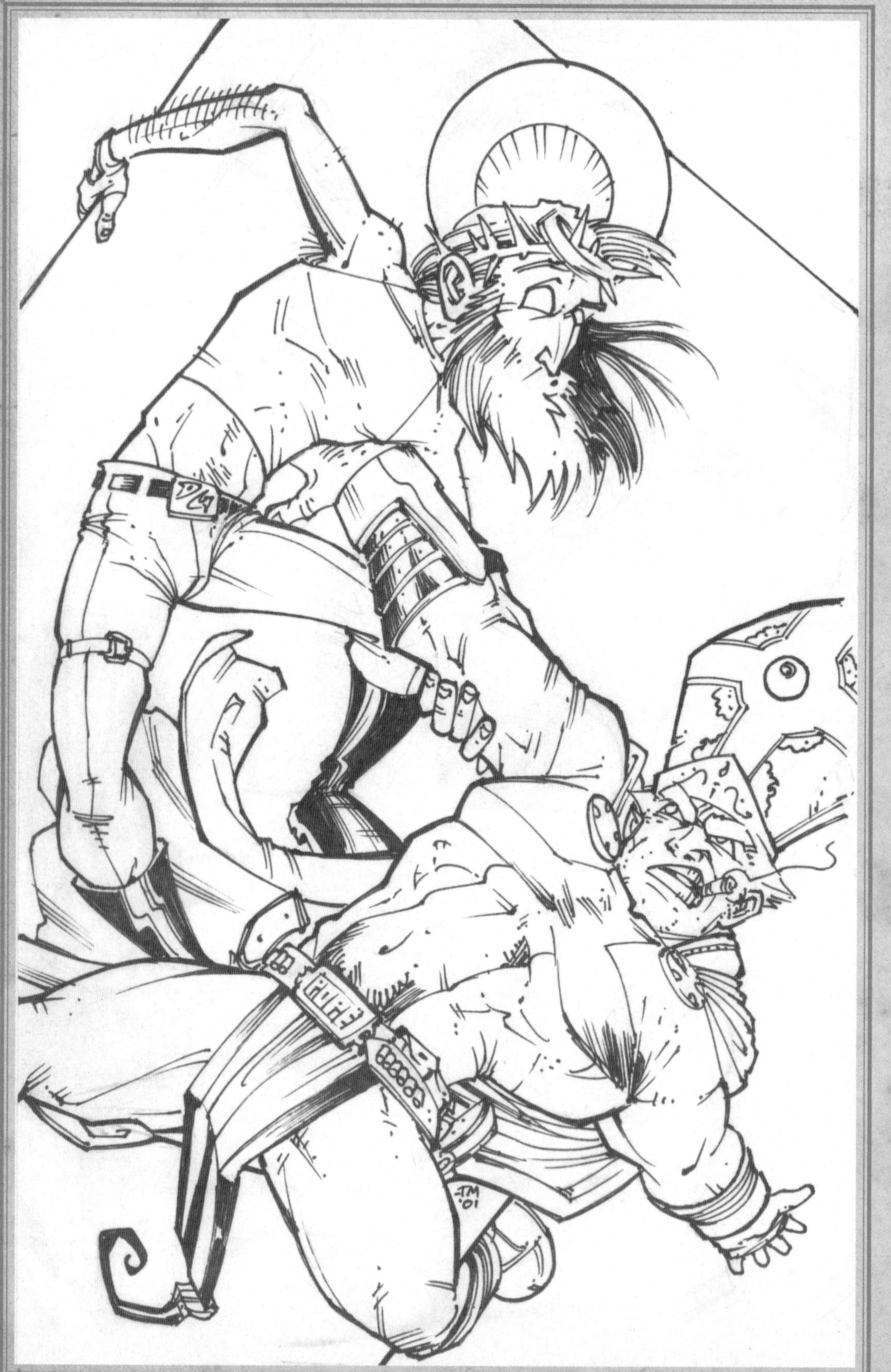

When I put together ads for these books, I usually talked Tony into doing all kinds of new art to be used only in the ads. I had always heard that the retailers like to see more than just covers when they flip trough the Previews catalogue, so I tried to oblige with extra art. Besides, it gave me all kinds of art to run in the trades! The one on the left page was masterfully colored by Hi-Fi's Brian Miller and used in Double Take #1. The one with Pope and Jesus as balloons was for our June 2000 ad for Mayhem #1 and Inkpunks #1, it appeared next to the title "Funk-O-Tron is expanding!" Get it? We were publishing more books that month--it was funny! I swear. Nobody noticed where Jesus' hose is going. Also on the page is art for the Shorts 1 and 2 ads.

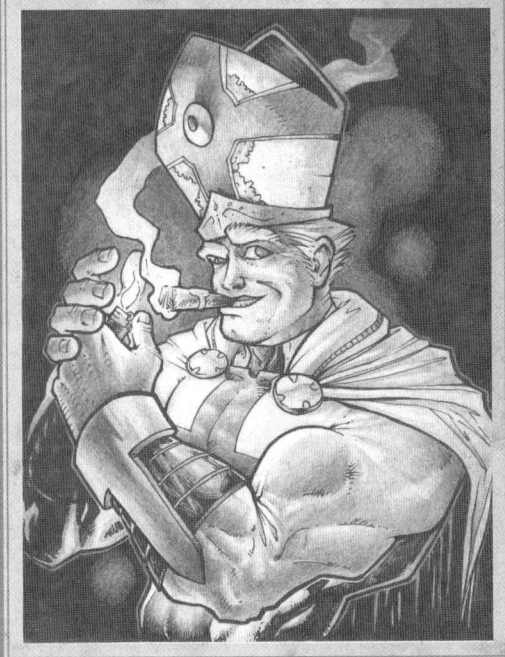

The following two pages were done completely by Tony for Battle Pope: Shorts #1. I'll never admit how funny I think they are. Well, okay fine... they're REALLY damn funny. You happy now, you goddamn vultures?

TIRED OF BEING PICKED ON?

NOBODY PICKS ON A "HOLY MAN!"

SPTOOIE! QUIT SHOVELING THAT SAND IN OUR FACES!
THAT GUY'S THE WORST SAND CASTLE MAKER ON THE BEACH!
LISSEN HERE, FATTY! I'D EAT YOUR FAT FACE - ONLY YOU'RE SO FATTY, I'D PROBABLY GET THE SQUIRTS FROM ALL YOUR FAT!
...FATTY!
WHY THAT DIRTY SO-AND-SO! ONE DAY, I'LL MOIDALIZE THAT BUM! ...I'M NOT THAT FAT!
DON'T SWEAT IT, PIGLET! GO GET SOME PIE!
OUR FATHER WHO ART IN HEAVEN, DAG NABBIT! I'M SICK AND TIRED OF NOT BEING ABLE TO SCORE! WHAT MORE DO THEY WANT? ISN'T THE HAT ENOUGH?!!
Prayin' with the Good Book!
HOT DAMN! THANKS TO A LITTLE PRAYER AND A LOTTA STEROIDS, I'M READY TO DOLE OUT ASS-WHOOPIN'S FOR THE LORD!
LATER
Tight, firm ass!
...OH YEAH? I STILL GOT ONE FAT THING YOU CAN MUNCH ON, YA LOUSY SON OF A BITCH! HAWHAW!
POP!
YOU BRUTALLY DISMEMBERED THAT GUY JUST TO ASSERT YOUR MANHOOD! PLEASE TAKE ME NOW!
THAT'S RIGHT, YA SUPERFICIAL SKANK! LET'S FIND AN ALLEY, I'LL SHOW YA WHY MY HAT'S FULLA RUBBERS!

Battle Pope
My goddamn knees can't touch!

I WAS PICKED ON, TOO - NOT ANY MORE!

That's right nerds, I understand exactly what it's like to be "picked on." I was a dumpy "347 pound weakling." I was "ashamed" of my "body" and I ate a lotta "Twinkies." The nuns wouldn't hop in the sack with me, and the altar boys put up a helluva fight. But that shit all changed for me, and we'll change it for you.. Join the clergy and become a "Holy Man!" We'll have you stacked fatter'n biscuits and built sturdier than a brick shithouse! ...And you have God's word on that! ...And I mean, who's word is better than that, eh?

GOD HAS HELPED MANY FIND PEACE AND AVOID DAILY THRASHINGS.

Nobody would hit a priest, right? Now you know why! Ever see those kung-fu movies? That's the kinda crazy shit we do! Those bastards are tough as nails! Become grotesque and obscenely muscular! Score with young, delicate men!

Don't delay -- REPENT TODAY!!!

Battle Pope
1942 University Avenue
Suite 305
Berkeley, CA 94704

THIS AD IS A *JOKE*. FEEL FREE TO SEND US MONEY, THOUGH...

Dear Funkotron: I'm giving you everything I own and leaving for a life of priesthood where I will learn to kick ass for the Lord!

____

____

____

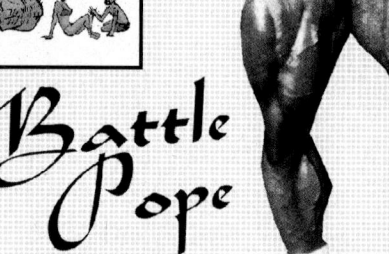

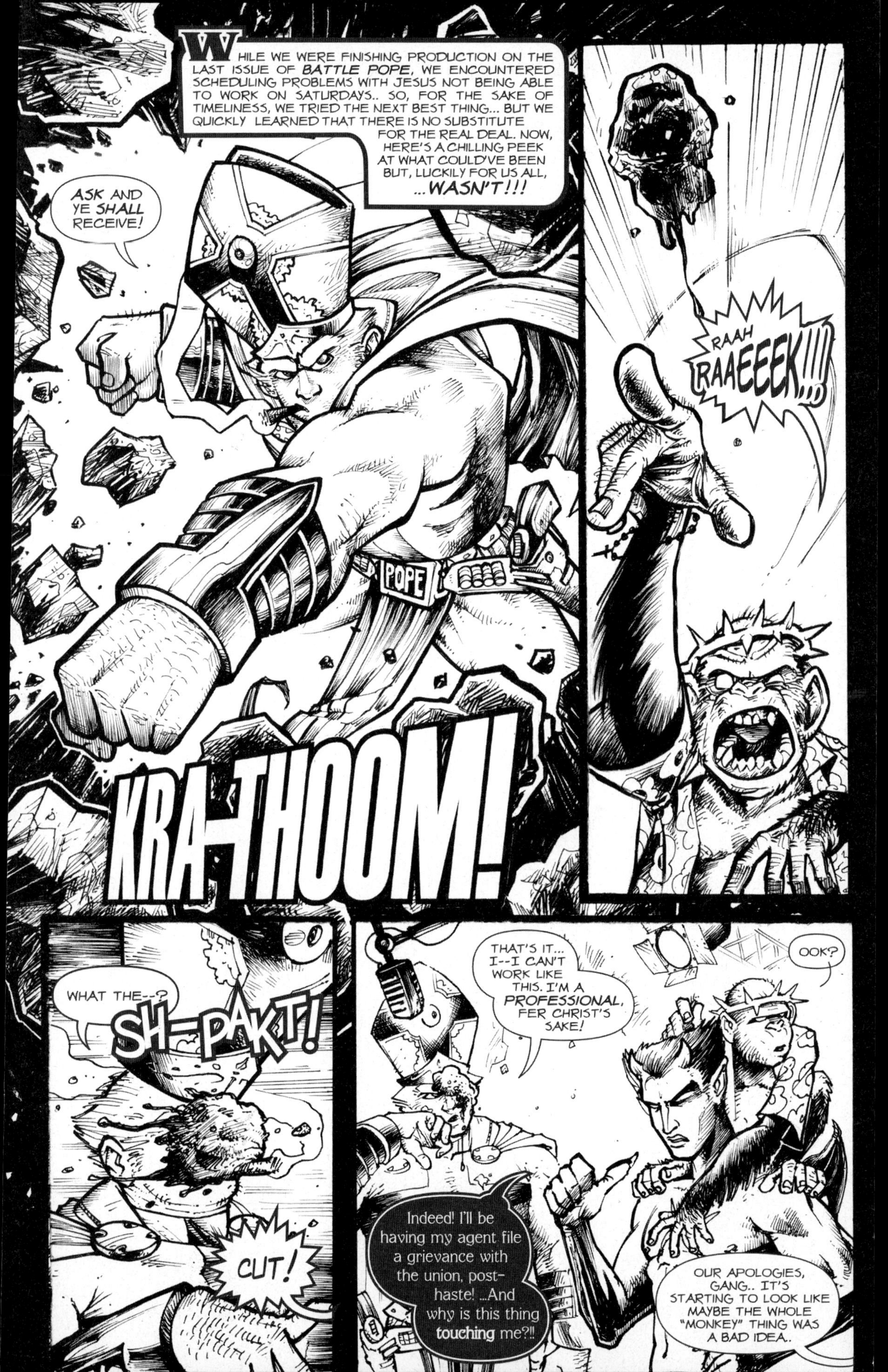
WHILE WE WERE FINISHING PRODUCTION ON THE LAST ISSUE OF BATTLE POPE, WE ENCOUNTERED SCHEDULING PROBLEMS WITH JESUS NOT BEING ABLE TO WORK ON SATURDAYS.. SO, FOR THE SAKE OF TIMELINESS, WE TRIED THE NEXT BEST THING... BUT WE QUICKLY LEARNED THAT THERE IS NO SUBSTITUTE FOR THE REAL DEAL. NOW, HERE'S A CHILLING PEEK AT WHAT COULD'VE BEEN BUT, LUCKILY FOR US ALL, ...WASN'T!!!
ASK AND YE SHALL RECEIVE!
KRA-THOOM!
RAAH RAAEEEK!!!
WHAT THE--?
SH-PAKT!
CUT!
THAT'S IT... I--I CAN'T WORK LIKE THIS. I'M A PROFESSIONAL, FER CHRIST'S SAKE!
OOK?
Indeed! I'll be having my agent file a grievance with the union, post-haste! ...And why is this thing touching me?!!
OUR APOLOGIES, GANG.. IT'S STARTING TO LOOK LIKE MAYBE THE WHOLE "MONKEY" THING WAS A BAD IDEA.

It's always fun, for me at least, to go back over the photocopies of Tony's pencils and see what he changed in the inks. He's always tweaking and making things better, while adding more little details and whatnot.

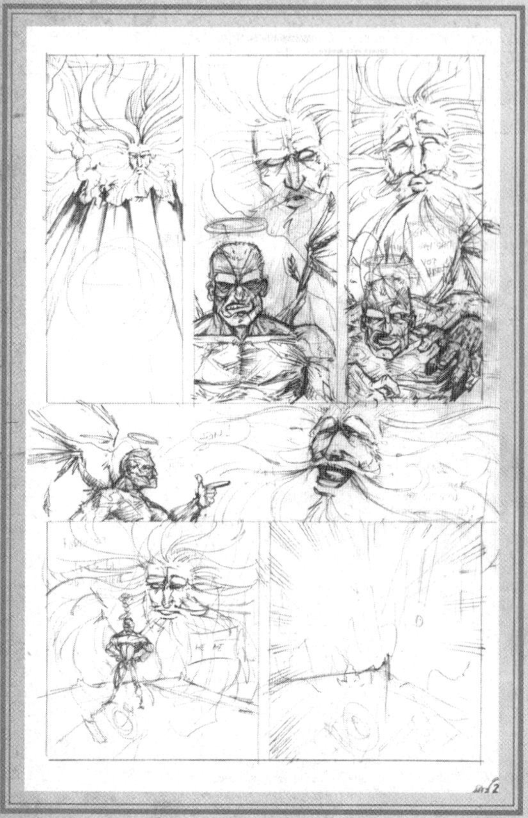

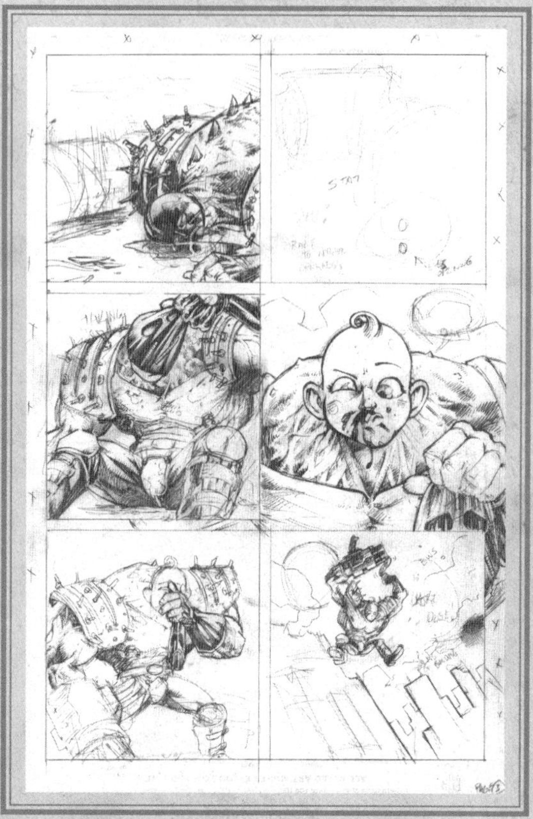

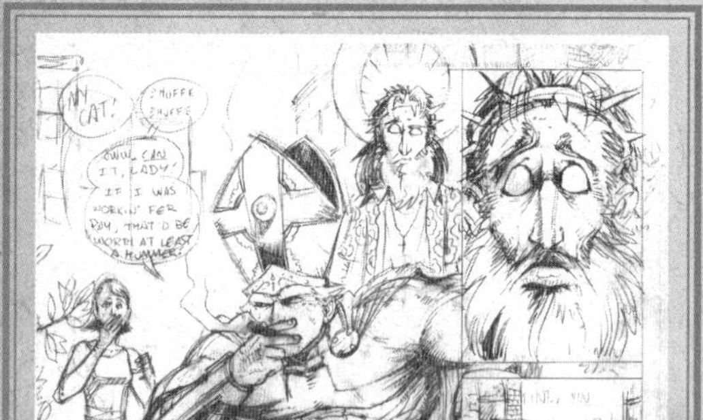
MY CAT!
IF I WAS WORKIN' FER PAY, THAT'D BE WORTH AT LEAST A HUMMER!
SHITHOLE TERRACE

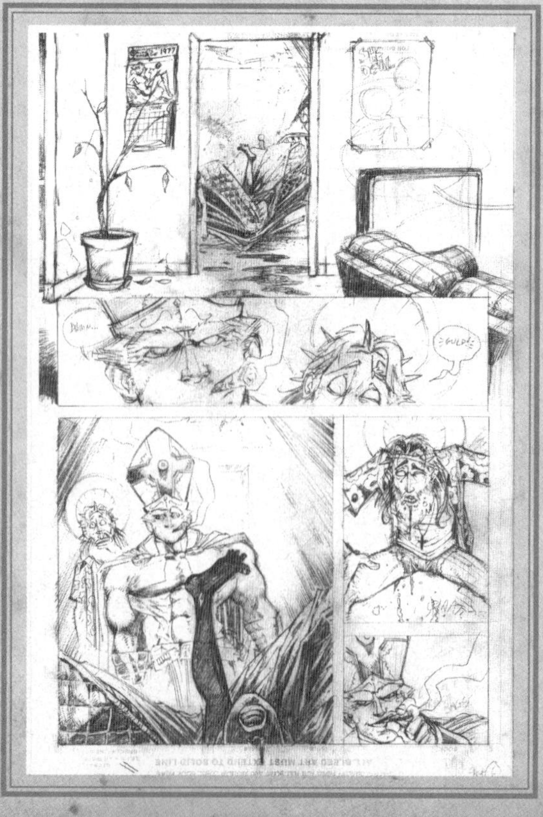

Shown here are some of the pages Tony inked in this trade that were not drawn by him or Matt. Tony is a hell of an inker, so much so that he can take pages that are obviously sub-par, such as the two I did shown here, and turn them into near masterpieces. Also on the page are two of Mark Kidwell's pages featuring the first appearance of Mark. I don't know if anyone has noticed, but most of the side characters in Battle Pope are named after the first artist to draw them.

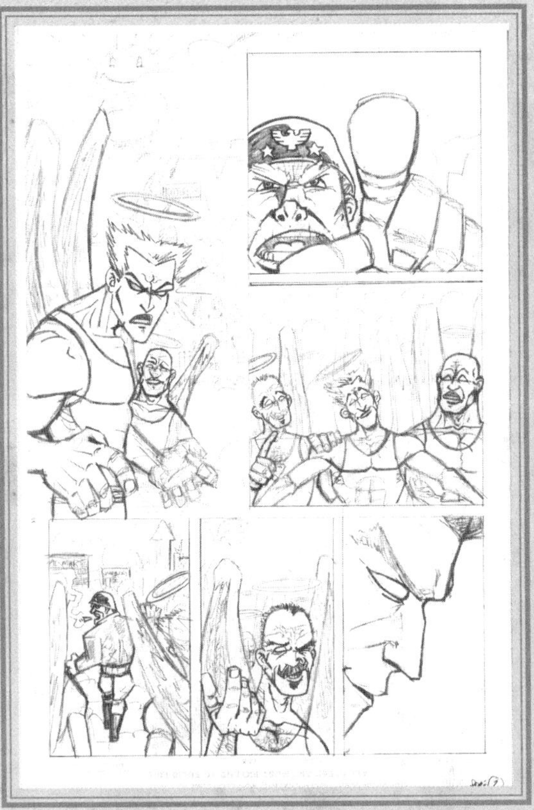

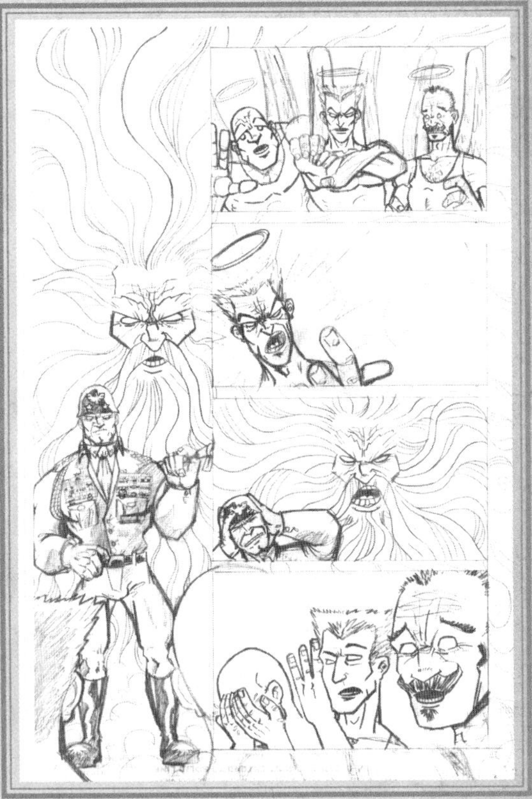

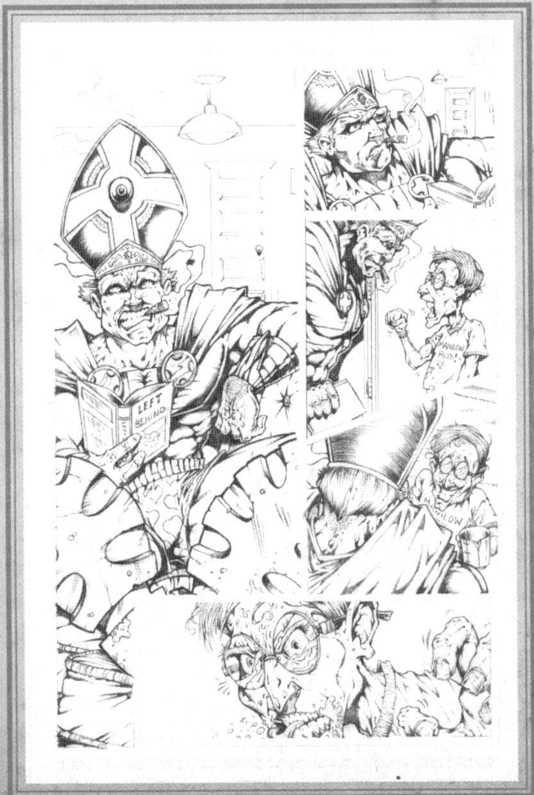

LEFT BEHIND

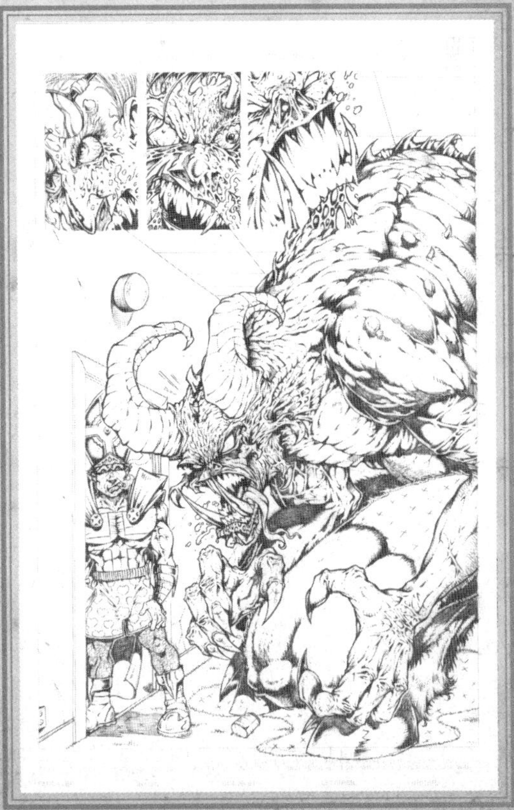

When I finished the plot for an issue of Battle Pope, I sat down and laid the entire book out on typing paper that was folded half, so what I had when I was done was a half-sized crudely drawn comic. From this, I would write the script and send the whole thing off to the artist(s). I used to draw these on the actual boards that I would give to Tony, until I realized that it was more of a hassle for him to erase as he drew and not leave anything out. Of course, doing them separately left me with stacks upon stacks of Battle Pope mini-comics to clutter up my studio. Compare the pages below to the ones printed in the book, you'll see all the things the artists did or didn't change... and how bad this book COULD have looked.

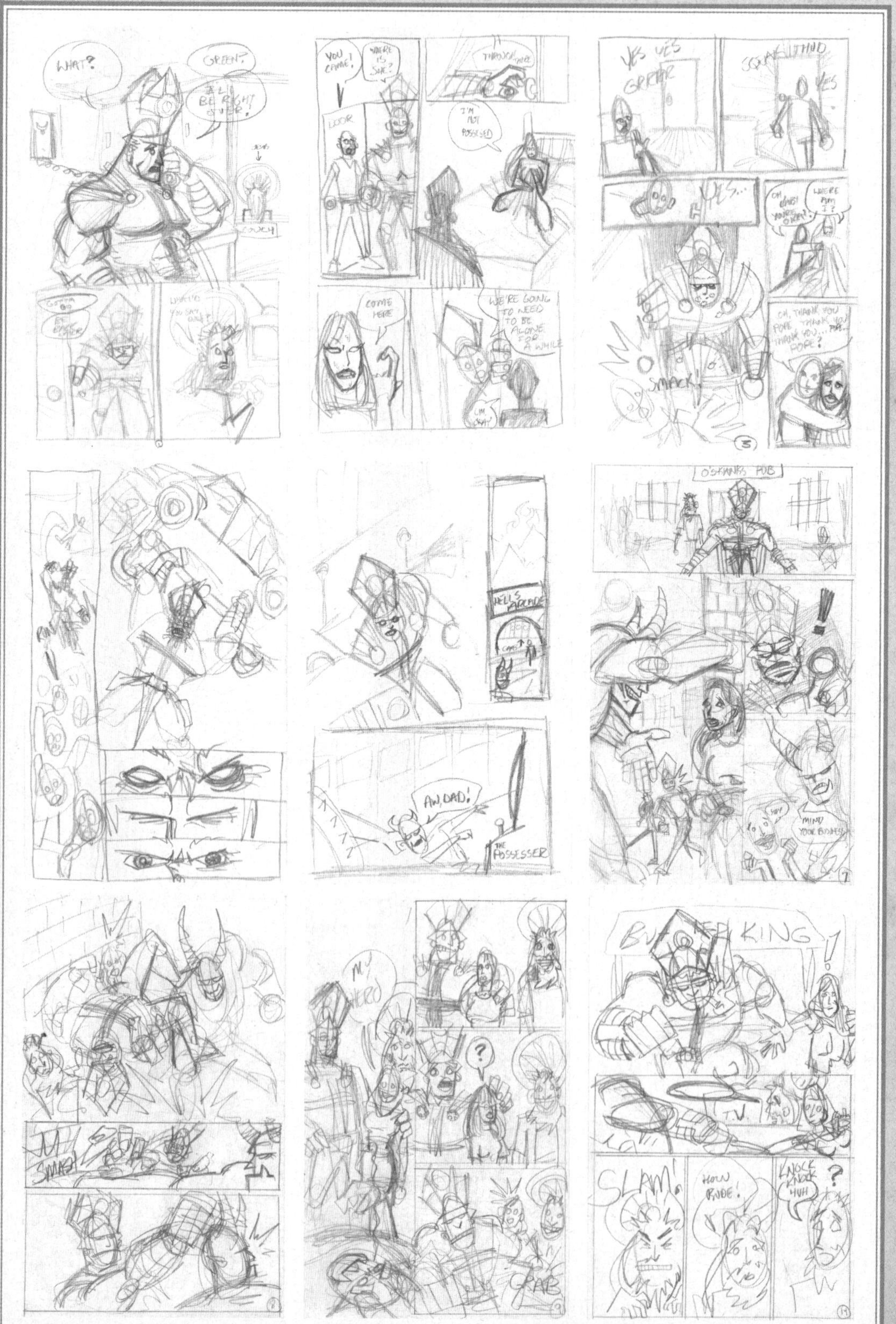
WHAT?
GREEN!
I'LL BE RIGHT OVER!
COUCH
YOU CAME!
WHERE IS SHE?
THROUGH THERE
DOOR
I'M NOT POSSESSED
COME HERE
WE'RE GOING TO NEED TO BE ALONE FOR A WHILE
YES YES GREATER
YES
YES...
WHERE AM I?
SMACK!
OH, THANK YOU POPE THANK YOU THANK YOU... POPE!
HELL'S ARCADE
AW, DAD!
THE POSSESSER
O'SHANKS PUB
!
MIND YOUR BUSINESS
SMASH
MY HERO
?
GRAB
KING
!
T.V.
SLAM!
HOW RUDE!
KNOCK KNOCK
HUH
?

More of my cruddy layouts.

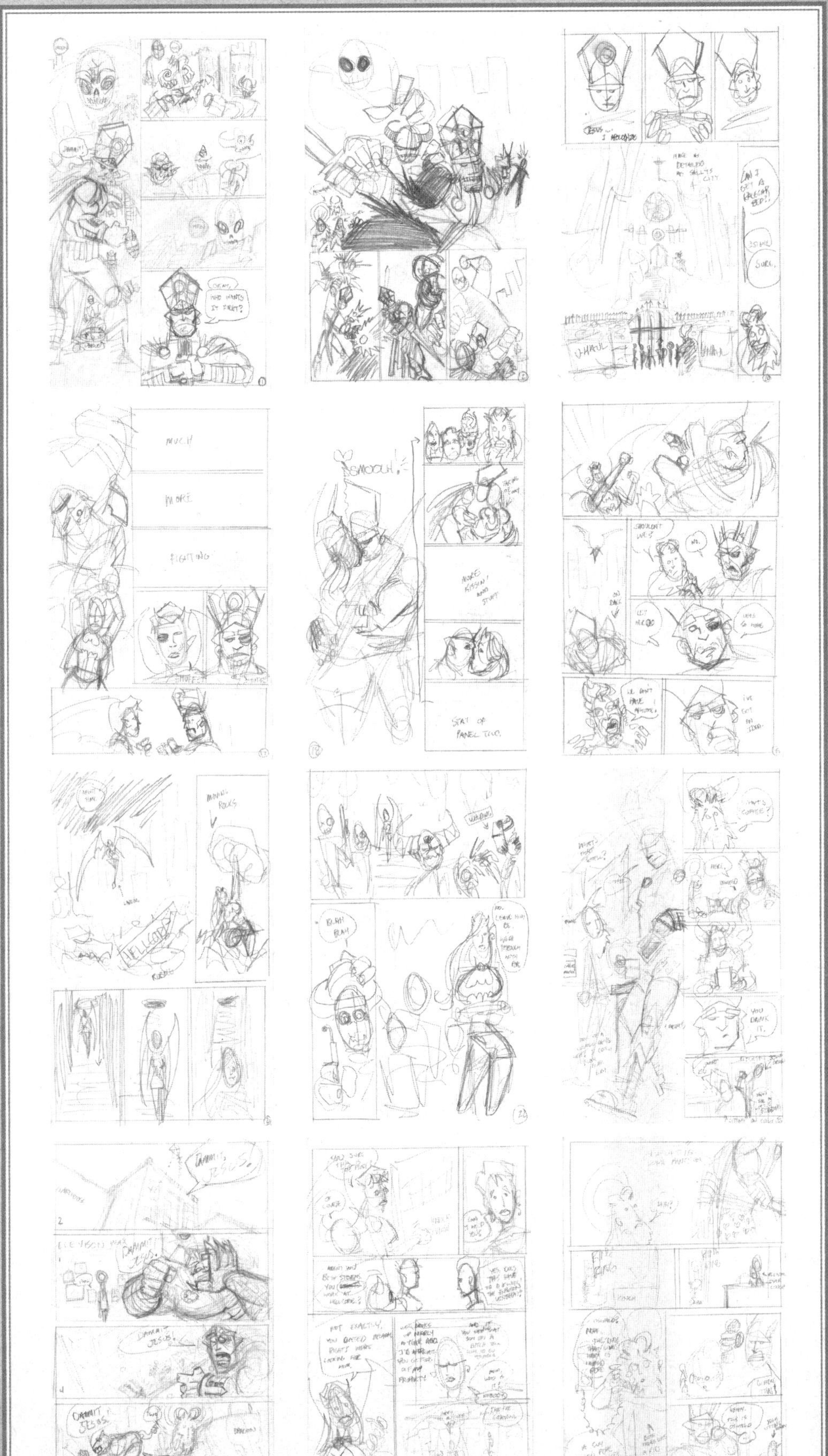

OKAY, WHO WANTS IT FIRST?
MUCH
MORE
FIGHTING
SMOOCH!
DAMMIT, JESUS!
U-HAUL

Here we have my layouts for the covers to issues 7 and 8. I wanted these covers to be very action packed, and "mayhem" filled. I think Matt did a bang-up job putting these together.

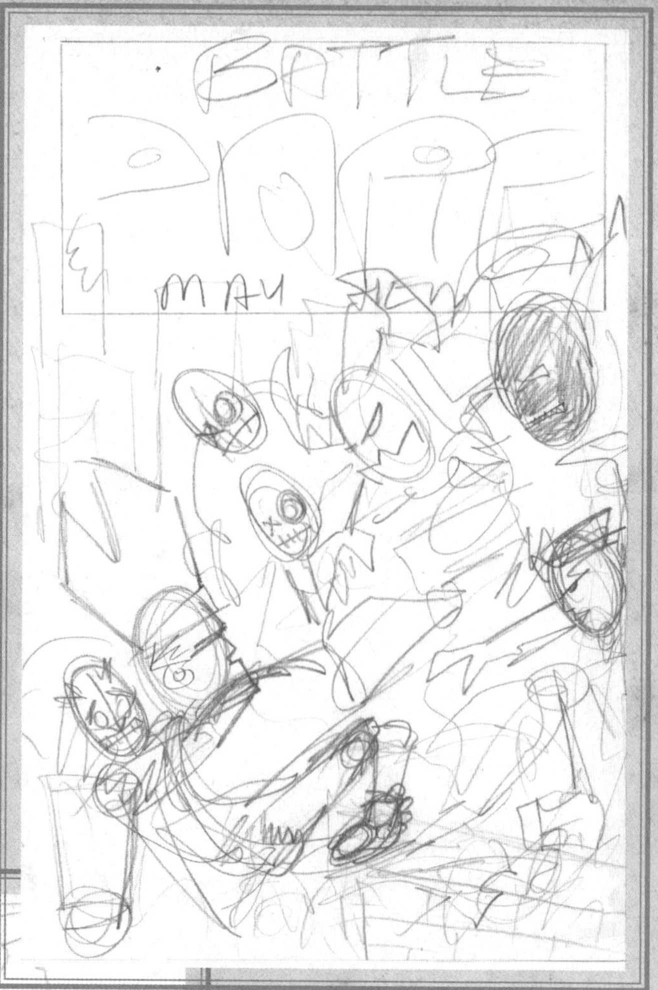
BATTLE
MAY

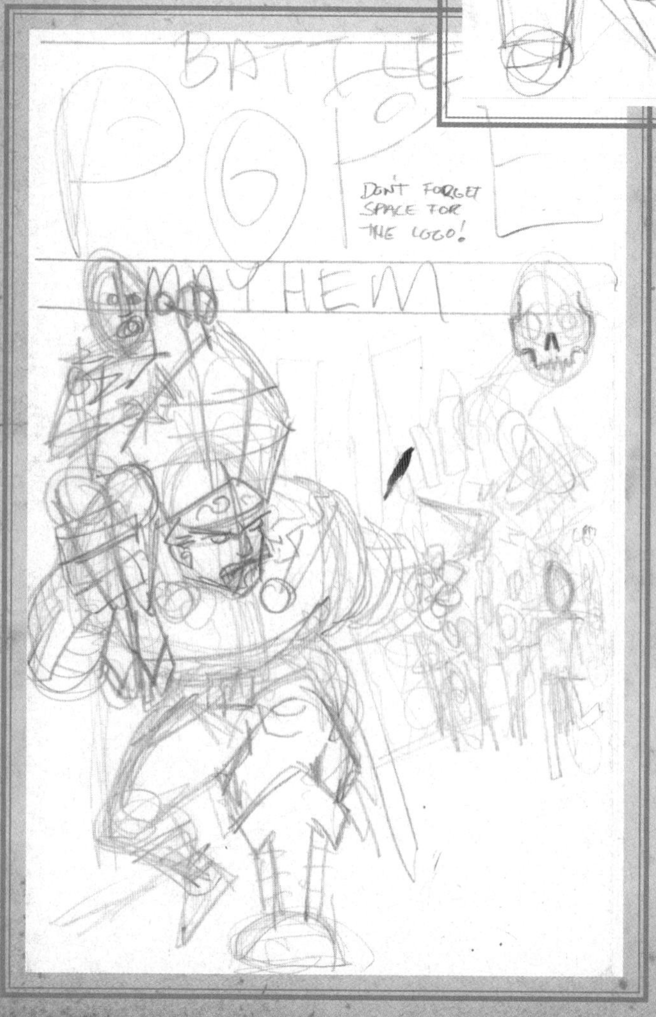
BATTLE POPE
DON'T FORGET SPACE FOR THE LOGO!
MAYHEM

I thought it would be cool if Pope and Jesus had a motorcycle at one point. I thought Jesus with a pilot's helmet and goggles would be a funny visual and that Pope would look bad-ass on a motorcycle. In the end I realized it'd be too cliché and decided against it. As of yet, I have NEVER shown them in a vehicle of any kind. However, it doesn't seem feasible that they would be walking everywhere, so at SOME point, I'll have to show them in a car... right now I'm thinking El Camino... the car that SCREAMS class.

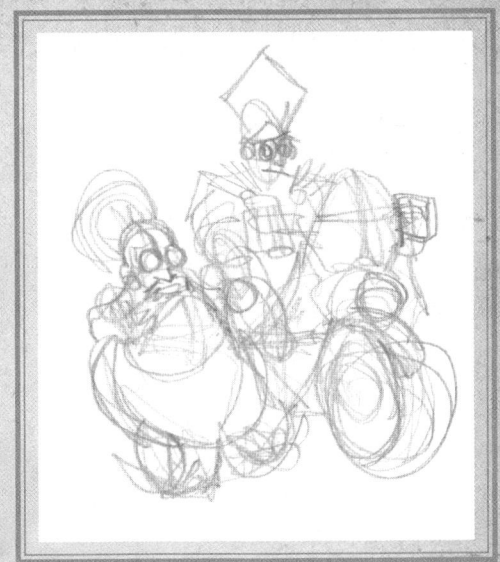

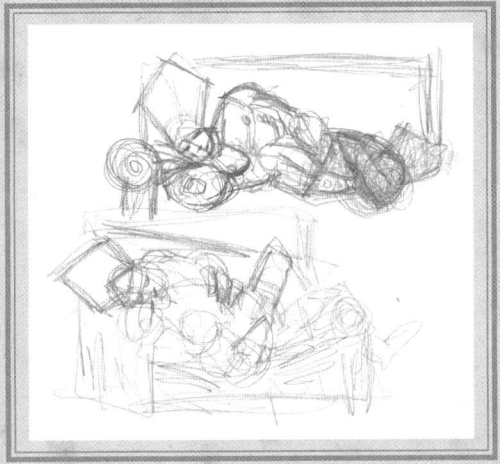

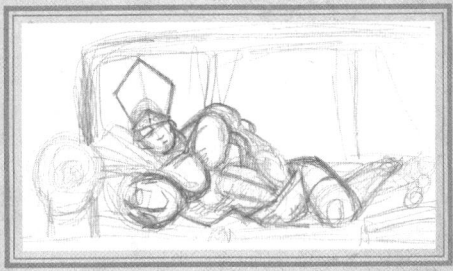

Because there were going to be six different artists working on Battle Pope Shorts #1, and most of the stories showed Pope's apartment, I decided that I had better do a rough layout so that nobody would draw anything in the wrong place. It also helped me get a feel for the place when I wrote issues 7 and 8. It's funny to me how everyone contributed to this apartment by drawing little details in the rooms that we incorporated into the final design. Such as the "She-Devil" poster that Brian Despain drew, and the nude woman art that Matt Roberts drew on the wall behind the couch. Tony added the old mechanics calendar from 1977 and the dead tree. All of these pages were drawn at the same time, so even though some appear before others, the apartment was being finalized simultaneously and I had to keep an eye on all the pages coming in to make sure no wall was duplicated incorrectly... of course, after I spent all this time trying to keep everything consistent, I drew the refrigerator in the wrong places on MY pages!

DRESSER
BED
BEDROOM
BATHROOM
CLOSET
SINK
PHONE
COUNTER
CHAIR
TRASH
FRIDGE
COUCH
TV
KITCHEN
TABLE
SHELVE?
DOOR

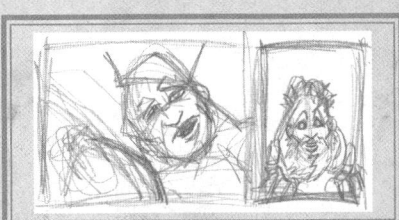

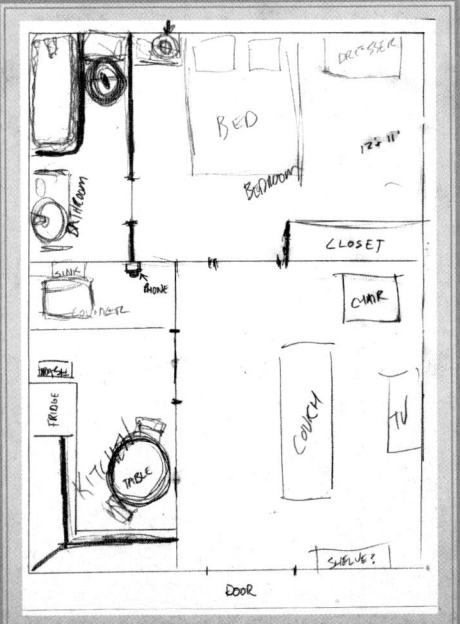

I did this little gag as a page in Battle Pope: Shorts #1 (issues 5 and 6 of the color series). It's a little send-up to my dad, and I don't know if anyone else thinks it's funny at all. My dad always used to say his crap smelled like roses after he came out of the john. If I ever complained about the smell, he would reply, "You smell those ROSES?" My dad is totally cool.

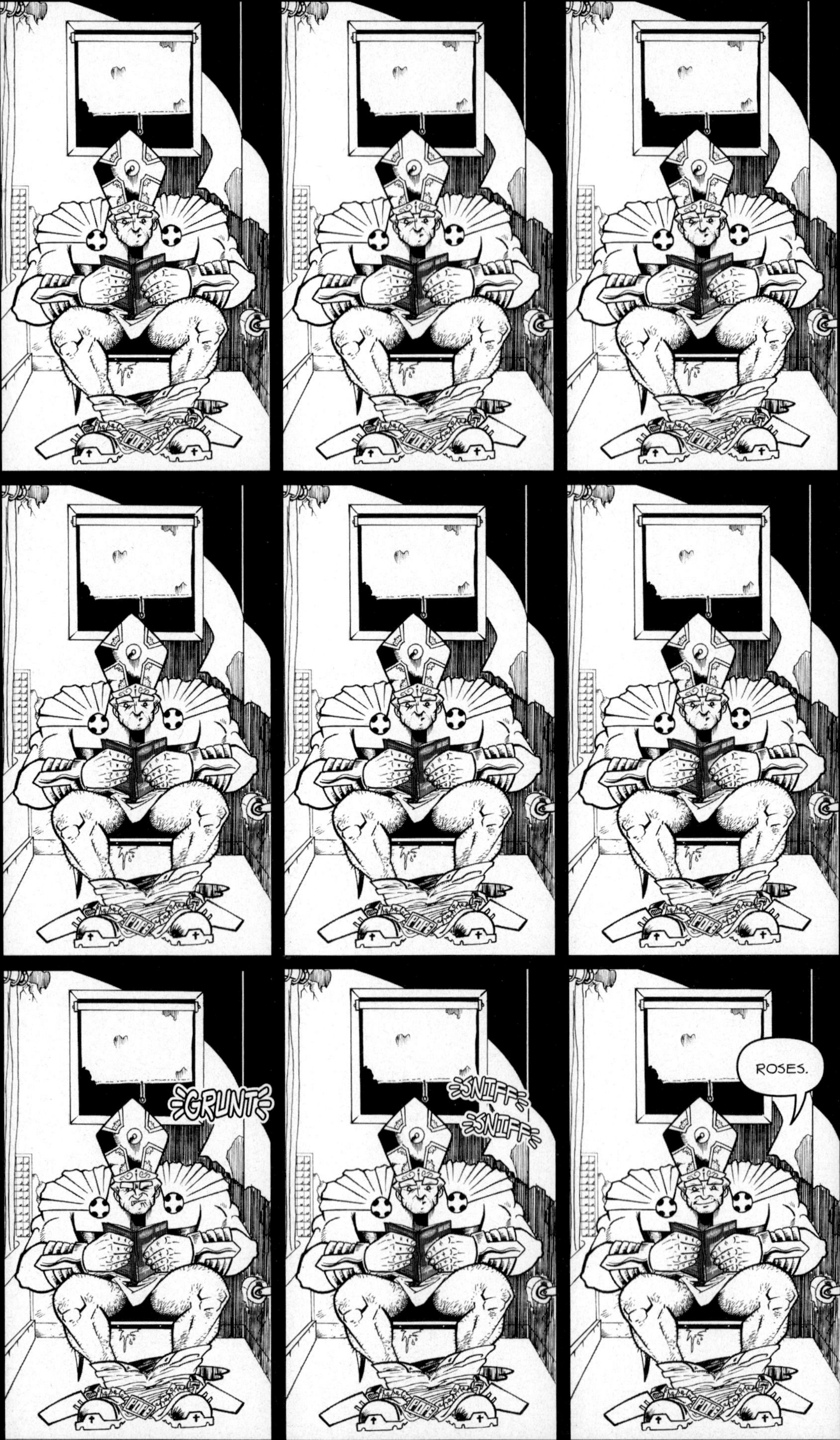
GRUNT
SNIFF
SNIFF
ROSES.

Here's Matt's pencils for the covers to this collection and issue 7. Matt Roberts is one of the best artists I've ever worked with. If he wasn't a proud member of the United States Air Force, I like to think we'd have done more comics together. I'd love to work with Matt again some day. His work on these Battle Pope issues was absolutely STUNNING.

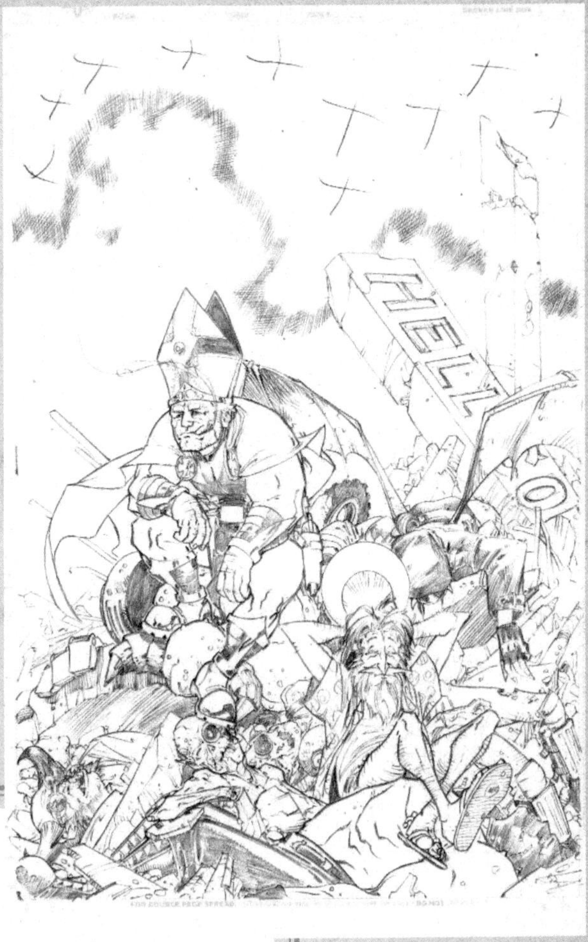
HELL

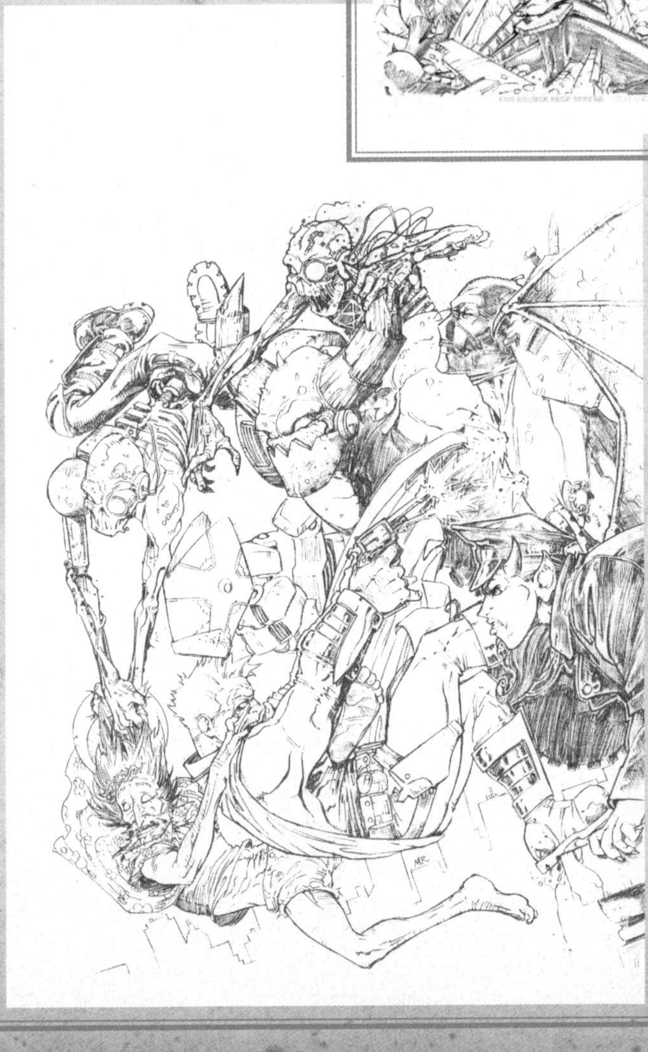

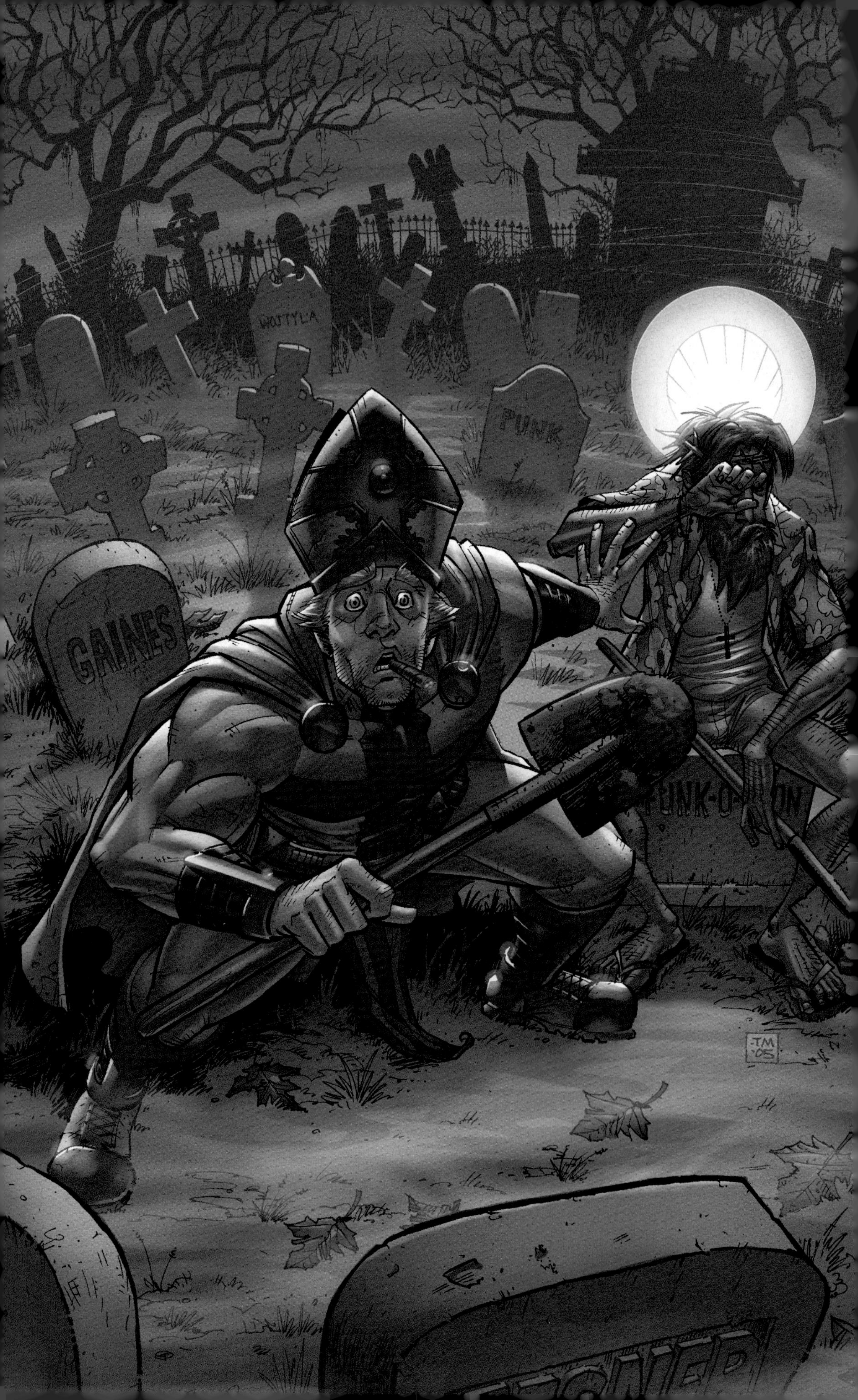
WOJTYLA
PUNK
GAINES
TM '05

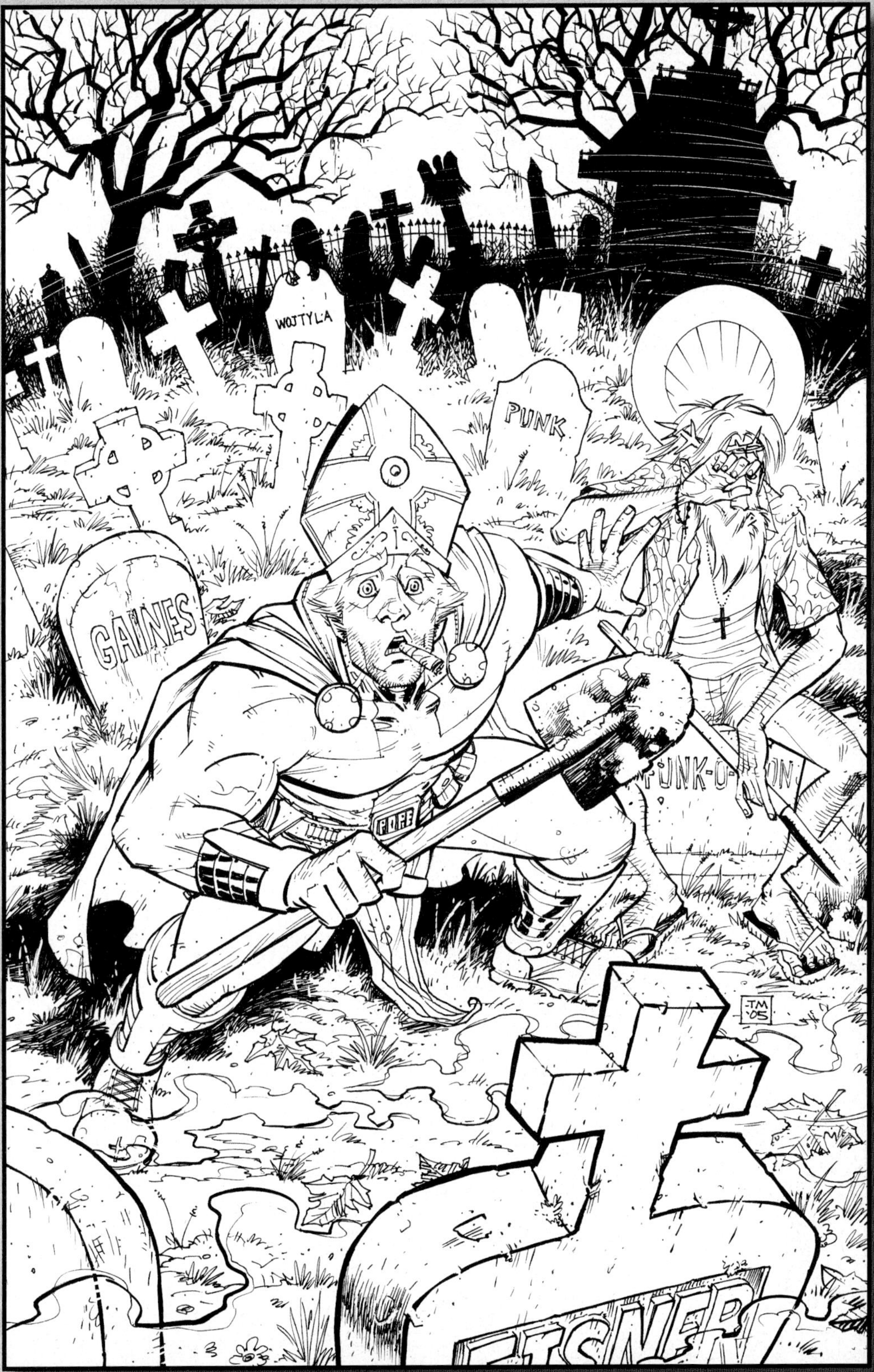
WOJTYLA
PUNK
GAINES
POPE
TM '05

There is no older cover for issue 5, because issue 5 was actually just half of Battle Pope: Shorts #1. So, well, we wouldn't really have anything to print here for comparison if it weren't for Tony's little flub-up. When he drew the new cover for this issue, he did a little Will Eisner tribute on the gravestone in the foreground--topped with a nice Christian cross--but everyone's hero, Will Eisner was jewish... so it had to be taken out in photoshop. Great cover though, by Tony... I really liked this one a lot.

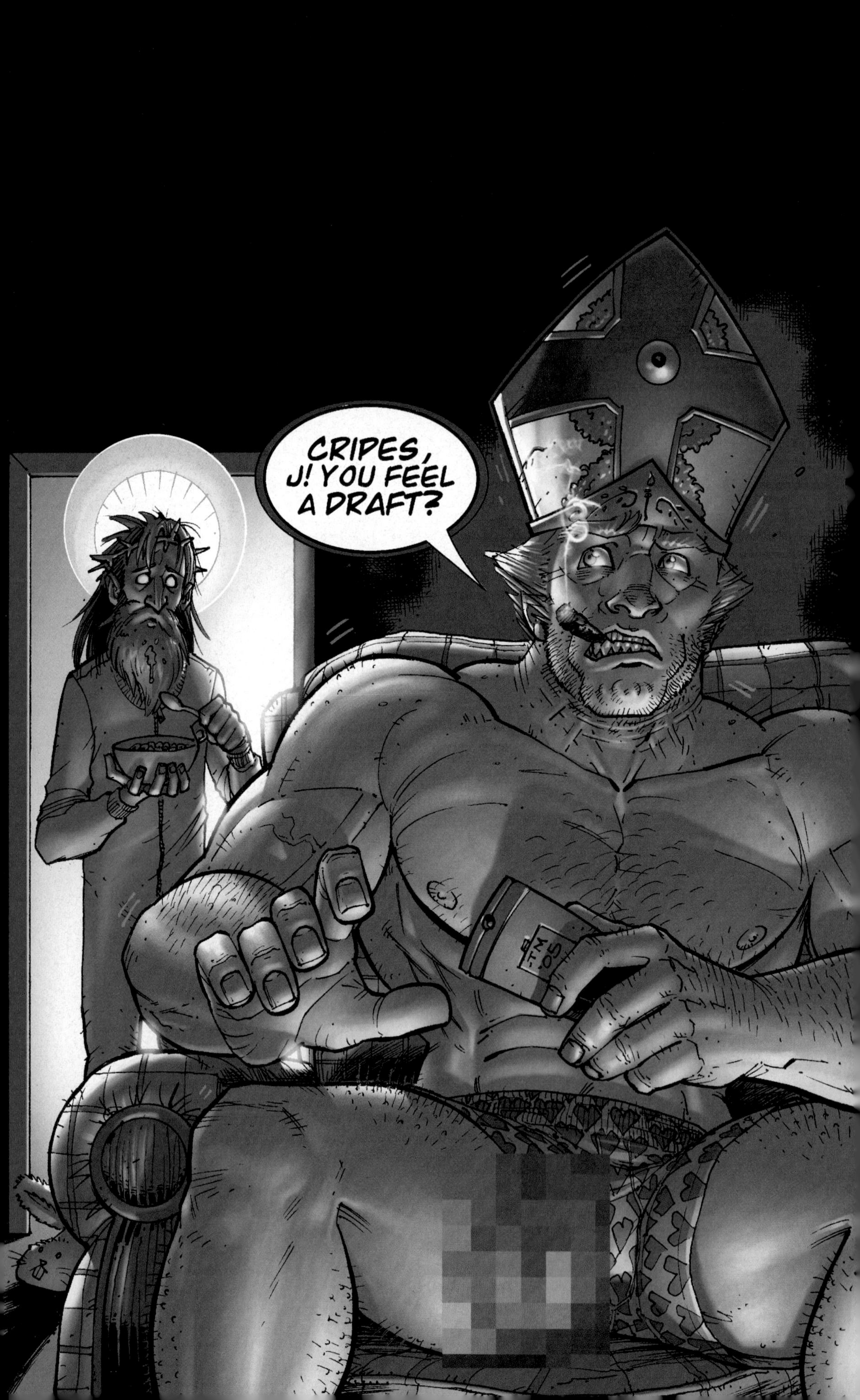
CRIPES, J! YOU FEEL A DRAFT?

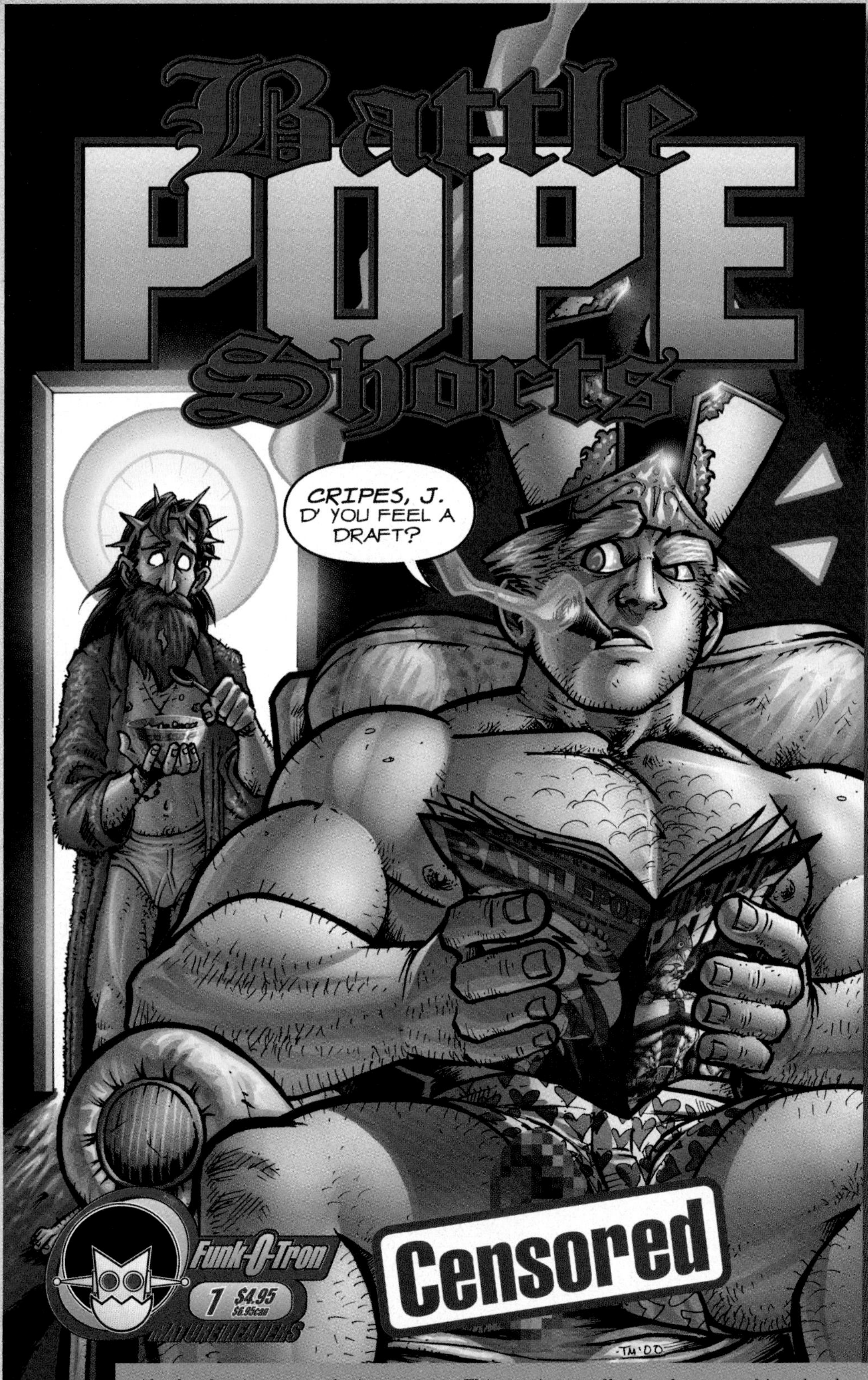
Battle
POPE
Shorts
CRIPES, J.
D' YOU FEEL A
DRAFT?
Funk-O-Tron
7 $4.95
$6.95can
MATURE READERS
Censored
TM'00

Ah, the classic, censored wiener cover. This one is actually based on something that happened to me with me grandfather when I was younger. He came outside and sat next to me on his picnic table one time when my family was visiting--he was wearing boxer shorts, as he often did, but his testicle was hanging out of the bottom of them. I ignored it--because I was polite, but then he noticed it, pushed it back in and said; "My damn nut was hanging out of my shorts--why didn't you TELL me? No wonder I felt a draft." My grandfather is probably the coolest dude on Earth.

I should also point out that the first version of this cover is the first thing Val Staples ever colored on Battle Pope. He offered to do the one cover for free as a portfolio piece, and I'm still to this day tricking him into coloring far more than he ever imagined he would.

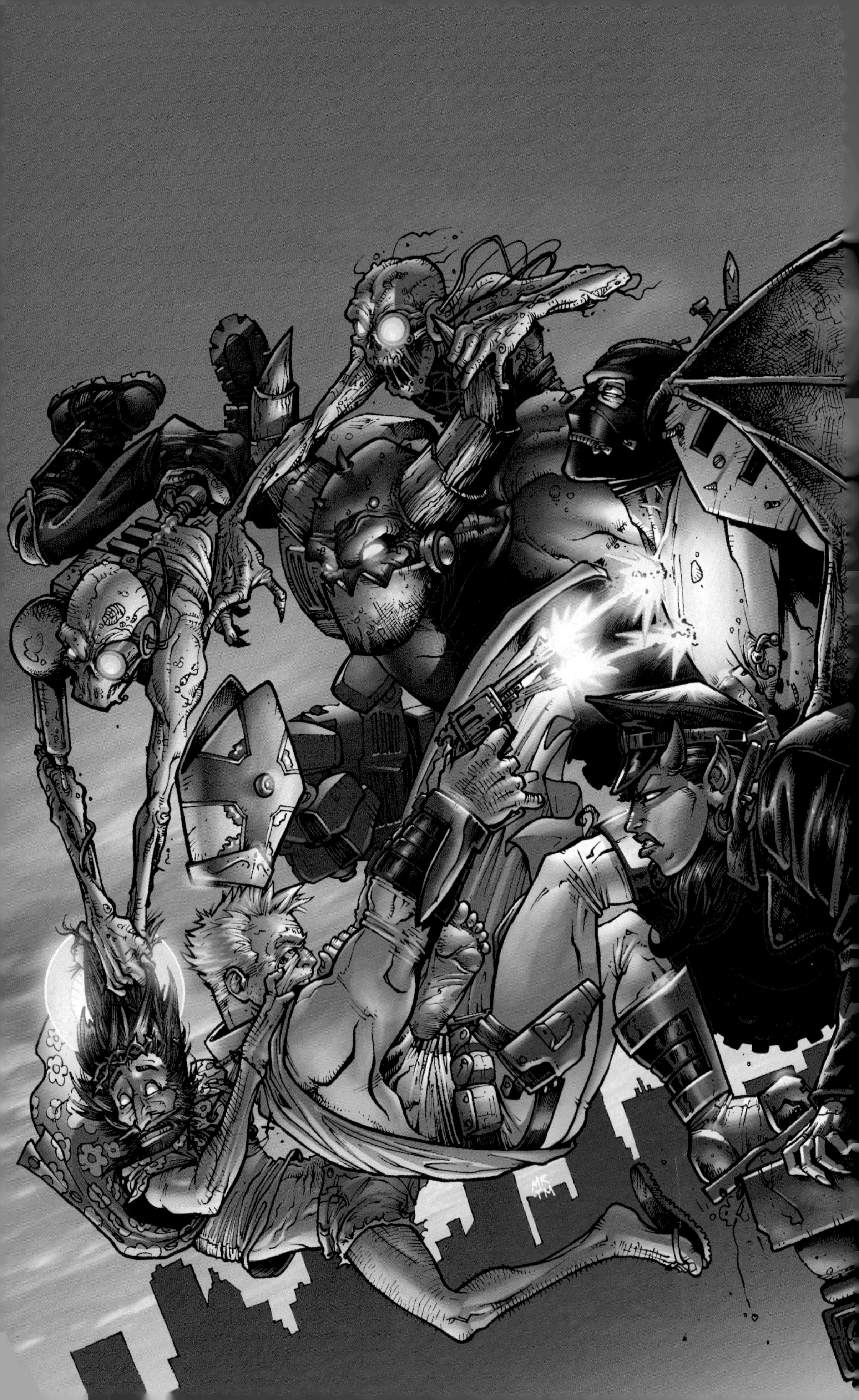

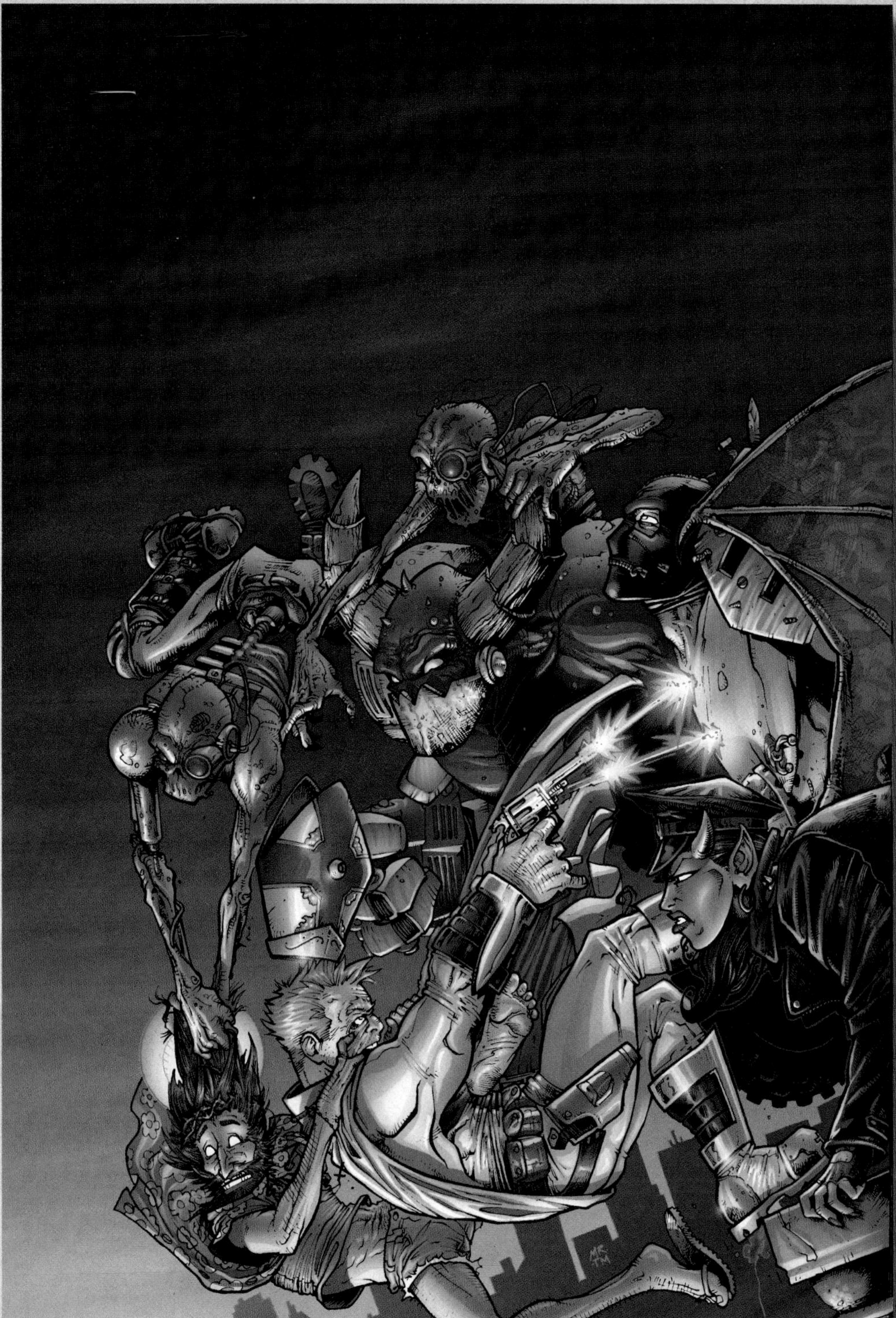

The line art is the same, sure, but for these covers Val Staples went in and recolored them from scratch. Val Staples was an important part of the Battle Pope team since the minute he colored the cover to Shorts #1. His flashy, and professional, coloring brought a higher sense of quality to the book, I thought. When he started coloring the covers I thought the book looked much more like a real, professional comic-book and not a book by two guys in Kentucky who had never done this before. Val really saved us.

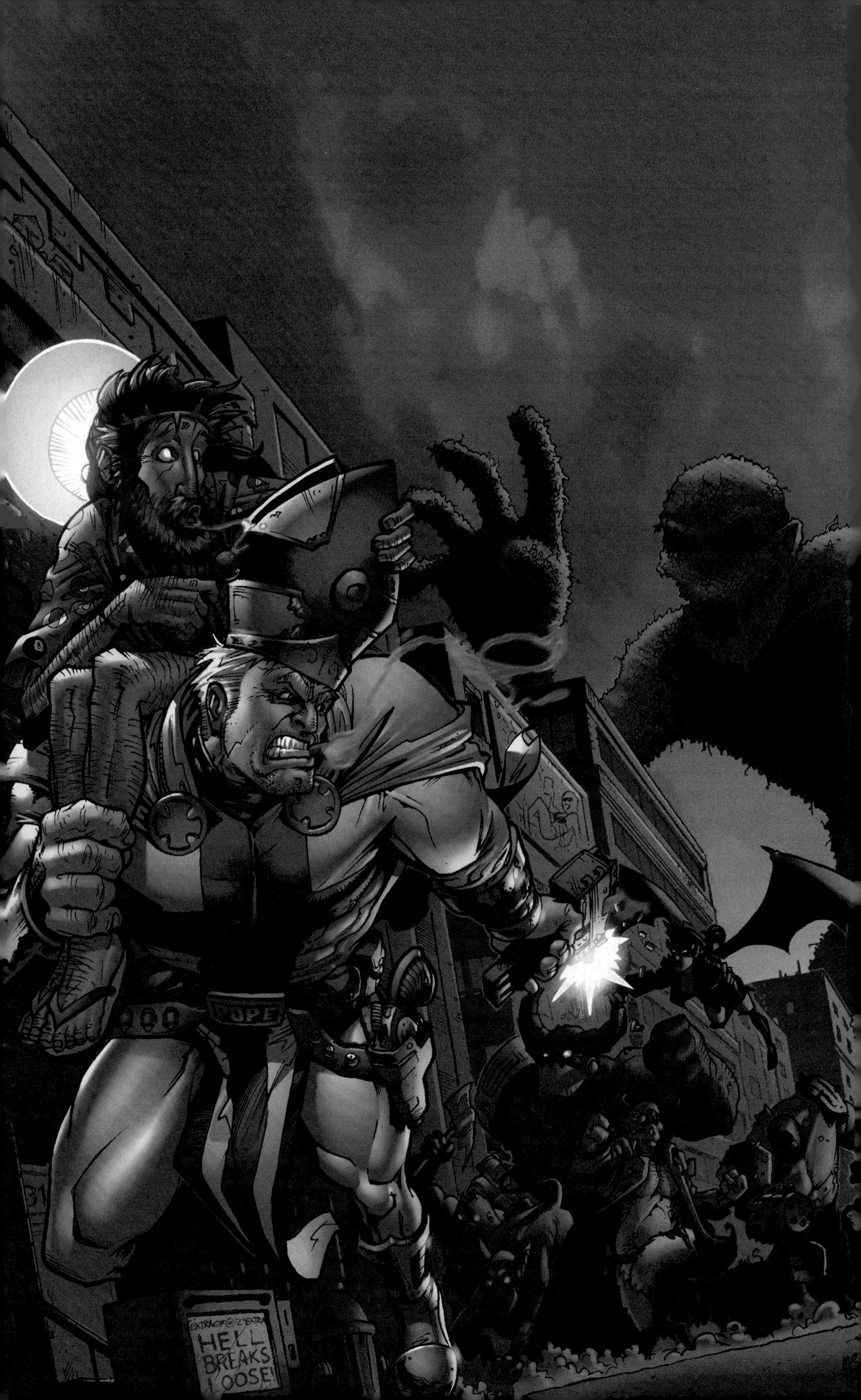
POPE
HELL BREAKS LOOSE!

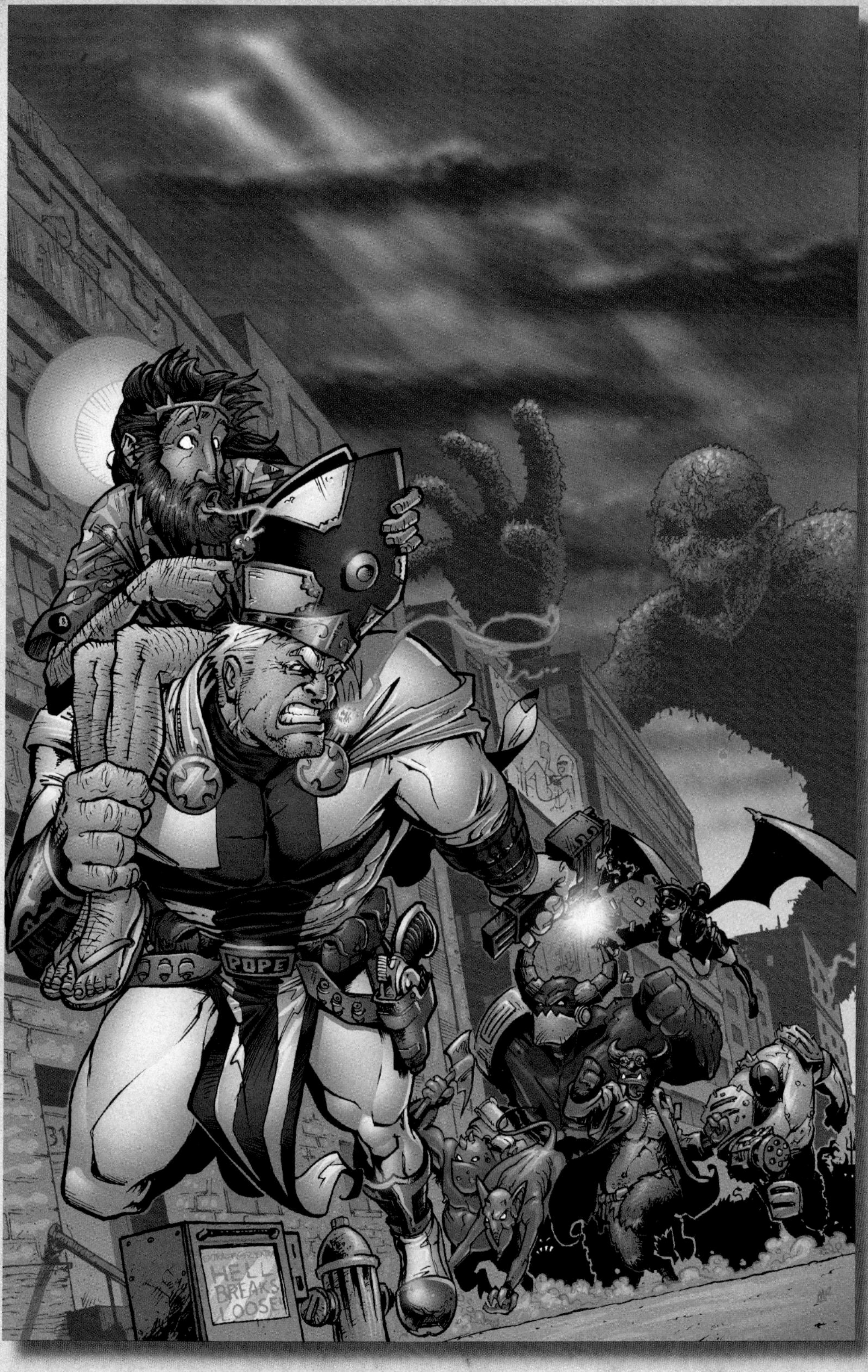
POPE
HELL
BREAKS
LOOSE

And finally the cover to issue 8 and the original version used for Battle Pope: Mayhem #2. I didn't even know Val had done that cool light shooting through the clouds thing on the original because it was always covered by the logo. Pretty neat. These two covers by Matt Roberts (for issues 7 and 8) are among my favorites for the series. Matt was a class act.

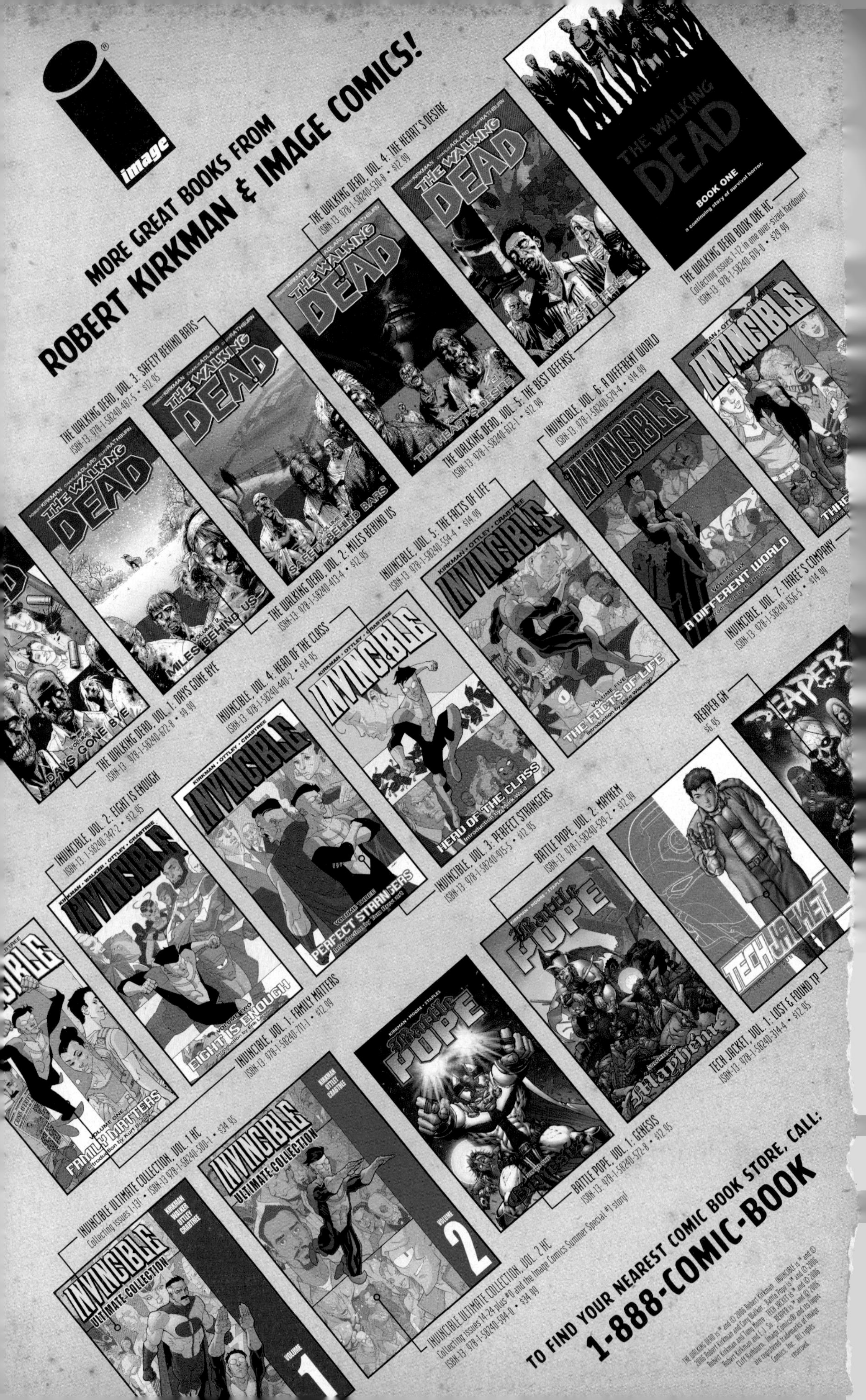

MORE GREAT BOOKS FROM
ROBERT KIRKMAN & IMAGE COMICS!
THE WALKING DEAD, VOL. 1: DAYS GONE BYE
ISBN-13: 978-1-58240-672-8 • $9.99
THE WALKING DEAD, VOL. 2: MILES BEHIND US
ISBN-13: 978-1-58240-413-4 • $12.95
THE WALKING DEAD, VOL. 3: SAFETY BEHIND BARS
ISBN-13: 978-1-58240-487-5 • $12.95
THE WALKING DEAD, VOL. 4: THE HEART'S DESIRE
ISBN-13: 978-1-58240-530-8 • $12.99
THE WALKING DEAD, VOL. 5: THE BEST DEFENSE
ISBN-13: 978-1-58240-612-1 • $12.99
THE WALKING DEAD BOOK ONE HC
Collecting issues 1-12 in one over-sized hardcover!
ISBN-13: 978-1-58240-619-0 • $29.99
INVINCIBLE, VOL. 1: FAMILY MATTERS
ISBN-13: 978-1-58240-711-1 • $12.99
INVINCIBLE, VOL. 2: EIGHT IS ENOUGH
ISBN-13: 1-58240-347-2 • $12.95
INVINCIBLE, VOL. 3: PERFECT STRANGERS
ISBN-13: 978-1-58240-915-5 • $12.95
INVINCIBLE, VOL. 4: HEAD OF THE CLASS
ISBN-13: 978-1-58240-440-2 • $14.95
INVINCIBLE, VOL. 5: THE FACTS OF LIFE
ISBN-13: 978-1-58240-554-4 • $14.99
INVINCIBLE, VOL. 6: A DIFFERENT WORLD
ISBN-13: 978-1-58240-579-4 • $14.99
INVINCIBLE, VOL. 7: THREE'S COMPANY
ISBN-13: 978-1-58240-656-5 • $14.99
INVINCIBLE ULTIMATE COLLECTION, VOL. 1 HC
Collecting issues 1-131 • ISBN-13: 978-1-58240-500-1 • $34.95
INVINCIBLE ULTIMATE COLLECTION, VOL. 2 HC
Collecting issues 14-24 plus #0 and the Image Comics Summer Special #1 story!
ISBN-13: 978-1-58240-594-0 • $34.99
BATTLE POPE, VOL. 1: GENESIS
ISBN-13: 978-1-58240-572-8 • $12.95
BATTLE POPE, VOL. 2: MAYHEM
ISBN-13: 978-1-58240-529-2 • $12.99
REAPER GN
$6.95
TECH JACKET, VOL. 1: LOST & FOUND TP
ISBN-13: 978-1-58240-314-4 • $12.95
TO FIND YOUR NEAREST COMIC BOOK STORE, CALL:
1-888-COMIC-BOOK
THE WALKING DEAD is ™ and © 2006 Robert Kirkman. INVINCIBLE is ™ and © 2006 Robert Kirkman and Cory Walker. Battle Pope is ™ and © 2006 Robert Kirkman and Tony Moore. TECH JACKET is ™ and © 2006 Robert Kirkman and E. J. Su. REAPER is ™ and © 2006 Cliff Rathburn. Image Comics® and its logos are registered trademarks of Image Comics, Inc. All rights reserved.